INDONESIA'S RISE

Seeking Regional and Global Roles

INDONESIA'S RISE

Seeking Regional and Global Roles

Vibhanshu Shekhar

INDIAN COUNCIL OF WORLD AFFAIRS

PENTAGON PRESS

Indonesia's Rise: Seeking Regional and Global Roles
by Vibhanshu Shekhar

ISBN 978-81-8274-817-0

First Published in 2014

Published by
PENTAGON PRESS
206, Peacock Lane, Shahpur Jat,
New Delhi-110049
Phones: 011-64706243, 26491568
Telefax: 011-26490600
email: rajan@pentagonpress.in
website: www.pentagonpress.in

Branch
Flat No.213, Athena-2,
Clover Acropolis,
Viman Nagar,
Pune-411014
Email: pentagonpresspune@gmail.com

Printed at Avantika Printers Private Limited.

to Brooke

CONTENTS

ACKNOWLEDGEMENT

This book has been written over the course of the last three years in three different geographical settings – India, Indonesia and the United States of America. In all of these places, Indonesia's rise is being debated and discussed vigorously. I have, in the process of writing this book, benefitted immensely, not only from these debates and discussions, but also from various people who made this book possible. Therefore, it is imperative that their roles and contributions be sincerely acknowledged.

Let me start with the Indian Council of World Affairs, New Delhi, India where the idea of this book was conceived and where the bulk of the manuscript was written during my research fellowship (February 2011-July 2013). The then Director General Ambassador Sudhir T. Devare agreed to support and sponsor my book project on Indonesia's rise. The Council also nominated two mentors – Professor Man Mohini Kaul and Ambassador Navarekha Sharma, who offered critical inputs in the research process. The Council's Director General, Ambassador Rajiv K. Bhatia provided constant moral support and sanctioned a field work to Indonesia. Furthermore, the book received important intellectual inputs from the Director (Research), ICWA, Dr Vijay Sakhuja, the former Director, ICWA, Ms Manika Jain, and my colleagues – Sandipani, Nivedita, Asif, Athar, Fazzur, Vikas, Sanjeev, Gnanagurunathan, Angira, Pankaj, Zakir, Saurabh and Dinoj. The staff at the ICWA library, including the main Librarian, Mr Rai facilitated my research at the library. Two anonymous referees provided valuable inputs in giving final shape to the book.

While conducting field research in Indonesia in November 2012, the book received valuable inputs from various people. Dr. Rahima Ima Abdulrahim, Executive Director of the Habibie Center, hosted me at the

Center on the recommendation of Professor Dewi Fortuna Anwar. The Center facilitated the process of data collection in various libraries throughout Jakarta and through interviews. The interviews were conducted with three sets of people: (a) senior officials in the Department of Foreign Affairs, Republic of Indonesia, (b) senior professors in universities, and (c) journalists. Some of the names are Professor Dewi Fortuna Anwar, Ambassador Pitono Purnomo, Director General, Policy Analysis and Development Agency, Department of Foreign Affairs, Jakarta, Ambassador Hasjim Djalal, Ambassador Rizali Indrakesuma, Indonesia's Ambassador to India, Dr. Endy M. Bayuni, Senior Editor, the *Jakarta Post*, Jakarta, Dr. Hariyadi Wirawan, the University of Indonesia, Jakarta, Dr. Connie Rahakundini Bakrie, the University of Indonesia, and Mr. Veeramalla Anjaiah, Senior journalist, the *Jakarta Post.*

While giving final shape to the book in the US, I participated in various meetings and conferences at the United States-Indonesia Society, the Sigur Center for Asian Studies, George Washington University, and the Center for Strategic and International Studies in Washington D.C. and interacted with researchers, scholars and practitioners. These meetings and interactions provided important insights into some of the salient aspects of themes discussed in the book. However, this list would remain incomplete without acknowledging the contribution of Margaret Brooke Beasley, who took up, perhaps, the most daunting and uninteresting task in writing a book – editing the entire manuscript.

Vibhanshu Shekhar

PREFACE

The idea of rising powers has gained traction in the last decade due to a sudden spurt in the number of rising powers across the globe and their overwhelming impact on global politics. They are agents of change, global growth, development and well-being for a vast segment of humanity that has been long living in hardship and poverty. These powers are redefining the agenda of global politics and outlining what their roles should be in these debates and discussions. However, their impact has been felt most acutely and directly in their respective regions, for example Brazil in South America and China in Asia.

One can imagine the depth and intensity of change in a region that has seen the rise of not just one but three powers – China, India and Indonesia. Their rise has placed the whole region at the forefront of global strategic discourses, set in motion processes of regional growth and integration, and given birth to new alignments of power and security challenges in the Asia-Pacific. The Asia-Pacific region never before felt so much empowered and vulnerable at the same time.

At the epicentre of the Asia-Pacific lies rising Indonesia – the fourth most populous country in the world, the third largest democracy, the largest ASEAN player, the largest Muslim democracy, one of the most moderate Islamic societies, and an important civilizational force in Asia. During the short span of two decades, Indonesia has risen, fallen and risen again. At least, the writers seem to make us believe so. This also amplifies how fleeting and quick these processes can be and how rigorously and frequently ideas and arguments are being debated and revisited.

A decade ago, while conducting my doctoral research, I was examining Indonesia's conception of security, the sources of its internal vulnerabilities and how the whole country was drifting very fast towards chaos and crisis. The incipient democracy was teetering; the state was in disarray; the military was discredited; the civic institutions were proving dysfunctional; law-enforcement agencies were learning to behave with the civilians; and the social fabric was experiencing cracks and ruptures in almost every corner. Indonesia was being seen as a vast breeding ground of terror networks and operatives.

Ten years later, I am again writing on Indonesia. However, this is a different time, a different Indonesia and therefore a different story altogether. This book is not a story of Indonesia's vulnerabilities, but rather its growing capabilities and desires to make its presence felt in regional and global politics. Indonesia is gradually consolidating its pluralistic democratic foundations and is emerging, with its sustained economic growth and huge natural resources, as an important economic player in the Asia-Pacific. It has resumed its critical responsibilities of steering the regional cooperative processes and taking the region towards peace and stability under the umbrella of ASEAN. The international community finds more than a lesson or two to take from the success story of Indonesia.

In this backdrop of a changing world, the growing Asia-Pacific, and rising Indonesia, this book seeks to examine various aspects of Indonesia's success story, outline its changing outlook and roles in the region and the world, and analyse emerging contours of Indonesia's long-term strategy as a rising power. In this vein, the book touches upon evolving complexities of the relationships, power projections and regional and global cooperation. While doing so, this book seeks to offer a balanced perspective by casting light on both domestic drivers and derivatives, and systemic pulls and pressures.

Vibhanshu Shekhar

ABBREVIATIONS

ABMI	Asian Bond Market Initiative
ABRI	Indonesian Armed Forces
ACSC	ASEAN Civil Society Conference
ADB	Asian Development Bank
ADIZ	Air Defence Identification Zone
ADMM+	ASEAN Plus Defence Ministerial Meeting
AEC	ASEAN Economic Community
AMM	ASEAN Ministerial Meeting
ANTAM	Aneka Tambang
APEC	Asia-Pacific Economic Cooperation
APF	ASEAN People's Forum
APSC	ASEAN Political and Security Community
APT	ASEAN Plus Three
ARF	ASEAN Regional Forum
ASCC	ASEAN Social and Cultural Community
ASEAN	Association of Southeast Asian Nations
BAP	Bali Action Plan
BDF	Bali Democracy Forum
BLT	Extended Unconditional Cash Transfer
BRICS	Brazil, Russia, India, China and South Africa
CECA	Comprehensive Economic Cooperation Agreement
CEPEA	Comprehensive Economic Partnership in East Asia
CII	Confederation of Indian Industry
CMI	Chiang Mai Initiative

CMIM	Chiang Mai Initiative Multilateralisation
COP 15	15th Conference of the Parties
CORPAT	Coordinated Patrolling
CSIS	Centre for Strategic and International Studies
CTBT	Comprehensive Test Ban Treaty
DoC	Declaration of the Conduct of the Parties
DPR	People's Representative Council
EAS	East Asia Summit
ESCAP	Economic and Social Council of Asia and the Pacific
EU	European Union
FICCI	Federation of Indian Chambers of Commerce and Industry
FOREX	Foreign Exchange
FPI	Islamic Defenders Front
FTA	Free Trade Agreement
GDP	Gross Domestic Product
GHG	Green House Gas
IBSA	India, Brazil and South Africa
IFCC	Inter-governmental Follow up and Coordination Committee on Economic Cooperation among Developing Countries
IMF	International Monetary Fund
IOR-ARC	Indian Ocean Rim Association for Regional Cooperation
ITEC	Indian Technical and Economic Cooperation
JCM	Joint Commission Meeting
JWG	Joint Working Group
KKN	Corruption, Collusion & Nepotism
KOPASSUS	Indonesian Special Forces
KPK	Corruption Eradication Commission
LNG	Liquified Natural Gas
MDG	Millennium Development Goals
MEF	Minimal Essential Force
MONUC	United Nations Organization Mission in the Democratic Republic of Congo
MONUSCO	United Nations Organization Stabilization Mission in the Democratic Republic of the Congo

MoU	Memorandum of Understanding
MP3EI	Master Plan for the Acceleration and Expansion of Indonesia's Economic Development
MPR	People's Consultative Assembly
NAASP	New Asian-African Strategic Partnership
NALCO	National Aluminium Company
NAM	Non-Aligned Movement
NATO	North Atlantic Treaty Organisation
NEFOs	New Emerging Forces
NTPC	National Thermal Power Corporation
NTS	Non-Traditional Security
OECD	Organisation for Economic Co-operation and Development
OIC	Organisation of Islamic Countries
OLDEFOs	Old Established Forces
ONUC	United Nations Operation in the Congo
PAN	National Mandate Party
PD	Democratic Party
PDI-P	Indonesian Democratic Party-Struggle
PKB	National Awakening Party
PKS	Prosperous Justice Party
PLA	People's Liberation Army
POLRI	Indonesian Police
PPP	United Development Party
PPP	Purchasing Power Parity
RCEP	Regional Comprehensive Economic Partnership
ReCAAP	Regional Cooperation for Combating against Armed Robbery and Piracy
REDD	Reducing Emissions from Deforestation and Forest Degradation in Developing Countries
SAREX	Search and Rescue Operations
SARS	Severe Acute Respiratory Syndrome
SLOCs	Sea Lanes of Communications
TNI	Indonesian National Army
TPP	Trans-Pacific Strategic and Economic Partnership

UN	United Nations
UN-HABITAT	United Nations Habitat
UNAMSIL	United Nations Mission in Sierra Leone
UNCLOS	United Nations Convention on the Law of the Seas
UNEF	United Nations Emergency Force
UNEP	United Nations Environment Programme
UNFCCC	United Nations Framework Convention on Climate Change
UNGA	United Nations General Assembly
UNIKOM	United Nations Iraq–Kuwait Observation Mission
UNIMOG	United Nations Iran-Iraq Military Observer Group
UNMIBH	United Nations Mission in Bosnia and Herzegovina
UNOSOM	United Nations Operation in Somalia
UNPROFOR	United Nations Protection Force
UNSC	United Nations Security Council
UNTAC	United Nations Transitional Authority in Cambodia
UNTAG	United Nations Transition Assistance Group
WTO	World Trade Organisation

INTRODUCTION

Rarely in history does a country undergo such an extreme transformation within a short span of time as Indonesia has experienced during the last fifteen years. The pendulum of Indonesia's future has swung from the threat of imminent disintegration at the end of the 20th century[1] to the prospect of being a pivotal state in the global and regional strategic discourses at the end of the first decade of the 21st century.[2] Indonesia is today the third largest democracy and the largest Muslim democracy in the world, an important player in the continental geopolitics of Asia, and the most significant pillar of ASEAN-driven security and economic architectures. In other words, the country is poised to play an important role in the strategic discourses confronting both the region and the world. Its moderate, democratic and secular credentials entitle the country to an important role in global politics as a potential interlocutor for any inter-civilisational dialogue between the Western and Muslim worlds. In fact, Indonesia's rise is a recipe that is finding a global flavour and taste.

Indonesia's strategic outlook during the 21st century augments new activism in its foreign policy with the twin focus of an active role in global affairs and projection as a pivotal power in regional strategic discourses. While the new outlook necessitates redefining strategic priorities, the changing dynamics of global politics expects greater contribution from the third largest democracy and the fourth most populous country in the world. Indonesia exudes a new-found confidence as a rising power, both in terms of its capacity and ambitions in its search for what its foreign minister, Marty Natalegawa calls a "dynamic equilibrium" in global and regional politics. He argues, "In our consensus DNA, we will position ourselves as a bridge builder by mapping out issues of common interest, and reinforcing, regionally and globally, a strong voice in international affairs."[3] The long-standing *bebasdanaktif* (open and active) foreign policy of Indonesia is undergoing a comprehensive churning, introducing, in the process, new priorities and policies reflective of changing geo-political realities of the Asia-Pacific.

The Rising Power Debate

The debate on rising powers, also referred to as new, major, emerging, or aspiring, is gradually acquiring greater salience and substance as new theoretical formulations emerge. Though the debate is not new, it has intensified during the last fifteen years with the emergence of new rising powers, casting light on four sets of questions – definitional and conceptual aspects, the choices and behaviour of rising powers, the impact on the existing international order, and the elasticity of the existing structure of power to accommodate the interests of these powers.[4] These debates and discussions have not only enriched the research on rising powers, but have also been able to give a definitive shape to this category of rising powers, with distinct roles and choices within the international system.

Any authoritative definition of the term 'rising power' remains elusive, due to conceptual problems associated with the term 'rising,'contestation over what constitutes and qualifies as a rising power, disagreement over their common traits and behaviour, and the changing character of power in the 21st century.[5] While power itself remains a contested concept, the ambiguity that inheres in the term 'rising' adds a considerable degree of confusion to any attempt or debate towards defining the term rising power. There is no agreement beyond a relatively stronger military and economic growth and prosperity about the constituent elements of a rising power. Even though China, India and Indonesia are debated and discussed as rising powers, their outlooks, characteristics, strategic choices and behaviour have been varied. Similarly, international responses and debates over their rise have been viewed and assessed differently. While the rise of China has been viewed as a matter of concern and a source of instability, the rise of India and Indonesia have been seen mainly through their balancing effect on the rise of China and in terms of their positive impact on the international system.

There is a general agreement among scholars that power, both as an idea as well as a tool of analysis, remains a contested and nebulous concept, constantly changing and acquiring new dimensions.[6] While it may be too early to announce and accept the 'end of power,'[7] the concept of power certainly has undergone considerable transformation. Various terms denoting different aspects of power have come in vogue since the end of the World War II, such as military power, material power, ideational power, normative power, hard power, soft power, and smart power.[8] The realist scholars, representing its different sub-schools – classical, structural, neo-classical, or offensive realism – identify whether small, middle, emerging, rising or great power, in terms of material capacities or assets (military and non-military) possessed by any country.[9] John Mearsheimer identifies power as material capacities a state possesses and divides it into two categories – military and latent power.[10] While the notion of military power is self explanatory, latent power refers to 'the socio-economic ingredients that go into building military power; it is largely based on a state's wealth and the overall size of its population.'[11] Paul M. Kennedy attributes the rise and fall of great powers to the 'correlation over the longer term between productive and revenue-raising capacities on the one hand and military strength on the other.'[12]

However, these capabilities should not be examined separately in order to assess the strength of a state; rather a holistic assessment of a state's capabilities should be performed.[13] Kenneth N. Waltz argues,

> The economic, military and other capabilities of nations cannot be sectored and separately weighed. States are not placed in top ranks because they excel in one way or another. Their rank depends on how they score on all of the following items: size of population and territory, resource endowment, economic capability, military strength, political stability and competence. States spend a lot of time estimating one another's capabilities, especially their abilities to do harm. States have different combinations of capabilities which are difficult to measure and compare, the more so since the weight to be assigned to different items change with the time.[14]

The idea of understanding power as the composite value of capabilities has received new impetus from the two-fold debate over the inclusion of non-material capabilities within the domain of power and the willingness of a state to be able to use the capabilities to project power. Non-material capacities are identified in terms of soft power, cultural and civilisational contribution to the world, and overall influence.[15] While writing in 1990, Joseph Nye argued, "The sources of power are, in general, moving away from the emphasis on military force and conquest that marked earlier eras. In assessing international power today, factors, such as technology, education, and economic growth are becoming more important, whereas geography, population, and raw materials are becoming less important."[16] Besides, a state could project its significance in global politics by showcasing its normative, cultural, or civilizational strength. For some, the rise of power is not necessarily only about expressing and advancing the country's strategic interests, but also an articulation of one's identity. In other words, a country could be known and valued by both its material as well as ideational strength, and together they could form the composite power of a country in international politics.

It is understood that power should not be viewed in absolute terms. It is rather relational or relative in nature since its exercise involves the ability of one entity to get things done from another entity that the latter, otherwise, would not want to do. Randall Schweller correlates the rise of a power with the relative increase in the state's political, military and economic power with economic resources acting as 'a preliminary to expansion and war.'[17]

In the backdrop of these debates, a rising power can be loosely understood as *an indeterminate and intermediate category of states between established great powers and middle powers, experiencing sustained rise in its composite capabilities (both material as well as non-material) in relation to its own strength in any time frame in the past, strength of the existing powers in the international system, or in relation to the state's capacity to influence the international debate and agendas of the regional and global politics*. The relative nature of the rise of power can be discerned at any or all of the three levels.[18] It can go on to become a great power or slip down in the hierarchy to the level of regional or middle power. The decline of Soviet Russia is a good example of the transient nature of the status of a power. In other words, the position of a rising power remains temporary and uncertain.

Moreover, there can be more than one rising power at any given time in global politics with different levels of capacities and willingness to influence the international system. Paul Kennedy refers to eight great powers during the period of the late 19th and early 20th century (Britain, the US, Germany, France, Russia, Italy, Japan and Austria-Hungary) and underscores the huge gap between the strongest and weakest great powers.[19] Kenneth Waltz identified eight major states, which sought to 'coexist peacefully or contended for mastery' during the period of more than 300 years from the Treaty of Westphalia until the 1970s.[20] Mearsheimer refers to four powers before World War II – the UK, Germany, the US and Russia – and three great powers in Asia in the 21st century – China, Japan and India.[21] Randall

Schweller asserts that there can be more than two rising powers at a time, but the intensity of impact on the international system or on existing power may vary depending on extent of power and influence vis-à-vis the existing great power.[22] For example, the United States, as an established power, may feel more threatened with the rise of China than with the rise of Brazil, India or Indonesia.

One of the commonly accepted methodologies for identifying a rising power is following international recognition about the status, role and influence of a particular power in global politics. International recognition can occur in several ways. It can happen in the form of an acknowledgement of a rising power by the leadership or government of an established great power or several other major powers. This acknowledgement may relate to growing military and economic capabilities of a state, its leadership role in regional relations, and its substantive contribution to global politics. The US proposal of the G-2 as a dialogue framework with China in 2009 and in 2013 can be seen as an accommodative offer from the established great power to the preeminent rising power. In fact, the international community may demand an active role of a rising power in shaping the international debates on key global challenges. A state's place of prominence in the key international decision-making agencies may also attest to its rising power status. For example, permanent membership on the United Nations Security Council, membership in the G-20 or greater voting rights in the International Monetary Fund can be indicators of the prominent status of a power and its global prominence and system-influencing capacity. These forms of recognition can also act as indicators for identifying the extent and intensity of the influence a rising power can exercise on the global structure of power.

Having highlighted the complexities in defining the term rising power, the second puzzle placed before us is about the choices and behaviours of a rising power, its short-term and long-term strategic goals, the implications of its rise for the existing international structure of power, and the evolving dynamics of relations between the international system and the rising powers. What do these rising powers seek to achieve and why do they choose what they choose? What kind of ways and means do these rising powers select to secure their strategic interests and long-term objectives? In sum, the global debate on rising powers has focused on (a) their choices and behaviours, (b) drivers shaping their strategic choices and behaviours, (c) emerging dynamics of relations between the rising powers and the international system, and (d) responses of established powers to the rise of other powers.

One can discern two perspectives, overlapping and sometimes mutually reinforcing, from the rising power debates: (a) the global debate on the rising powers from the viewpoint of their impact on the international system and the latter's responses to the rise; and (b) the debate within the rising country regarding its strategic choices and behaviours, both at the short- and long-term levels, and how best to benefit from the existing global order. The contents and contexts of the two debates often overlap, with one set of discourses influencing the other. To put it in the specific context of rising powers of Asia, it is not just the international community that is debating the rise of China, India and Indonesia and its implications for the system; their own strategic communities are also debating how to best project their rise, advance their strategic interests, and benefit from the prevailing international order. While the first set of debates has taken place globally, the second set of debates is occurring mainly domestically.

In contrast to the intensity of the international debate, which has depended on the level of impact a particular rising power has been able to make on the international system, the intensity of the domestic debate has depended on the capacity and growth of intellectual discourse within the country. Viewed from this perspective, the global debate highlights the growing influence of a particular rising power and its global recognition, while the level of robustness of the domestic discourse represents the regional and global aspirations of a rising power. For example, though China, India and also Indonesia have been characterised as rising powers, the level of intensity and the robustness of both the global and domestic debate in and upon these three powers have varied, with China drawing the maximum attention and Indonesia just beginning to draw global attention.

Theoretical formulations as a part of the global debate have followed two broad trajectories of the International Relations discipline: first, a systemic-level view with global structural factors shaping the rising powers' relations and positions within the existing international structure of power, and second, a state-centric view with domestic drivers – ideas, culture, identity, interests – shaping a particular power's relations with the international world. The first approach involves primarily two schools – realism and liberalism. While the majority of the realist scholars stress the inevitability of conflict between the established power and the challenger, the liberal school highlights the accommodative and integrative capacities of the liberal order.[23] In fact, the debate has occurred along two poles of argumentation – utter destruction emanating from the inevitability of an ascendant power challenging the established power versus the robustness of an international order strengthened by both the existing and rising powers at the same time.

Some of the realist scholars view rising powers as 'dissatisfied powers' seeking to acquire more power and resources and thereby inevitably bringing them into conflict with the existing great powers.[24] These arguments have come primarily from two key realist perspectives – the power-transition school and offensive realism – while locating the whole debate in the context of the rise of China and its impact on the existing international structure of power. It has been argued that the rise of China has been entwined with a sense of fear and an uncertainty as to whether it is a peaceful or conflict-prone process.[25] Ronald Tammen and Jacek Kugler predict Sino-US conflict in the future, using the power-transition theory.[26] The theory postulates that "wars occur at the global level when a dissatisfied challenger sees an opportunity to take on the pre-eminent international leader."[27] Mearsheimer argues that 'great powers tend to have aggressive intentions and they aim to maximise their share of world power.'[28] Such a situation is destabilising and leads to an inevitable confrontation between the established and ascendant powers. Mearsheimer contends that 'the US and China are likely to engage in an intense security competition with considerable potential for war.'[29] Robert Gilpin's idea of hegemonic war falls into a similar pessimistic picture about the rising powers and power transition in world politics.[30]

These pessimistic views have invited more optimistic reactions from their rival school of liberalism that emphasises the integrative capacities of the international liberal order and equally powerful desires of the rising powers to be an important part of the international order. Such scholars contend that the rise of a power does not necessarily mean a violent transition, and not all power transitions have led to war.[31] There are historical precedents where power transition has occurred peacefully. For example, Britain ceded the mantle of global leadership peacefully to the US, and the rise of Japan did not pose a challenge to American supremacy.[32] To quote John Ikenberry, "the global hierarchy today is different than global hierarchies of the past – it is harder to overturn and easier to join."[33] Also, the rising powers are not necessarily pursuing a 'balancing strategy,' but rather 'a strategy of integration into the Western liberal order.'[34] It is argued that these rising powers are not trying to threaten the existing order for change it, if necessary by force, to serve their interests. They want to reform, instead of change, the system since they are underrepresented, and this decision is situational rather than inevitable.[35] The world has seen the tendencies, on the part of both the established as well as rising powers, to accommodate the interests of each other. The rationale for accommodation, according to this approach, lies in the power and logic of interdependence.

The above-mentioned perspectives have examined rising powers primarily from systemic perspectives, where attributes of the international system and the dynamic of relations with the system shapes the behaviour of a rising power. Jeffrey Legro, however, finds them to be linear projections unable to fully explain why and when a rising power behaves the way it does.[36] Instead of power transition, he locates the rising power behaviour in the context of purpose transition and emphasises the role of ideas and domestic variables instead of systemic factors in shaping the choices and behaviour of a rising power.[37] Putting the debate in the specific context of China, Legro argues that the behaviour of China will ultimately be determined by national ideas prevalent within China about how to achieve foreign policy goals. These ideas, according to him, "empower certain domestic interest groups over others, generate expectations against which the performance is assessed, and either facilitate or impede the possibility for a new strategy to emerge."[38]

Also, mere possession of power does not designate a state as a great power. Even though capacities are known to considerably influence foreign policy behaviour, a particular power, driven by its own ambitions and constraints, might choose a different role.To quote Paul Kennedy, "an economic giant could prefer, for reasons of its political culture or geographical security, to be a military pigmy, while a state without great economic resources could nonetheless organise its society as to be a formidable military power."[39] Both Germany and Japan have, notwithstanding their capabilities, made the choice not to strengthen their respective militaries and pursued a somewhat different culture of national security.[40] In other words, a state must have the willingness or aspirations to mobilise its capabilities to advance its strategic interests and project its role as a system-shaping actor.

It is in these contexts that domestic variables have begun to factor prominently in the debate over drivers shaping the choices and behaviour of rising powers. In fact, several writings have looked at the choices and behaviours of rising powers from an inside-out perspective, with a focus on domestic drivers and priorities of rising powers.[41] For them, domestic variables, such as ideas, culture, identity, ideologies, interest groups, and the political elite play a critical role in shaping the choices and behaviours of the rising powers.[42] Moreover, these choices are construed as projections of their identity that they seek to present to the international community.[43] These projections can often be a reflection of prevailing worldviews within the domestic realm of a rising power. These world-views, referred to by Henry Nau as 'foreign policy schools of thought,' are essentially 'conceptual frameworks for thinking about the world,' differing 'in terms of the scope, goals, and means of foreign policy – whether a country aspires to be a global or local actor, seeks ideological or material goals, or prefers hard or soft power to achieve these goals.'[44]

The above-mentioned analysis offers us three key reference points – the composite capabilities of a state, international recognition, and a state's ambitions and actual behaviour – to analyse the outlook and characteristics of a rising power. In light of these reference points and discussions over the choices and behaviours of a rising power, the following traits can be put forth to identify a rising power. A rising power:

- must have adequate material and non-material resources to support its regional and global roles;
- directly influences regional politics;
- projects indirectly its normative power or non-hegemonistic characteristics onto global politics;
- maintains a relatively stronger military and is engaged in internal balancing;
- seeks to maximise its interests by suitably modifying the international structures of representation; and
- is guided by the power of national ambitions and absorptive capacities and structures of the international system.

Even though a rising power may not have the same capacity to shape the global system as the existing great powers, it interacts with the global system in a particular fashion, and in the process, influences decisions affecting the global system. Given their limited capability to directly influence global politics, rising powers tend to more aggressively deploy their normative power or non-hegemonic characteristics to project their global image. This can be said to be true of Indonesia.

Debating Indonesia's Rise

One of the most significant changes characterising the geopolitical reality of the Asia-Pacific during the first decade of the twenty-first century was the emergence of Indonesia as a rising power. Various scholars have used different expressions – 'Asia's third Giant,' 'a rising power,' 'a global swing state,' 'one of Asia's leading powers,' 'a regional pivot,' and probably 'the world's first Muslim and democratic superpower' to highlight the country's new-found status in regional and global politics.[45] These articulations of Indonesia's new-found status have focused on the considerable growth in Indonesia's composite capabilities, its ambitions to play a greater role in global politics and growing international recognition for its new roles.

The current debate on Indonesia's rise has two distinct but mutually reinforcing angles – systemic and domestic. The systemic-level debate has concerned itself with the implications of the rise for the international system and Indonesia's contribution to the strengthening of the international system. Unlike the case of China, there is hardly any writing on Indonesia's rise that raises concerns for the safety, longevity or stability of the global order. In fact, the entire debate has focused on how best to utilise the positive momentum generated by the rise of democratic Indonesia. Recent US-based writings have identified rising Indonesia as one of the most significant opportunities for US foreign policy, and a critical partner in strengthening the liberal international order.[46] Democratic Indonesia, along with other 'global swing states' (Brazil, India and Turkey), 'possesses the capability and the legitimacy to bolster the interlocking web of norms, institutions, rules, and relationships that has for six decades preserved peace among the great powers, fostered economic prosperity, and facilitated the spread of freedom.'[47] At the height of the Arab Spring in 2011, rising Indonesia was viewed as a model democracy for the Middle East to emulate.[48] Reinforcing these two assumptions, Ted Piccone has argued that 'Indonesia's democratic progress and Muslim identity have important implications for broadening the legitimacy of global democracy and human rights order.'[49] President Obama, during his visit to Indonesia in November 2010, called upon Indonesia to play a much more active role in global politics. Furthermore, almost every important global player and every nation-state in the Asia-Pacific is cajoling Indonesian leadership to take a pro-active role. Indonesia, as a member of the G-20, is sitting at the high table deliberating the political and economic future of the world.

At the same time, the rise of global swing states like Indonesia has prompted a subtle shift in the international debate towards how best to accommodate and represent the interests of these rising powers in the global order, especially in international multilateral institutions, such as the United

Nations, World Bank, International Monetary Fund, World Trade Organisation, and so on. Active participation of these powers in the G-20 deliberations over arresting the negative fallout of the global economic crisis reflects complementary and reinforcing equations between the democratisation of the international order and greater contribution from these rising powers. Moreover, the successful conclusion of the WTO negotiations at the Bali Summit in December 2013 attests to Jakarta's active diplomatic role in making the global order work and maintaining its relevance amidst changing characters and players of global politics. It is argued that Indonesia with its capability and legitimacy, represents promising opportunities in the US effort to defend and strengthen the international order.[50]

These systemic-level debates have received vital reinforcements from the domestic-level debates taking place in Indonesia. The domestic debate has focused, in addition to the above-mentioned issues, on Indonesia's rightful place in the international system, the projection of its power and the expression of its long-term foreign policy goals. There is a growing realisation among Indonesian policy makers that Indonesia as a confident, democratic and powerful Asia-Pacific player needs to go beyond the confines of traditional wisdoms of foreign policy if it wishes to best capitalise on one of the momentous politico-strategic global shifts taking place in its close geographical proximity. Since this book has highlighted different aspects of the domestic debates regarding rising Indonesia's global and regional roles in various chapters, only a snippet of these debates is presented below in the form of identifying emerging contours of Indonesia's strategic worldview and its strategy of deployment of smart power to advance Jakarta's global prominence.

Emerging Contours of Indonesia's Strategic Worldview

As Indonesia responds to these developments, it has begun to lay down rules of Jakarta's long-term strategic engagement in the Asia-Pacific and the world. These components can be identified as the evolving strategic outlook of a rising power. Indonesia's articulation of its long-term strategy in the Asia-Pacific is an outcome of a combination of three developments: (a) the growing significance of the Asia-Pacific in global politics, (b) a fundamental shift taking place in Asia-Pacific geopolitics, and (c) the emergence of Indonesia as an important regional pivot and global player.

Jakarta's new-found confidence is also manifested in the willingness of its leaders to conceptualise distinct roles for the country in the 21st century – fuelling new ideas and principles of foreign policy, generating an atmosphere of doctrinal discourse, and enriching and strengthening both the content and context of Indonesia's strategic world-view. Indonesian leaders have been known for their penchant for new doctrines and catch-phrases to define Indonesia's strategic priorities and foreign policies – Sukarno's Old Established Forces (OLDEFOs) versus New Emerging Forces (NEFOs), Hatta's *Bebas Dan Aktif*, Suharto's advocacy of regional resilience and *Musyawarah* and *Mufakat*, SBY's 'Million Friends Zero Enemies', and Marty Natalegawa's 'Dynamic Equilibrium.' Such an approach can be traced back to the Javanese tradition of leaders exhibiting their words of wisdom. Indonesia's Foreign Minister, R M Marty Natalegawa, while assuming the charge of ASEAN chair, suggested the vision of developing "Dynamic Equilibrium" in the regional and global strategic landscape. These debates and discussions have brought forth several important components of Indonesia's strategic choices and dilemmas as a rising power.

First, rising Indonesia's dilemmas are not about how to change the international system (Jakarta has actually been a beneficiary of the liberal international order), but rather about how to best position itself in the fast-changing international order and leverage the evolving great power politics for both the short-term as well as long-term strategic interests at the regional and global level. In this capacity as an important regional and global player, Jakarta has called for reforms in the existing international order and the global representative bodies. The doctrine of 'dynamic equilibrium' is essentially an expression of a rising power with the objectives of (a) playing a greater role in the regional and global strategic discourses, (b) negotiating parity in its strategic engagement with important global players, and (c) acting as an interlocutor and mediator in the issues of both intra-regional and international challenges.

Second, there is a growing realisation that 21st century global politics and the geopolitics of the Asia-Pacific are going to be fundamentally different from that of the 20th century. Marty Natalegawa, the Indonesian Foreign Minister, while discussing the emerging contours of global politics, characterised it as one marked by the Cold Peace, instead of Cold War. The contours are already emerging. Two distinct characteristics are the rise of Asian powers and the Global South. Today's global politics is being influenced considerably by the resurgence of the Global South, with developing countries of Asia, Africa and Latin America registering a wave of growth and prominence. Their rise has opened up new avenues for dialogue and cooperation, not only within the developing world, but also between the East and West and the North and South, with the objective of balanced global growth and development. This is also evident from the growing significance of the G-20 in lieu of the G-8 as the premier platform for deliberation over global issues. Indonesia has sought to utilise its elevated position as a member of G-20 to not only strengthen the solidarity of the sub-alterns, but also push for the greater acceptability of its global role within the family of Global South. The current leadership of Indonesia has consistently pushed forth this aspect of Indonesia's global projection.

Third, understanding and addressing the changing characters of regional geopolitics lies at the heart of rising Indonesia's regional diplomacy. The more fundamental question facing Indonesian regional diplomacy is now a rising power like Indonesia should assert its own strategic ambitions, pursue its economic interests, and create conditions for peace and stability in the region. The Asia-Pacific reign not only brings opportunities of cooperation and prosperity, but also poses challenges to regional peace and stability. The geo-political realities of the Asia-Pacific have undergone fundamental transformation, epitomised by the rise of new power centres – China, India, Indonesia and Japan – in close geographical proximity, its emergence as an important axis of global political and economic discourses, its growing vulnerability as a hotbed of major power rivalries, and the consequent undermining of the ASEAN-led regional cooperative processes. While Asia is witnessing the rise of new powers in close proximity, the ASEAN institutions appear to be the lone rangers working towards maintaining regional peace and stability. The limitations of the ASEAN-driven regional security architecture, whose conception and agenda lies in managing the big-power relations in East Asia, forecasts a volatile Asia where major powers are left to themselves to manage their affairs. Major powers and players are engaged in strategic manoeuvrings to ensure that the emerging regional architecture maximizes its interests and facilitates its growing ambitions. As the regional politics of the Asia-Pacific is drifting towards uncertainty, instability, and multipolarity, Indonesian leadership has come to believe that its best interest lies in a multipolar power structure that places Indonesia in a position of prominence in regional geopolitics and gives much greater room for balancing between different regional powers and players. Moreover, it offers an important opportunity to continue its leadership role within

Southeast Asia that is gradually witnessing great power jostling for strategic influence. In the new matrix of power relations that is beckoning the Asia-Pacific, Indonesia finds itself holding important aces while the Great Game unfolds in the region.

Fourth, Indonesia, while deliberating the prevailing strategic scenario in Southeast Asia, has focused on four important issues – time-bound realisation of the ASEAN community, the issue of the South China Sea, Myanmar, and the smooth development of the ASEAN regional architecture. Indonesia, as an important leader in ASEAN-driven multilateralism, the most powerful ASEAN member, and an important Asian player, faces the dilemma between providing leadership to the ASEAN process and convincing the Asian biggies to work together at the ASEAN table, as well as engaging Asian and global players independently as a regional power. Indonesia has long emphasised (a) the centrality of ASEAN in the East Asian Community-building processes, (b) the involvement of all major Asian players in the ASEAN cooperative processes, and (c) effective ASEAN deliberation over key challenges facing the continent. ASEAN remains the most important regional platform for Indonesia's regional foreign policy articulation.

Fifth, non-traditional sources of security challenges have weighed heavily in the domestic debates of the Indonesian strategic community. The issues of terrorism, maritime security and climate change remain key security concerns for the country.

Finally, Indonesia's rise has, once again, stirred up a substantial debate within the country about what constitutes Indonesia's strategic culture that shapes the country's foreign policy behaviour. Broad contours are emerging out of the debates and discussions among the national elite and strategic community, as they are getting more and more engaged in the churning of the historical-cultural traditions and normative foundations of Indonesia's strategic engagement with the outside world. Though these values and beliefs have long existed, the national elite and strategic community of Indonesia have begun debating these values and beliefs shaping their foreign policy choices. These elements of strategic culture address critical issues of the role and vision of the leadership, its long-term strategy in regional and global politics, its national and international identity, and the country's national security, threat perceptions, responses to those threats, strategic doctrine, and long-term foreign policy goals. The pursuit of strategic autonomy in the form of *Bebasdan Aktif* foreign policy, the projection of the country as the largest and moderate Muslim democracy in the world, and the country's somewhat intrinsic character of underbalancing while assessing its national security and threat perceptions, emerged as important reference points in the debate on Jakarta's strategic culture.

Deploying 'Smart Power' or Using Power Smartly?

Some argue that mere possession of hard or soft power does not guarantee a corresponding level of influence in international politics. What plays a critical role in defining the power of a state is its ability to optimally utilise its material and non-material capabilities in strengthening and justifying its foreign policy behaviour. This brings us to what is referred to by Joseph Nye Jr. as 'smart power.'[51] He points out, "A smart power narrative for the twenty-first century is not about maximising power or preserving hegemony. It is about finding ways to combine resources into successful strategies in the new context of power diffusion and the rise of the rest."[52] Though he is discussing the strategy of the United States, he refers to the small power diplomacy of Singapore as the best example of the usage of smart power.[53]

The foreign policy behaviour of rising Indonesia represents a somewhat 'smarter' projection of its hard material and soft non-material power. While speaking at Harvard University, President Yudhoyono characterised the 21st century as 'the century of soft power' and laid out nine imperatives to create a new world through such soft power. For the first time, after the departure of Sukarno, Jakarta has begun exhibiting activism in global political deliberations, as manifested in the willingness of its leaders to conceptualise distinct regional and global roles for the country in the 21st century. Democratic Indonesia's long-term foreign policy priorities represent a sustained effort to create a desired outcome by highlighting its practical importance and positioning its normative stance in tune with the changing realities of the global order. Remarkably, Indonesia is not deploying its military resources in its projection as a rising power. In fact, Indonesia's under-fed and under-developed military profile remains conspicuous, with its absence from Indonesia's success story as a rising power. Indonesia has tried to project its benign aspirations and has somewhat neglected the second requirement for the rise of a power. As a result, while Indonesia may find a platform in the international fora for its role and normative expressions, it may not find corresponding prominence in terms of hard-core military and strategic calculations at the regional and global level. Nonetheless, Indonesian leadership, both in terms of the nature of the assertion of its power and the process of conversion of its capability into influence or global attention, has been projecting smartly the growth in its economic power and the normative capital emanating from its democratic outlook.

Conceptual Framework of the Book

Any discussion about Indonesia's rise highlights perhaps the most pertinent question – what has caused and triggered Indonesia's rise? Is Indonesia's rise an outcome of the changing realities of global and regional politics in the 21st century? Is the rise merely a reflection of what is argued as 'the rise of the rest' where the rise of the Asian century and its constituent units is nothing but a part of the larger global continuum and therefore a product of larger global processes, which have occurred since the end of the Cold War? Is Indonesia's rise an outcome of the growth in the capabilities as well as ambitions of the political leadership of democratic Indonesia? In other words, is Indonesia's rise simply a reflection of the larger global trend and a product of systemic developments, or is it rooted in its unique domestic transformation and the changing geo-political realities of the region? Answers to these questions entail a deeper probe into the evolving linkages between domestic transformation within Indonesia, changing geo-political realities of the Asia-Pacific region, and larger systemic processes at play.

This book identifies power as the central instrument of analysis contextualising Indonesia's rise within two variables of changing global and regional structures of power and the relative growth in Indonesia's capabilities and ambitions. A particular state might act differently under the influence of (a) structural-systemic constraints imposed by the prevailing regional and global structure of power, or (b) composite capabilities and national ambitions shaped by elite-consensus and its strategic culture. While the systemic factors reflect the prevailing regional and global structure of power and the specific position of a particular player in the given structure of power, domestic factors exist in the form of the country's capabilities, civilisational world-view, political culture, the ruling elite, ideology, and other sets of societal-political norms. The foreign policy of rising Indonesia in the 21st century is the making of both of these processes. In other words, Indonesia's rise is a reflection of both what the country represents and offers and the growing global and regional demand and space for such commodities. With these two variables as important drivers of Indonesia's strategic behaviour in the Asia-Pacific, this research draws from theoretical insights of neo-classical realism and critical geopolitics.

There is a near consensus among the experts on Indonesia that domestic politics has always influenced Indonesian foreign policy as expressed through its historical politico-strategic beliefs, values and norms. President Yudhoyono's call for a set of codified laws at the international level to prevent insult to religious beliefs and blasphemous practices was essentially an attempt to capitalise on the cultural sensitivity of domestic constituencies. The role of domestic catalysts can be seen at two levels – relative growth in the composite capabilities of the state, and the growing expressions of its ambition to play a greater role in global and regional politics. Jakarta is gradually coming out of a cumulative domestic crisis, consolidating its democratic foundations and continuing its upward economic trajectory in a time of global crisis and subsequent recovery. With a FOREX reserve of more than US$100 billion, sustained annual GDP growth of the more than 6 per cent, a fast-growing middle class, its status as the fourth largest democracy of the world and the largest Muslim democracy, a stable political order, a nuanced and well-trained diplomatic apparatus, and a successful leadership, Indonesia is presenting itself and seen globally as an important power during the first decade of the 21st century.

This book makes following arguments:

- Indonesia's rise is an outcome of (a) an altered global and regional structure of power, and (b) domestic consolidation and expression of its growing ambitions.
- Indonesia as a rising power reflects new confidence and ambition to project its pivotal role in the new-emerging geopolitics of the Asia-Pacific in the 21st century.
- Rising Indonesia's regional diplomacy has followed two-fold strategies of leveraging power politics and accelerating the regional integrative processes to secure its strategic interests consolidating.
- As Jakarta projects its normative capital, promises to be a critical reinforcing factor in the global order, and actively participates as a responsible citizen in global debates, it claims greater space in global politics that its leaders think rightfully belongs to their country.
- As India and Indonesia engage each other as rising powers, they are identifying a common global agenda, giving shape to a common 'Delhi-Jakarta Paradigm' over larger normative and practical issues facing both the global and regional orders.
- Rising Indonesia's success story faces formidable internal challenges in the form of growing Sunni majoritarianism, the culture of

underbalancing, compulsions of coalition politics and the challenge of corruption.

This book is divided into seven chapters. The first chapter discusses important drivers of Indonesia's rise. These drivers relate to fundamental changes taking place in domestic, regional and global settings, facilitating Indonesia's pivotal positioning in the world in the aftermath of its worst politico-economic crises and democratic transition. While the second chapter discusses Indonesia's changing regional strategic environment in which it finds itself boxed in, the third chapter deals with rising Indonesia's responses to regional challenges. These two chapters analyse (a) evolving politico-strategic trends in the Asia-Pacific, (b) rising Indonesia's regional diplomacy, and (c) Indonesia's own turf – Southeast Asia and ASEAN. Moreover, the chapter attempts to document how a rising Indonesia is articulating its new strategic priorities and what that means for Asia-Pacific geopolitics, great power relations in the region, and regional peace and stability. The fourth chapter discusses different aspects of Indonesia's global diplomacy. Moreover, it also spells out basic tools of diplomacy that rising Indonesia has deployed while seeking its place of prominence in the changing global order. The fifth Chapter outlines various dimensions of growing strategic engagement between the two rising powers – India and Indonesia. This chapter also explores the question of what their cooperation means for the regional strategic atmosphere and in what ways they can contribute to global politics. Indonesia's success story is far from complete and carries trends towards disappointment. In this context, the sixth chapter discusses key challenges facing the country that can derail Indonesia's success story. Finally, the seventh chapter locates the discussion of Indonesia's rise and its strategic behaviour in the 21st century in light of the country's own evolving strategic culture. It also throws light on current debates taking place within the country regarding its strategic doctrine, threat-perceptions, the changing perception of Indonesia towards its regional boundary and its identity, and its long-term strategic priorities.

ENDNOTES

1. John R. Bolton, "Indonesia: Asia's Yugoslavia," *Far Eastern Economic Review,* vol. 162, no. 13 (1 April 1999), pp. 31; David Rohde, "Indonesia Unravelling," *Foreign Affairs,* vol. 80 (2001), pp. 110-124; Jusuf Wanandi, "Indonesia: A Failed State?" *The Washington Quarterly,* vol. 25, no. 3 (Summer 2002), pp. 135-146; David Armstrong, "The Next Yugoslavia? The Fragmentation of Indonesia," *Diplomacy & Statecraft,* vol. 15, no. 4 (2004), pp. 783-808.
2. Daniel M. Kliman, "Global Swing States and U.S. Strategy," *GMF Policy Brief,* August

2013, http://www.gmfus.org/wp-content/blogs.dir/1/files_mf/1377879312Kliman_GSSandUSStrategy_Aug13.pdf (accessed on 22 December 2013); Anthony Reid (ed.), *Indonesia Rising: The Repositioning of Asia's Third Giant* (Singapore, ISEAS, 2012); Santo Darmosumarto, "Indonesia: A New 'Middle Power'," *The Jakarta Post,* 30 October 2009; Jessica Brown, "Jakarta's Juggling Act: Balancing China and America in the Asia-Pacific, *CIS Foreign Policy Analysis,* no. 5, 3 February 2011,http://www.cis.org.au/publications/foreign-policy-analysis/article/2342-jakartas-juggling-act-balancing-china-and-america-in-the-asia-pacific (accessed on 18 May 2013).

3. "Indonesia Wants Regional Bloc to be 'Strong Voice'," *Bangkok Post,* 17 December 2010 http://www.burmanet.org/news/2010/12/17/bangkok-post-indonesia-wants-regional-bloc-to-be-strong-voice/ (accessed on 18 May 2013).
4. Andrew F. Hart and Bruce D. Jones, "How do Rising Powers Rise?" *Survival,* 52, no. 6 (2010): 63-88; Randall L. Schweller, "Managing the Rise of Great Powers: History and Theory," in Alastair Iain Johnston and Robert S. Ross, *Engaging China: The Management of an Emerging Power* (New York: Routledge, 1999), pp. 1-31; John J. Mearsheimer, The Tragedy of Great Power Politics (New York: W.W. Norton, 2001); Henry R. Nau and Deepa M. Ollapally (eds.), *Worldviews of Aspiring Powers: Domestic Foreign Policy Debates in China, India, Iran, Japan, and Russia* (Kindle Edition) (Kindle Locations 4-6: Oxford University Press, 2012); Andrew Hurrell, "Hegemony, Liberalism and Global Order: What Space for Would-be Great Powers?," *International Affairs,* vol. 82, no. 1 (January 2006), pp. 1-19; Hanns W. Maull, "The Rise of New Powers: Implications for the Transatlantic World," in Daniel S. Hamilton and Kurt Volker, *Transatlantic 2020: A Tale of Four Futures* (Washington, DC: Center for Transatlantic Relations, 2011), pp. 71-92; Pinar Tank, "The concept of "rising powers"," *NOREF Policy Brief,* June 2012, http://www.peacebuilding.no/var/ezflow_site/storage/original/application/aa7c23bf5887ab060f1af737a39a000a.pdf (accessed on 02 November 2013).
5. Andrew F. Hart and Bruce D. Jones, op.cit.
6. Charles V. Kegley Jr. and Eugene R. Wittkopf, *World Politics: Trend and Transformation* (New York: Worth Publishers, 1999), pp. 383-88; Joseph S. Nye, Jr., *The Future of Power* (New York, Public Affairs, 2011, pp. 3-24.
7. Moises Naim, *The End of Power: From Boardrooms to Battlefields and Churches to States, Why Being In Charge Isn't What It Used to Be* (Philadelphia: Basic Books, 2013).
8. Joseph S. Nye, Jr., op.cit., pp. 3-24.
9. Kenneth N. Waltz, "Theory of International Politics (Massachusetts: Addison Wesley, 1979), p. 131; John J. Mearsheimer, op.cit.; Randall L. Schweller, op.cit., p. 2.
10. John J. Mearsheimer, ibid, p. 55.
11. Ibid.
12. Paul Kennedy, *Rise and Fall of Great Powers* (London: Unwin Hyman, 1988), p. xvi.
13. Kenneth N. Waltz, op.cit.,
14. op.cit., p. 131.
15. Joseph S. Nye, Jr., op.cit., pp. 3-24.
16. Ibid, p. 208.
17. Randall L. Schweller, op.cit., p. 2.
18. Albert Iain Johnston and Randall Schweller quoted in Joshua Itzkowitz-Shifrinson, "Assessing China's Rise: Power and Influence in the 21st Century" *Massachusetts Institute of Technology Workshop Report,* 27-28 February, 2009, http://web.mit.edu/ssp/publications/conf_reports/china_rising_workshop_report.pdf (accessed on 10 October 2013).
19. Paul Kennedy, op.cit., p. xvi.

20. Kenneth N. Waltz, op.cit., p. 131.
21. John J. Mearsheimer, op.cit.
22. Randall L. Schweller, op.cit., p. 2.
23. A brief description of these debates can be seen in M. Taylor Fravel, "International Relations Theory and China's Rise: Assessing China's Potential for Territorial Expansion," *International Studies Review*, vol. 12, no. 4 (December 2010), pp. 505–510.
24. John J. Mearsheimer, op.cit.; Ronald L. Tammen, and Jacek Kugler, "Power transition and China-US conflicts," *Chinese Journal of International Politics*, vol. 1, no. 1, 2006, pp. 35–55.
25. Thomas J. Christensen, "Fostering stability or creating a monster? The rise of China and U.S. policy toward East Asia" *International Security*, vol. 31, no. 1 (Summer 2006), pp. 81–126.
26. Ronald L. Tammen, and Jacek Kugler, op.cit., pp. 35–55.
27. Ibid, p. 39.
28. John J. Mearsheimer, op.cit., p. 168.
29. John J. Mearsheimer, "The rise of China will not be peaceful at all," *The Australian*, 18 November 2005.
30. Robert Gilpin, *War and Change in World Politics* (New York: Cambridge University Press, 1981), pp. 186-210.
31. G. John Ikenberry, "The Rise of China and the Future of the West: Can the Liberal System Survive?," *Foreign Affairs,* vol. 87, no. 1 (January-February 2008), http://www.foreignaffairs.com/articles/63042/g-john-ikenberry/the-rise-of-china-and-the-future-of-the-west (accessed on 14 November 2013).
32. Ibid.
33. G. John Ikenberry, "The Rise of China: Power, Institutions and the Western Order," in Robert S. Ross, Feng Zhu (eds.), *China's Ascent: Power, Security, and the Future of International Politics* (Ithaca: Cornell University Press), p. 90.
34. Quddus Z. Snyder, "Rising Powers and International Politics: A liberal systemic perspective," *APSA 2010 Annual Meeting Paper*, 2010, http://papers.ssrn.com/sol3/papers.cfm?abstract_id=1643369 (accessed on 14 November 2013).
35. Ibid.
36. Jeffrey W. Legro, "What China will Want: The Future Intentions of a Rising Power," *Perspectives on Politics,* vol. 5, no. 3, September 2007, p. 505.
37. Ibid.
38. Ibid.
39. Paul Kennedy, op.cit., p. xvi.
40. Peter J. Katzenstein (ed.) *The Culture of National Security: Norms and Identity in World Politics* (New York: Columbia University Press, 1996).
41. Jeffrey W. Legro, *Rethinking the World:Great Power Strategies and International Order* (Ithaca, NY: Cornell University Press, 2005); Henry R. Nau and Deepa M. Ollapally (eds.), *Worldviews of Aspiring Powers: Domestic Foreign Policy Debates in China, India, Iran, Japan, and Russia* (Kindle Edition) (Kindle Locations 4-6: Oxford University Press, 2012).
42. Jeffrey W. Legro, Rethinking the World: op.cit.; Henry R. Nau and Deepa M. Ollapally, op.cit.
43. Henry R. Nau and Deepa M. Ollapally, ibid.
44. Henry R. Nau, "Introduction Domestic Voices of Aspiring Powers," in Henry R. Nau and Deepa M. Ollapally (eds.), op.cit.

45. Richard Fontaine and Daniel M. Kliman, "International Order and Global Swing States," *The Washington Quarterly*, vol. 36, no. 1 (Winter 2013), pp. 93-109; Daniel M. Kliman, "Global Swing States and U.S. Strategy," op.cit.; Anthony Reid, op.cit.; Dewi Fortuna Anwar, "A Problem of Mixed Messages," *The Asialink Essays 2012,* vol. 4, no. 6 (August 2012), p. 2; Anindya Novyan Bakrie, "US Pivot to the Region has Changed the Game," *The Jakarta Globe,* 03 January 2012, http://www.thejakartaglobe.com/columnists/us-pivot-to-the-region-has-changed-the-game/488796 (accessed on 18 September 2012); Lie Nathanael Santoso, "Defining Indonesia's Need for a Grand Strategy," *The Jakarta Post,* 19 August 2011; Ted Piccone, "Global Swing States and the Human Rights and Democracy Order," *GMF Global Swing States Working Paper*, November 2012, http://www.brookings.edu/~/media/research/files/papers/2012/11/27%20global%20 swing%20 states%20piccone/27%20global%20swing%20states%20piccone.pdf (accessed on 22 December 2013); Joshua Keating, "The Stories you Missed in 2010," *Foreign Policy Special Report*, 28 November 2010, http://www.foreignpolicy.com/articles/2010/11/29/the_stories_you_missed_in_2010?page=0,0#sthash.hzXnJn9J.dpbs (accessed on 22 December 2013).
46. Richard Fontaine and Daniel M. Kliman, ibid; Daniel M. Kliman, ibid; Ted Osius, "Global Swing States: Deepening Partnerships with India and Indonesia," *Asia Policy*, no. 17 (January 2014), http://www.nbr.org/publications/asia_policy/AP17/Advance/AP17_SwingStates_110413.pdf (accessed on 22 December 2013).
47. Ibid, p. 93.
48. Joshua Kurlantzick, "Is Egypt the Next Indonesia?," *Council on Foreign Relations*, 07 February 2011, http://blogs.cfr.org/asia/2011/02/07/is-egypt-the-next-indonesia/ (accessed on 20 December 2012); "The Indonesian example: Remember 1998," *The Economist*, 07 February 2011, http://www.economist.com/blogs/asiaview/2011/02/indonesian_example (accessed on 20 December 2012).
49. Ted Piccone, ibid.
50. Richard Fontaine and Daniel M. Kliman, op.cit., p. 98.
51. Joseph S. Nye, Jr., op.cit., pp. 207-234.
52. Ibid, p. 208.
53. Ibid.

1

INDONESIA'S RISE: DOMESTIC, REGIONAL AND GLOBAL DRIVERS

> "I envision a century-old Indonesia standing on three great pillars that make up a great modern state: a strong and just economy, a stable and modern democracy, and a thriving civilization."– *Susilo Bambang Yudhoyono*[1]

Indonesia's rise is an outcome of both domestic consolidation and systemic changes taking place at the regional and global level. While the domestic transformation has strengthened the country's capabilities and international image, international changes have offered opportunities for Jakarta's regional and global projections. Highlighting Indonesia's rise, its President, Susilo Bambang Yudhoyono declared, "Indonesia is the world's third largest democracy, the largest economy in Southeast Asia, a key growth area in the world economy, and soon we will have one of the largest productive work focus in Asia."[2]

During the last ten years, the domestic outlook of Indonesia has been marked by its continued economic growth, growing young middle class, a relatively stable and decentralised polity, and its gradual emergence as a confident democracy with civilian leadership. Indonesia is known and appreciated not only for its growing economy and its fast-expanding middle class market, but also for being the largest Muslim democracy in the world and one of the most liberal and moderate Muslim societies in the world. Moreover, its successful democratic experience of the past fifteen years after more than thirty years of authoritarian rule raises hope for the democratisation of non-democracies and offers a blueprint as to how to tread the democratic path. The nation-state is steadily heading towards civilian supremacy and institutionalised politics. Large-scale political reforms have taken place, including decentralisation and provincial autonomy. Democracy is well-entrenched in the country, and an average Indonesian takes democratic politics as granted, something germane to their societal-political ethos. Similar confidence is evident among the Indonesian leaders. President Yudhoyono attributes Indonesia's rise to the country's domestic consolidation in the form of sustained economic growth and stable democratic politics.[3] To quote him, "I do believe that in order to play some roles regionally and internationally, any country must have certain capacity. And in the case of Indonesia, this capacity is derived from our domestic consolidation."[4] Today, Indonesians themselves are not worried as much about the future of democracy as about corruption, governance and economic development.

In addition to domestic and democratic consolidation, several developments of regional and global significance have pushed Indonesia towards playing an active role in international politics. One such development is the rise of Asia that has fundamentally altered the geopolitics of the Asia-Pacific. In this new politico-strategic landscape, ASEAN institutions have emerged as a critical regional interlocutor, providing an overarching cooperative framework involving stakeholders of the region. Indonesia within ASEAN finds itself at the fulcrum of these parallel processes. Moreover, regional trends are both prompting and forcing Indonesia to become pro-active. The limited capabilities of smaller powers in Southeast Asia and the limitations of ASEAN as a regional grouping have promoted Indonesia to a pro-active leadership role in regional affairs to ensure that the region and the regional grouping does not merely become a playground of major powers. At the same time, the regional dynamics of power politics has allowed Indonesia to project itself as an important balancer between the pulls and pushes coming from different powers. As a whole, the evolving dynamic of power politics in the region has offered Indonesia both a challenge and an opportunity to project itself as an important voice in regional geopolitics.

The rise of Asia has coincided with the rise of the Global South or what is referred to as the 'rise of the rest.' This process has not only strengthened the voice of the developing countries like Indonesia, but also presented them an important opportunity to negotiate the terms of relationships between the developed North and developing South. Rising Indonesia as a member of the developing world and a leader of the Non-Aligned Movement (NAM) stands prominent in the success stories of the developing world. Indonesia's sustained economic growth during the global economic crisis since 2008 presented the country as a safe and reliable investment destination and a promising market.

Indonesia as a Success Story: Growth amidst Global Crisis

Equipped with strong economic fundamentals, Indonesia, the largest ASEAN economy, is poised to emerge as an important economic player from the Global South. Many writings have emphatically added another "I" (Indonesia) to the existing acronym of BRICS.[5] Indonesia is more than a trillion dollar economy (GDP PPP) and ranks 15th among the world's largest economies. The Asian Development Bank (ADB) Vice-President, Stephen P. Groff declared in June 2013 that the Indonesian economy, on an average, recorded around 5.9 per cent growth during the preceding five years.[6] The economy is expected to grow at the rate of 7-8 per cent after 2013, making Indonesia one of the ten largest economies in the world by 2025.[7] By 2030, Indonesia will be the 7th largest economy, with 135 million members of the consuming middle class and with 71 per cent of the cities producing more than 86 per cent of GDP, warranting huge demand for resources, market and skilled labour.[8] Given its robust economic outlook, membership of the G-20, and chairmanship of ASEAN, the World Economic Forum agreed to hold the annual meeting of World Economic Forum on East Asia in Jakarta in June 2011.

The Indonesian economy has registered remarkable resilience and growth, driven by gradual politico-economic reforms, rapid growth of the middle class, a young workforce, strong domestic and external demand, a relatively efficient financial sector, increased foreign investment, and political stability. The exchequer is filled, foreign investment is returning at a faster pace to the country, local Indonesians are investing more and banks are better organised and disciplined. The stable democratic government has embarked on gradual reforms in different sectors, correcting anomalies in the financial sector that plunged the economy into crisis in 1997.

The growing confidence of Indonesian leadership also manifests in the idea of "the Jakarta Consensus," proposed by President Yudhoyono on 5 September 2010. The consensus asserts a distinct Indonesian model of development based on (a) political stability and law enforcement,

(b) balanced roles for the government and the market, (c) integration into the global market without succumbing to the multinational corporations, (d) growth with equity, (e) a developed domestic market, and (f) a multiparty presidential system.[9] Echoing similar confidence, the Indonesian Ambassador to the US, Dino Pati Djalal, while speaking in the US on the "Promise of the 21st century," focused on some of the issues mentioned above including, governance.[10]

Indonesia has shown resilience while the advanced economies have been going through shocks at regular intervals. The economy is being driven by large-scale domestic consumption, as well as demand coming from the rising economies of China and India, which allowed the country to shift its market away from the economies-in-crisis of the West. A better picture of Indonesia's economic performance can be seen in the following table comparing select ASEAN economies. The Indonesian economy has maintained 6 plus percentage growth since 2007, with the exception of the year of 2009 when the global economy took a major down turn due to crisis in the advanced economies of America and Europe. Even during the crisis years, the Indonesian economy posted substantial GDP growth while other stronger and industrialising ASEAN economies were registering contraction in their economies marked by negative or no growth.

Table 1.1: Annual GDP growth in select ASEAN economies (2007-2012)[11]

Select ASEAN Economies	2007	2008	2009	2010	2011	2012
Brunei	0.2	-1.9	-1.8	2.6	2.2	2.2
Indonesia	**6.3**	**6.0**	**4.6**	**6.2**	**6.5**	**6.2**
Malaysia	6.3	4.8	-1.5	7.2	5.1	5.6
Philippines	6.6	4.2	1.1	7.6	3.6	6.8
Singapore	9.0	1.7	-0.8	14.8	5.2	1.3
Thailand	5.0	2.5	-2.3	7.8	0.1	6.5

While the World Bank, in its report in March 2011, accorded a positive outlook to the Indonesian economy, other agencies have predicted an upward trajectory for the economy in the coming years in both domestic and external sectors. The country's external Debt-to-GDP ratio came down from 159 per cent in 1998 to approximately 20 per cent in 2010.[12] At the same time, Indonesia's FOREX reserves went up from US$22 billion in 1998 to more than US$90 billion in 2010.[13] During this period, Indonesia emerged as one of the most favoured investment destinations in the world. Insight Global, one of the global rating agencies, upgraded Indonesia from a 'speculative territory' to an 'investment grade economy.'[14] The total FDI in Indonesia registered a steep hike from approximately US$5 billion to US$13 billion.[15] A similar trend was noticeable in the portfolio investment sector.

The Indonesian Middle Class Takes the Centre-Stage

Domestic consumption has proved to be a key factor in Indonesia's continued growth story. More than 60 per cent of the GDP in 2010 was generated by domestic consumption, and it is reported that this percentage could reach upto 65 per cent in the next 20 years.[16] Indonesia's growth story world not be complete without discussing what is perhaps the most important stimulus of domestic demand – its fast-growing young and mobile middle class. The World Bank has designated more than 50 per cent of the Indonesian population as the middle class, consuming between US$2-20 a day.[17]

Though it is generally agreed that the middle class is at the root of Indonesia's success story, opinions vary regarding its socio-economic background and professional outlook, and therefore, the exact number of this class. While writing in the mid-1950s, an eminent Dutch scholar, Justus M. van der Kroef, identified five different groups that could form part of the Indonesian middle class: (a) the group of industrial entrepreneurs, (b) the distributing middle class entrepreneurs, (c) the middle class concerned with transport and communication services, (d) artisan entrepreneurs with their own shops, serving a local market, and (e) the professional middle class.[18] Since then, the general definition of the middle class, its outlook and its membership have changed considerably.

New criteria are being applied today to define the middle class. As per the World Bank classification, anyone spending between US$2-20/day can be considered as a part of the middle class.[19] By this calculation, the total number of Indonesian middle class members is 50 million and this number may go up to 150 million by 2014, representing one of the world's fastest growing markets.[20] An alternative conception identifies the Indonesian middle class as having grown during the last ten years from 81 million to 131 million, with approximately 26 million middle class consumers being added every year.[21] As per yet another definition, any household possessing the troika of a television set, a refrigerator and an automated vehicle would fall into the middle class grouping.[22] The number of households owning this combination went up from 25 per cent of households in 2006 to 42 per cent by the end of 2011.[23]

The Indonesian middle class today is more urban, techno-savvy, skilled, independent, powerful, and somewhat consumerist. Many of its members are western-educated and English-speaking, allowing greater interaction between local and international businesses.[24] They are driven by their new-found consumption capacities and modern urban outlook. This middle class is not only fuelling domestic demands, but also pushing the country towards greater urbanisation. More and more people with consumption capacities are moving towards the urban areas. As a result, Indonesia is experiencing one of the fastest rates of urbanisation in the world, with 50 per cent of its population living in urban areas.[25] Moreover, the process of greater urbanisation and the rise of new middle class are adding dynamism to the national economy by stirring up greater consumption of and demands for real estate, leading to a new construction boom in the Indonesian cities.[26] As the cities are growing both in terms of population as well as in numbers, they are witnessing vertical pattern of urban growth while accommodating the influx of people.

Indonesia is also enjoying the demographic dividend resulting from the country's vast and growing young workforce. By one standard, 61 per cent of Indonesia's population was below the age of 35 in 2010, an important source of domestic demand that is driving Indonesian economy today.[27] While speaking at the Delhi Dialogue in New Delhi in March 2011, the Indonesian Commerce Minister, Mari Elka Pangestu, labelled approximately 30 per cent of the country's population as 'young work-force.'[28]

The consumption-driven growth model is, so far, driving the national economy and keeping it insulated from the international crisis. It is yet to be seen whether such a trend can keep the economy going in the long run or will generate its own problems, such as growing gaps between the rich and poor, and between the cities and rural areas. Additional concerns are the inflationary pressure on the national economy and resulting price rise.

Democratic Consolidation under 'Civilian and Secular Leadership'

Perhaps the most talked about component of Indonesia's rise is its successful transition from an unstable, chaotic and dysfunctional political system during the late 1990s to one of the most successful examples of the democratic experience in a multi-ethnic, predominantly Muslim, and developing nation. Indonesia has viewed itself and been characterized in an applauding fashion by many countries of the world as the largest Muslim democracy and the third largest democracy after India and the US.[29] It has conducted three fair and free elections in 1999, 2004 and 2009 that saw participation of more than fifty political parties, the incumbency of three presidencies, the impeachment of one president, the continued logjam in the legislative functions as a result of coalitional democracy, and the election of each and every leader at the grass-roots level in a democratic manner. The country is scheduled to witness another mammoth democratic exercise in different stages in 2014 when Indonesian voters will be electing their President and parliamentarians.

Indonesia has followed a multi-party, presidential form of democratic politics since the downfall of Suharto in May 1998. Presidents are directly elected by the people, and their election is not contingent on the party's numerical strength within the People's Representative Council (DPR). In other words, a President can run the government even if his or her party does not hold a majority in the legislature. So far three Presidents – Abdurrahman Wahid, Megawati Sukarnoputri and Susilo Bambang Yudhoyono – have led the country, and none of them ever enjoyed a majority in the national legislature. The election of a presidential candidate depends not on the strength of the party and its cadre, but rather the leadership charisma and mass appeal of the individual candidate. The PDI-P leader, Megawati Sukarnoputri, despite representing the largest political party in the national legislature, lost the Presidential election in 2004 to a new-comer, Susilo Bambang Yudhoyono. He presided over the country for five years (2004-2009) with approximately 50 seats in a more than 500-seat legislature. President Yudhoyono has been in office for ten years, making him the longest serving democratically elected president in the history of independent Indonesia.

The continued functionality of the elected presidency, which does not have a majority in the legislature, reflects the durability of the democratic structure of the country. In fact, the presidency, in the absence of majority, has functioned primarily as a coalition-based and consensus-driven executive, highlighting the growing strength of the Indonesian democracy and maturation of its political structures. The current Yudhoyono government (2009-2014) is based on a six-party coalition comprising of more than two-third of the seats in the DPR. Notwithstanding their inexperience in facing democratic dysfunctionality within the legislature, the minority executive has been able to function, introduce gradual reforms and work through a coalition-based majority.

Over the years, large-scale political reforms have taken place, which have democratised the political processes and diminished the role of nominations and the military in the legislative bodies. Even a conservative report like the Economist Intelligence Unit's Democracy Index, which characterises Indonesia as a flawed democracy, admits that citizens are enjoying political rights and civil liberties and notes improvement in freedom of the press and economic freedom. Elections are free and fair, and the national legislature is filled not with nominated favourites of the Executive, but rather democratically elected representatives. The military has no representation within the national legislative body and it is no longer nominated to the DPR. There is no restriction on the number of political parties contesting national and provincial elections. In contrast with the three arbitrarily clubbed political groupings of Suharto's era, candidates are fielded in the elections by individual political parties, whose statures are regulated by a fairly independent election commission. The 1999 national election saw an outburst of political parties, and more than forty political parties have contested each election since then.

Though the number of political parties has gone up considerably, national politics has remained dominated by seven important political parties – Democratic Party (PD), GolKar, Indonesian Democratic Party-Struggle (PDI-P), Prosperous Justice Party (PKS), National Mandate Party (PAN), United Development Party (PPP), and National Awakening Party (PKB). A break-up of the numerical strength of these seven parties in the DPR as per the 2009 elections is given below.

Table 1.2: Seats of Seven Political Parties in the DPR after 2009 General Elections

Political Parties	Seats in the DPR
Democratic Party	148
GolKar	106
Indonesian Democratic Party-Struggle (PDI-P)	94
Prosperous Justice Party (PKS)	57
National Mandate Party (PAN)	46
United Development Party (PPP)	38
National Awakening Party (PKB)	28
Total Seats in the DPR	**560**

The three largest political parties follow a somewhat secular or non-confessionalised politics. Two political parties – PAN and PKB – represent moderate Islamic politics and acted as vanguard of the democratic movement in the country in 1997-98. Democratic Party and PKS are new political entities and have focused more on issues of governance, efficiency and anti-corruption. Two other political parties – PKS and PPP – have pushed a diverse Islamic agenda within the country. They have begun to gain influence in the national political scene during the last two elections.

Indonesia's democratically elected governments appeal to wider domestic and international audiences, exercise greater politico-economic power and provide a stable political structure. They enjoy greater political and societal legitimacy today than they did either at the time of independence or during the early *Reformasi* era following the fall of General Suharto. The current Yudhoyono government enjoys wider support within the national legislature and exudes political confidence in running the government, highlighting its stable character.

Declining Role of the Military and Greater Civic Space

The military is gradually ceding its control over civic and political space to the civilian leadership, and in the process, further strengthening democratic institutions of the country. Renamed as the Indonesian National Army (TNI), the Indonesian Armed Forces (ABRI) saw a calibrated effort on the part of the civilian and democratic political leadership to end its presence in two of three vital areas – central legislatures, law-enforcement and provincial politico-administrative structures. The military does not have any *de jure* presence in the legislative bodies – the DPR and MPR (People's Consultative Assembly) – and the system of large-scale nominations that ensured the military's presence in the legislature has been done away with. President Yudhoyono, a former military general, has assiduously followed and promoted civilian politics during the last ten years. In principle and in practice, the infamous '*Dwifungsi*' (dual role) of the TNI does not exist anymore. Moreover, the Indonesian army, since 2001, has been stripped of its policing responsibilities within the country, thereby considerably reducing the army's presence in civic life. In an effort to institutionalise the law-enforcement business, the democratic leadership has created a separate department of POLRI (Polisi Republik Indonesia) and a mobile paramilitary brigade, and placed them in charge of internal defence.

The military has remained disciplined and shown little interest in reoccupying political positions. It has remained well within its limits in the provinces. However, the skeptics argue that the current discipline in the military has come primarily because a retired general is in power since it was missing during the regime of Megawati Sukarnoputri. It has been suggested that the litmus test will be the tenure of next presidency (2014-19) after the departure of Yudhoyono. The country has retained its infamous 'Territorial Command Structure,' which proved to be one of the most powerful instruments of central control over the provinces and an important reason for corrupt and oppressive practices of the Indonesian army in the provinces. Its continued existence has sustained the army's business interests in the resource-rich provinces and continued domination in the provincial politico-economic affairs. It is argued that a meaningful disciplining of the military can occur only after the dismantling of the territorial command structure.[30]

Decentralisation Strengthens Democracy in the Provinces

The democratic *bodypolitik* of Indonesia has seen significant transformation in the arena of centre-province relations that have come to largely define the national outlook of the country since independence. In order to empower the periphery and extend its democratic political processes to the provinces, Indonesia has embarked on the process of politico-economic decentralisation that aims at managing affairs locally. The process had taken off under the transitional government of B.J. Habibie, when popular unrest and calls for democratic change forced the regime to introduce a wide range of reforms, including the empowerment of local and provincial political processes.

The first major step was taken in 1999 when two laws were passed (Laws No. 22/1999 and No. 25/1999). While the first law aimed at regional governance, the second law aimed at giving fiscal powers to the regional governments. These laws provided a blueprint for the decentralisation programme. Since federalism continues to remain a taboo word in the country, greater emphasis has been laid on devolving power from the centre and empowering provinces, districts (*Kabupaten*) and villages (*Desas*). As per the new laws, regional representatives are democratically elected from among the local population. They are no longer accountable to the central government, but rather to the regional councils. Accordingly, the civil services in the provinces and central offices in the provinces, which were earlier managed by the central government, are being managed locally, including the recruitment process. Apart from a few areas such as defence, security, foreign policy, monetary and fiscal affairs, the majority of functions have been delegated to the provincial governments. Almost all the public service departments are administered provincially and accountable to local assemblies. The central government has also initiated a process of regional re-districting (*Pemakaran*), and as a result, the number of regencies and municipalities has doubled since the ascent of the democratic era. In addition to political and administrative decentralisation, the central government has also delegated financial powers to the regional bodies. Provinces also enjoy greater autonomy in terms of legislative functions and revenue generations.

Nevertheless, the danger remains that the process of decentralisation in the absence of institutionalisation of political behaviour and critical politico-administrative checks and balances can lead to chaos. The empowerment of the local elite and continuation of the military's territorial command structure brought about an unholy alliance between the military, the local political and religious elite and the business houses. This combination intensified ethno-communal violence in the outlying areas during the early years of the 21st century. Many of the writings on post-Suharto violence and instability consider decentralisation, regional re-districting and empowerment of the local political elite as important triggers for large-scale inter-ethnic and ethno-communal violence in the outlying provinces. On the other hand, it is asserted that the process of decentralisation has slowed down over the years. The majority of the provisions of the Laws No. 22 and 25 have not even been implemented. The lack of implementation has put a serious question mark over the subsequent government's intentions of actually introducing decentralisation in the provinces and empowerment of local people.

Rising Indonesia's Military Modernisation

Indonesia has, once again, embarked on the process of military modernisation under its democratic government. Though the Suharto regime initiated the programme of developing what is called 'strategic industries' during the 1980s, it failed to take off due to financial cut-back, retrenchment, lack of research and development capacities, international sanctions and governmental neglect.[31] The onset of the economic crisis in 1997-98 and the departure of Suharto and his technocrat successor, B.J. Habibie, forestalled any possibility of the revival of the military modernisation programme in the country.[32] Since then, Jakarta's military preparedness has been overlooked by the country's leadership.[33] In fact, it is argued that the Indonesian navy is capable only of managing its offshore territorial defence within its Exclusive Economic Zone.[34] It does not possess any capabilities of adjacent force projection and shipping protection, capabilities that are possessed even by much smaller ASEAN powers like Malaysia, Thailand and Singapore.[35] New realities of the 21st century – economic growth, better international image, major-power rivalries in the Asia-Pacific and Indonesia's growing strategic profile – have led to rethinking among the leadership, augmenting demands for sophisticated weaponry and better military training.

The military modernisation programme has focused on three important sectors – indigenous production, joint development, and procurement from overseas. An important component of Indonesia's military modernisation is the consolidation and advancement of Indonesia's indigenous defence industry, especially the revival of strategic industries. In order to achieve this objective, the Indonesian government has focused on greater financial allocation, restructuring of these industries, and the inclusion of joint-production and technology transfer provisions in bilateral agreements while engaging in the overseas procurement of defence weaponry.[36] Indonesia's budgetary allocation for defence spending more than doubled from US$2.38 billion in 2005 to US$5.75 billion in 2011.[37] Two countries seem to have figured prominently in Indonesia's overseas procurement or joint development of defence equipment – South Korea and Russia.

The Indonesian Defence Minister, Purnomo Yusgiantoro, declared that the reason behind the selection of South Korea as a partner for Indonesia's defence modernisation is the former's willingness to engage in joint production and technology transfer.[38] The Indonesian government placed an order for the procurement of three submarines from South Korea in January 2012 and signed a Memorandum of Understanding (MoU) with Seoul for the joint development of a fighter aircraft, for which Indonesia would pay 20 per cent of the development costs over a decade and receive 50 of them.[39] As a part of the agreement based on the agreement of joint-production and technology transfer, South Korea will produce the first submarine in its own shipyard with the participation of Indonesian technicians and the other two will then be produced in the Indonesian shipyard of PT PAL in Surabaya.[40] In fact, the Indonesian government had signed similar agreement with South Korea in October 2003 for the procurement of four submarines to be delivered by 2008.[41] However, the agreement did not materialise because of their high expense and the hard currency requirement.[42] The production of missile-guided frigates and amphibious assault ships for the Indonesian Navy has been made possible by the transfer of technology through the acquisitions of 7,300-ton Landing Platform Docks from South Korea-based Daesun Shipbuilding and Dutch-made Sigma corvettes.[43] Moreover, Indonesia also jointly develop 1,400-ton submarines with South Korea and C-705 anti-ship missiles with a range of 140km with China.[44]

The Indonesian government successfully test-launched a supersonic anti-ship missile, a Russian-built *Yakhont*, in April 2011, arguably with the objective of 'developing a sea-denial capability within archipelago, as a result of concerns over potential intervention or interference by larger powers as well as rivalry as with sub-regional peers, notably Malaysia.'[45] Indonesia received a US$1 billion Line of Credit for defence purchase from Russia in 2006 and decided to use one-third of the credit in buying 6 SU-30MK combat aircraft and two submarines.[46] The same year, Jakarta agreed to purchase two corvettes from the Netherlands at the cost of US$950 million.[47]

These developments highlight the growing focus of the Yudhoyono government on naval modernisation. Such an understanding seems to have been driven by the prevailing sentiment of strategic uncertainty in the Asia-Pacific, the greater naval modernisation of major regional powers, such as China and India, the escalation of the South China Sea dispute and Indonesia's maritime character. The Indonesian government drew international criticism in 2005 for its poor performance in the management of archipelagic waters when Lloyd's Agency declared the Strait of Malacca as unsecure and piracy-prone. Though Indonesia has initiated the process of its naval modernisation and maritime security has emerged as one of the most important items of the security agenda, the deployment and future positioning of the Indonesian navy has not received much attention. The current strategic thinking seems focused on the management of its territorial waters. For example, it has been pointed out that the main objective of the procurement of submarines is the protection of strategic maritime corridors, such as areas north of the Malacca Strait, the Natuna Sea, the Sulawesi Sea and the Bali Strait.[48] The 2005 plan of naval modernisation has aimed at developing a 'green water' navy by 2020 that would enable the country only in protecting its archipelagic territories and sea-lanes.[49]

Rise of the Asia-Pacific Facilitates Indonesian Ascent

A stable, growing, and powerful Indonesia is probably benefitting the most from the changing regional geopolitics of the Asia-Pacific. Not only has regional demand pushed the Indonesian economy towards a commodities boom, but also the changing strategic atmosphere has placed Indonesia in a pivotal position in the new-evolving dynamic of power politics in the region. Moreover, the rise and growth of the ASEAN-driven regional cooperative architecture and Indonesia's leadership role in the grouping has added new glamour to Indonesia's strategic profile in the region.

Regional Demand Fuels Rising Indonesia's Commodities Boom

The Asia-Pacific has emerged as the most dynamic and growing regions of the world. It is home to some of the biggest and fastest growing economies in the world, repositories of huge wealth and a productive work-force, and is gradually emerging as an epicentre of global economic and political transactions. With the combined GDP of US$39 trillion, the region contributes approximately 56 percent of global economic output, constitutes half of the world population, and contains the world's most dynamic trade and energy routes.[50] The first decade of the twenty-first century has seen the resuscitation of an 'Asian Century' discourse that entails the importance of Eastern Asia in global economics and the rise of China and India as new dynamos of global economic growth.[51] Immanuel Wallerstein highlights the growing significance of East Asia in the areas of production, commerce and finance and argues that the region's importance is set to grow further.[52] As stated by the President of European Central Bank, Jean-Claude Trichet, the Asia-Pacific, representing roughly half of the global population, contributed around 37 per cent of global GDP in terms of Purchasing Power Parity (PPP) and roughly 40 per cent of global growth came from Asia in 2007.[53] As per the World Bank October 2013 update, the region, despite economic slowdown, was predicted to still contribute 40 percent of global growth and one-third of global trade in 2013.[54]

The vast markets of China and India have emerged as shock absorbers and growth-drivers. The growing demands for fuel and oil from China and India have given an additional external push to Indonesia's commodities boom. The global economic crisis coincided with the 180 per cent rise of the export of both the non-renewable (mainly oil and gas) and renewable (vegetable oil) resource commodities from Indonesia.[55] Indonesia has already toppled Malaysia from the position as the biggest exporter of palm oil. The sharp decline in the share of Indonesia's traditional export market (Japan, EU, US and Singapore) from approximately 60 per cent of Indonesia's total exports in 2007 to 46.4 per cent in 2010 stands in contrast with a steep increase in Indonesia's exports to China and India that stood at 10.2 and 6.5 per cent respectively.[56] Indonesia's exports to India quadrupled and exports to China tripled during the crisis years of 2008-2009.[57] The respective economies of China, India and Malaysia have seen the largest growth in the percentage volume of Indonesia's exports during the last four years.[58] Many Indian companies, such as Tata Power, Mittal, and Reliance Power, have bought coal mining rights in Indonesia.

Indonesia as a Pivot in Regional Geopolitics[59]

The emergence of new power-configurations in the Asia-Pacific and growth of ASEAN-driven multilateral cooperative processes have offered Indonesia opportunities for regional leadership roles. Indonesia is emerging as a pivotal state in the strategic rivalries between the United States and China, China and India and between China and Japan.[60] Indonesia has one of the fastest growing economies of the region along with geographical advantages and strategic resources and finds itself being pampered by these competing players in the region.

Moreover, the rise of Indonesia as a pivotal state has re-positioned the country as an important interlocutor in the ongoing strategic debate within continental geopolitics. At the same time, the more fundamental question facing Indonesian foreign policy today is whether it should take sides in the new-evolving geopolitical equations in the continent or assert its own strategic ambitions and contribute, in the process, to the rise of an Asian multipolarity. The evolving structure of multipolarity in the Asia-Pacific offers Indonesia an important opportunity to continue its leadership role within a Southeast Asia that is gradually emerging as the main battleground in the region.

Since Indonesia does not share any long-standing territorial/boundary dispute with any other powerful Asian player (China, India and Japan), it is exercising greater leverage in charting its own independent foreign policy priorities without worrying about any tactical/strategic backlash in its own backyard. Such a position allows Jakarta to pursue a rational, pragmatic, and also hard-bargaining policy, turning its engagement with other important conflicting Asian powers to its advantage. Such an articulation is also in tune with President Yudhoyono's phrase of 'zero enemies, a million friends.' In other words, the emerging geopolitical realities of Asia offer a conducive atmosphere for Indonesia to pursue its short-term and long-term strategic goals.

Indonesia has also received attention due to its role as the informal leader of the ASEAN-driven cooperative processes. Indonesia's leadership role during the ASEAN's crisis in Phnom Penh in July 2012 received appreciation not only within ASEAN, but also from the important powers and dialogue partners of ASEAN. ASEAN forums not only involve the participation of important global and regional players, but also become a venue for great power rivalries and competition. The multilateral engagement has undergone significant transformation in terms of geo-political outlook, agenda of the policy and mandate of the institutionalized cooperation in the region. In fact, the idea of cooperation has never ever been so powerful and profound in the near history of the Asia-Pacific. Moreover, the nature of interactions has become much more complex, warranting a nuanced approach on behalf of ASEAN. For example, China is ASEAN's largest trading partner despite the fact that it shares territorial disputes with some of the ASEAN countries. Given the process of greater economic integration, the idea of collective vulnerability is taking deeper roots, again demanding collective responses that can be a complex process. The growth of the ASEAN mechanism has not only placed Indonesia in a beneficial situation, but also enhanced the strategic leverage, Indonesia can draw from its growing profile within the grouping and the region.

Global Push to Indonesia's Rise

Twenty-first century global politics is going to be fundamentally different from that of the 20th century, and contours are already emerging. Marty Natalegawa, the Indonesian Foreign Minister, while discussing the emerging contours of global politics, characterised it as one marked by the Cold Peace, instead of Cold War.[61] The centres of global transactions are shifting from the developed world towards the Developing countries of Asia, Africa and Latin America, registering a wave of growth and prominence in the Global South, in sharp contrast to economic stagnation and crisis in the advanced world. Nearly 85 countries recorded per capita income growth faster than the OECD average of 2.75 percent.[62] It is predicted that "the 'E7' of China, India, Brazil, Russia, Indonesia, Mexico and Turkey will, by 2050, be around 25 per cent larger than the current G-8 when measured in dollar terms at market exchange rates, or around 75 per cent larger in Purchasing Power Parity (PPP) terms.[63] This is also evident from the growing significance of the G-20 in lieu of the G-8 as the premier platform for deliberation over global issues.

The rise of the Global South has opened up new avenues for cooperation, new sets of responsibilities for the developing world to work together, and new opportunities for both the East-West and North-South dialogue. As a result, the idea of global development, eradication of poverty and the accomplishment of Millennium Development Goals appear more attainable today. These developments have placed Indonesia in an advantageous position to connect itself with the rising Global South as an important leader of the group, reinforcing the legacy of Sukarno, who once championed the cause of the developing countries of Asia and Africa.

Indonesia's moderate Islamic outlook and its image as the largest Muslim democracy have contributed to its significance in the global discourse on political Islam and the evolving dynamic of relationships between the Muslim world and the West. The 9/11 era brought forth the discourse on how Islam in general and political Islam in particular engages with both the international community and the West. Though the discourse remained dominated by the conceptualisations and parameters developed by the West, it cast light on Indonesia's nation-building project as a moderate Muslim democracy. Indonesian Muslim democracy has offered the West an important rallying point and reference point for the engagement between Islam and the West. As a result, Indonesia began emerging as a darling of the West-driven discourse on engaging Islam that, in turn, provided wider politico-strategic and diplomatic space for the projection of Indonesia's own international image.

Jakarta has begun discussing how it should conceive and pursue its long-term global priorities and posturing. For the first time since the departure of Suharto, Indonesia has begun exhibiting activism in global political deliberations, as evident from the country's active participation in the Climate Change, WTO, and G-20 negotiations. Its membership of the G-20 has not only accorded Indonesia an important place of prominence in global politics, but also given it a voice in the most important global discourses. Jakarta's new-found confidence is also manifested in the willingness of its leaders to conceptualise distinct global roles for the country in the 21st century. This element of Indonesia's strategic vision has found prominence in the articulations of the country's key decision makers.

Conclusion

Indonesia is riding on its new-found confidence that emanates from its domestic consolidation, its geo-strategic positioning in the Asia-Pacific and its new-emerging image and desire for identity-building at the global level. The pro-active and confident leadership has also found as conducive regional and global atmosphere for the projection of Indonesia's rise. While these trends continue to shape Indonesia's profile, the story is far from complete.

These developments carry within themselves seeds of change and challenges, which, if not handled carefully, may interfere with and complicate Indonesia's success story. For example, the growing trend towards religious radicalisation within Indonesia may disrupt both its domestic politics and its global positioning. Though the country has benefitted from the commodities boom and growing consumerism of the middle class, it might overheat the national economy and undermine the principal manufacturing sectors of the economy. Therefore, these drivers of change may also prove to be agents of crisis in the long run as shown in the chapter six. Similarly, though the evolving rivalries and power politics have provided a strategic leverage to Indonesia, they may jeopardise regional peace and compromise Jakarta's regional leadership if not addressed carefully and effectively. The critical factor lies with the role and direction of the leadership and their focus on the structural consolidation of the country and the dynamic of interaction with the systemic agencies.

ENDNOTES

1. Susilo Bambang Yudhoyono, "Indonesia in 2045: A Centennial Journey of Progress," *Strategic Review,* vol. 1, no. 1 (August 2011), p. 47.
2. Susilo Bambang Yudhoyono, "The Big Shift and the Imperative of 21st Century Globalism," Keynote Speech at World Economic Forum 2011, Davos, 27 January 2011, http://www.embassyofindonesia.org/press/docpdf/THE%20BIG%20SHIFT%20AND%20 THE%20IMPERATIVE%20OF%2021ST%20CENTURY%20GLOBALISM.pdf
3. Susilo Bambang Yudhoyono, "Speech at The Wilton Park Annual Address, Indonesia's Role as Regional and Global Actor," 2 November 2012, http://www.presidenri.go.id/index.php/eng/pidato/2012/11/02/2001.html (accessed on 12 December 2012).
4. Ibid.
5. Maureen Farrell, "Indonesia: The newest BRIC?," *CNN Money*, 15 October 2012, http://money.cnn.com/2012/10/15/investing/indonesia-bric/index.html (accessed on 27 December 2012); "Indonesia's Middle Class: Missing BRIC in the wall," *The Economist,* 21 July 2011, http://www.economist.com/node/18989153 (accessed on 27 December 2012).
6. Stephen P. Groff, "Economic Growth in Southeast Asia: Integration, Sustainability, and Capacity Development," *Asian Development Bank,* 28 June 2013, http://www.adb.org/news/speeches/economic-growth-southeast-asia-integration-sustainability-capacity-development (accessed on 07 December 2013).
7. Anoop Singh, "Indonesia Resilient Growth to Continue," *The Jakarta Post,* 2 May 2011, http://www.thejakartapost.com/news/2011/05/02/indonesia-resilient-growth-continue.html

(accessed on 28 December 2012).

8. Raoul Oberman, Richard Dobbs, Arief Budiman, Fraser Thompson and Morten Rosse, "The Archipelago Economy: Unleashing Indonesia's Potential," *Mckinsey Global Institute Report*, September 2012, http://www.mckinsey.com/insights/asia-pacific/the_archipelago_economy (accessed on 21 May 2013).
9. Aleksius Jemadu, "Parts Washington, Beijing and Delhi: The Jakarta Consensus," *The Jakarta Globe,* 13 September 2010, http://www.thejakartaglobe.com/opinion/parts-washington-beijing-and-delhi-the-jakarta-consensus/395920 (accessed on 20 January 2013).
10. Dino Pati Djalal, "Promise of the 21st Century," 16 March 2011, http://www.youtube.com/watch?v=IdGciEyAOGA (accessed on 20 January 2013).
11. "World Development Indicators – GDP Growth (Annual %)," *The World Bank Databank,* http://data.worldbank.org/indicator/NY.GDP.MKTP.KD.ZG/countries/4E-ID?page=1&order=wbapi_data_value_2009%20wbapi_data_value%20wbapi_data_value-first&sort=desc&display=default (accessed on 08 December 2013).
12. Simona Mocuta, "S&P Upgrades Indonesia's Sovereign Risk Rating to Just Below Investment Grade," *Global Insight,* 11 April 2011
13. Ibid.
14. Ibid.
15. Ibid.
16. "Accommodating the Growing Middle Class," *The Jakarta Globe,* 21 December 2012, http://www.thejakartaglobe.com/editorials/editorial-accommodating-the-growing-middle-class/562912 (accessed on 27 December 2012).
17. Verra and Fitriani, "Indonesia's Rising Middle Class: Tweeting To Be Heard," *RSIS Commentaries,* no. 104/2012, 19 June 2012, http://www.rsis.edu.sg/publications/Perspective/RSIS1042012.pdf (accessed on 27 December 2012).
18. Justus M. van der Kroef, "Entrepreneur and Middle Class in Indonesia," *Economic Development and Cultural Change*, vol. 2, no. 4 (1954), pp. 304-305.
19. Michael Andrew and Peng Yali, "The Rise of the Middle Class in Asian Emerging Markets," *KPMG Report,* April 2012, http://www.kpmg.com/cn/en/IssuesAndInsights/ArticlesPublications/Documents/Middle-Class-Asia-Emerging-Markets-201206-2.pdf (accessed on 27 December 2012).
20. "Indonesia's Middle Class: Missing BRIC in the wall," *The Economist,* 21 July 2011, http://www.economist.com/node/18989153 (accessed on 27 December 2012); Michael Andrew and Peng Yali, op.cit.,
21. "Hot Growth Markets in the Spotlight Indonesia: Hidden Treasure – Indonesia," *Ernst & Young*http://www.ey.com/Publication/vwLUAssets/Hot_growth_markets_in_the_spotlight_-_Hidden_treasure-Indonesia/$FILE/Hidden_Treasure_Indonesia.pdf, p. 2.
22. Debnath Guharoy, "Analysis: How big is Indonesia's middle-class today?," *The Jakarta Post,* 28 February 2012, http://www.thejakartapost.com/news/2012/02/28/analysis-how-big-indonesia-s-middle-class-today.html (accessed on 27 December 2012).
23. Ibid.
24. Joana Bundo, "The Middle Class Problem that Threatens Indonesia," *Asia House,* 19 December 2012, http://asiahouse.org/news-and-analysis/detail?id=141 (accessed on 28 December 2012); An Hodgson, "Indonesia's Rising Middle Class to Transform the Country's Consumer Market," *Euromonitor International,* 3 July 2012, http://blog.euromonitor.com/2012/07/indonesias-rising-middle-class-to-transform-the-countrys-consumer-market.html (accessed on 28 December 2012).
25. Shoeb K. Zainuddin, "Middle Class Growth Fuels Lippo," *The Jakarta Globe,* 06 November

2012, http://www.thejakartaglobe.com/business/middle-class-growth-fuels-lippo/554413 (accessed on 27 December 2012).

26. Ibid.
27. Joana Bundo, op.cit.,
28. Mari Elka Pangestu in Sudhir T. Devare and Vibhanshu Shekhar, *Delhi Dialogue III: Beyond the First Twenty Years of India-ASEAN Engagement* (New Delhi, Manohar, 2012).
29. Azyumardi Azra, "Islam, Indonesia and Democracy," *Strategic Review,* vol. 1, no. 1 (August 2011), p.73.
30. Marcus Mietzner, "The Politics of Military Reform in Post-Suharto Indonesia: Elite Conflict, Nationalism, and Institutional Resistance," *East West Centre Policy Studies*, no. 23, 2006, East West Centre, http://www.eastwestcenter.org/fileadmin/stored/pdfs/PS023.pdf (accessed on 30 December 2012).
31. "Chapter Ten: Current trends in Asia-Pacific defence industries," *The Military Balance*, vol. 109, no. 1, 2009, p. 458; "Revitalizing Indonesia's Defence Industrial Base: Agenda for Future Action," *RSIS Policy Report*, 05 July 2012, p. 3, http://www.rsis.edu.sg/publications/policy_report/Revitalizing_Indonesia_Defence_Industrial_Base_—_Agenda_for_Future_Action_5_July_2012.pdf (accessed on 30 December 2012).
32. "Chapter Ten: Current trends in Asia-Pacific defence industries," op.cit., p. 458.
33. "Revitalizing Indonesia's Defence Industrial Base," op.cit.,
34. James Goldrick and Jack McCaffrie, *Navies of South-East Asia: A Comparative Study* (New York, Routledge 2013), pp. 12-13.
35. Ibid.
36. "Revitalizing Indonesia's Defence Industrial Base, op.cit., p. 3.
37. Ibid.
38. Michael Johnson, "Indonesia looks to Africa, the Middle East to sell military equipment," *Asia-Pacific Defense Forum,* 05 October 2012, http://apdforum.com/en_GB/article/rmiap/articles/online/features/2012/10/05/indonesia-arms-export (accessed on 30 December 2012).
39. "Chapter Six: Asia," The Military Balance, vol. 111, no. 1, 2011, p. 207.
40. Michael Johnson, op.cit.
41. James Goldrick and Jack McCaffrie, op.cit., p. 84.
42. Ibid.
43. "Revitalizing Indonesia's Defence Industrial Base," op.cit., p.3.
44. Zakir Hussain, "Indonesia Seeks to Boost Arms Industry," *The Jakarta Globe,* 24 March 2012, http://www.thejakartaglobe.com/news/indonesia-seeks-to-boost-arms-industry/506923 (accessed on 30 December 2012).
45. "Chapter Six: Asia," op.cit., p. 206.
46. "East Asia and Australasia," *The Military Balance*, vol. 107, no. 1, 2007, p. 336.
47. Ibid.
48. Michael Johnson, op.cit.,
49. James Goldrick and Jack McCaffrie, op.cit., p. 86.
50. "The Importance of the Asia-Pacific Region," Voice of America Editorial, 24 September 2012, http://editorials.voa.gov/content/the-importance-of-the-asia-pacific-region/1514099.html (accessed on 11 23 December 2013).
51. Kishore Mehbubani, *The New Asian Hemisphere: The Irresistible Shift of Global Power to the East* (New York: Public Affairs, 2008); David Scott, "The twenty-first Century as Whose Century?", *Journal of World-Systems Research*, vol. 13, no. 2, 2008, pp. 104-108; Immanuel

Wallerstein, "East Asia and the World: The Decades Ahead", no. 157, Birmingham University, 15 March 2005, http://fbc.binghamton.edu/157en.htm

52. Immanuel Wallerstein, ibid,
53. Matthieu Bussière and Arnaud Mehl, "China's and India's Roles in Global Trade and Finance: Twin Titans for the New Millenium?" *ECB Occasional Papers*, no. 80, January 2008., European Central Bank, http://www.ecb.int/pub/pdf/scpops/ecbocp80.pdf
54. "East Asia Pacific Economic Update, October 2013 – Rebuilding Policy Buffers, Reinvigorating Growth," *The World Bank Economic Update,* October 2013, http://www.worldbank.org/en/region/eap/publication/east-asia-pacific-economic-update-october-2013 (accessed on 23 December 2013).
55. Laura Lipscobm et. al., "Indonesia: Select Issues" *International Monetary Fund Country Report,* no. 10/285, September 2010, http://www.imf.org/external/pubs/ft/scr/2010/cr10285.pdf (accessed on 30 December 2012).
56. "Indonesia: EU Bilateral Trade and Trade with the World," IMF (DoTS), DG TRADE, 8-Jun-11, http://trade.ec.europa.eu/doclib/docs/2006/september/tradoc_113391.pdf
57. Tom Wright, "Indonesia: Indonesia's Commodity Boom Is a Mixed Bag," *Corp Watch,* March 24th, 2008, http://www.corpwatch.org/article.php?id=14988 (accessed on 30 December 2012); Laura Lipscobm et. al., "Indonesia: Select Issues" *International Monetary Fund Country Report,* no. 10/285, September 2010, http://www.imf.org/external/pubs/ft/scr/2010/cr10285.pdf (accessed on 30 December 2012).
58. Laura Lipscobm et. al., op.cit.,
59. A detailed discussion of the regional environment shaping Indonesia's rise and its regional responsibilities is given in the chapter 2 of this book.
60. Norimitsu Onishi, "US and Chin vie to win over Jakarta: With Visit to Indonesia, Obama tries to secure strategic edge in region," *The International Herald Tribune*, 10 November 2010, p. 1; Sara Schonhardt, "US, China vie for influence among Indonesian riches," *Asia Times Online*, 06 May 2011, http://www.atimes.com/atimes/Southeast_Asia/ME06Ae02.html (accessed on 15 March 2012).
61. Ahmad Rizky Mardhatillah Umar, "A Critical Reading of 'Natalegawa Doctrine'," *The Jakarta Post,* 07 January 2011, http://www.thejakartapost.com/news/2011/01/07/a-critical-reading-'natalegawa-doctrine'.html (accessed on 21 May 2013).
62. Cited in Hardeep S. Puri, "Rise of the Global South and Its Impact on South-South Cooperation," World Bank Special Report, October 2010, http://siteresources.worldbank.org/WBI/Resources/213798-1286217829056/puri.pdf
63. Ian Taylor, "'The South Will Rise Again'? New Alliances and Global Governance: The India–Brazil–South Africa Dialogue Forum," *Politikon: South African Journal of Political Studies*, vol. 36, no. 1, 2009, p. 52.

2

MAPPING THE GEOPOLITICS OF THE ASIA-PACIFIC

The Asia-Pacific region, as it enters the 21st century, euphemistically referred to as the 'Asian century,' is emerging as a focal point of the global strategic discourse. The region represents a curious melee of multiple paradoxes. This is the region where prosperity coexists with abject poverty, democracy with authoritarianism, multiculturalism with majoritarianism, peace with conflict, and, above all, security with threats to survival. The region is home to both the richest and poorest places on earth, the smallest and the largest nation-states, the oldest civilizations and modern nation-states, developed and underdeveloped regions, and primitive and wired places. While China, India and Indonesia are emerging as the fastest growing economies, Myanmar and North Korea continue to remain pariah states. The region has emerged as both a new axis of prosperity as well as a new theatre of uncertainty and insecurity. The Asia-Pacific is one of the most dangerous theatres of rivalries and conflicts in this century of peace, progress and prosperity.

The Idea of the 'Asia-Pacific': A Nebulous Construct

Before identifying and examining the changing geopolitical realities of the Asia-Pacific in the 21st century, it is important to understand and define the region itself – the geographical canvas of the term as used in this book. According to Simon Dalby, "we must not limit our attention to a study of the geography of polities within pregiven, taken for granted, commonsense spaces, but investigate the politics of the geographical specification of politics."[1] In other words, regions as geopolitical classifications can be temporary discursive constructs driven by interests and power.

The Asia-Pacific region is an abstract notion and a context-specific, country-specific, and a time-specific construct. In other words, the geo-political boundary of the region has been constantly changing, often reflecting the strategic priorities of the countries and the organisations or actors trying to define it. It has incorporated newer members and actors, leading to the reformulation of its boundaries, its characteristics, and challenging, in the process, the very notion of its pre-ordained and static character.

The Asia-Pacific as a regional entity still remains a 'nebulous construct' reflecting an expanding geo-political canvas with an indeterminate membership and membership criteria. There does not seem to be any definitive geopolitical boundary of the region, and various countries and regional groupings define it differently. Different pan-Asia-Pacific international organisations have varied in the number of members, indicating their divergent regional focus and preferences. The APEC (Asia-Pacific Economic Cooperation) has 21 members, the ARF (ASEAN Regional Forum) has 27 members, and the ESCAP (Economic and Social Council of Asia and the Pacific) has more than 50 members. ASEAN seems to have identified the Asia-Pacific region with the ARF. The Foreign Ministers of the ASEAN member-states agreed during the 27th ASEAN Ministerial Meeting (AMM) in 1994 to make the ARF an 'effective consultative Asia-Pacific Forum for promoting open dialogue on political and security cooperation in the region.'[2] Does that mean that its understanding and canvas of the Asia-Pacific region changes with the entry of new members in the forum?

Though the APEC includes Thailand and Vietnam as its members, it does not include the intervening space of Cambodia and Laos. The admission of Russia into the APEC in 1997 is understood as a US concession to Russia after opposition to its entry into NATO and pressure from China, Japan and South Korea. While Australia, under the Labor leadership of Bob Hawke and Paul Keating, did not consider India to be a part of the Asia-Pacific during the 1990s and opposed Indian membership in the APEC, the same country under the similar Labor leadership of Kevin Rudd acknowledged India as an important player in the Asia-Pacific while floating a new Asia-Pacific Community in June 2008. Moreover, though not included in the ARF at the time of its inception, India was admitted to the Forum two years later, highlighting a further expansion of the ASEAN approach towards Asia-Pacific regionalism. Though Pakistan, as an ARF member, forms a part of the Asia-Pacific, the sub-region of South Asia did not figure in the APEC's definition of the Asia-Pacific until 2008.

Moreover, the region is experiencing the process of community-building with different core areas and overlapping boundaries, emerging out of divergent strategic priorities and foreign-policy focuses of constituent countries.[3] Dennis Rumley identifies four different scales of community-building processes in the Asia-Pacific:

> . . . (a) an overarching Pacific Rim or Pacific Basin concept which is an Asia and Pacific concept; (b) a less inclusive Asia-Pacific Economic Cooperation (APEC); (c) the scale of the Western Pacific states; and (d) a regional concept, which is exclusively Asian.[4]

Echoing similar vagueness, the former foreign minister of Singapore, Tommy Koh, while delivering a speech at the Asia-Pacific Community Conference held in Sydney in November 2009, highlighted two distinct processes of community building within the region – East Asia community building and Asia-Pacific community building.[5] While ASEAN+3, the EAS and the ARF are Asia-focused cooperative processes, the APEC is an essentially Pacific-focused initiative. These parallel processes also indicate the growing elasticity of geo-political boundaries, and the expansion of ASEAN-driven integrative processes. What differentiates these organisations and these cooperative processes are their geo-political canvas, the fulcrum of their activities, and their different composition.

Traditionally, Indonesia's articulation of the Asia-Pacific seems to have veered between the two regional conceptualisations of the ARF and the APEC, with the former focusing on the Asian part of the region and politico-strategic concerns and the latter focusing on the Pacific part of the region and economic objectives. Indonesia has sought to achieve three objectives within the ARF: '(a) enhance its international profile through its role and leadership in ASEAN as the primary driving force of ARF; (b) preserve and advance its national interest in various important political and security issues; and (c) encourage regional commitment to enhance cooperation in issues of mutual interest and common concern.'[6] On the other hand, Jakarta's main objectives in APEC have been to 'increase the Indonesian economic capacity, competitiveness and innovation and encourage the establishment of open market in Asia-Pacific.'[7] Almost three-fourths of Indonesia's total trade takes place with the APEC countries.[8]

Of late, the eastern part of the Indian Ocean has also begun to figure into the regional understanding of Indonesia as a region of growth, a source of vulnerabilities, and as a platform for greater regional and multilateral cooperation. Though the Indian Ocean figured in the country's strategic thinking, it did not receive much attention until December 2004 when the country was jolted by the devastating Tsunami that originated in the Indian Ocean. The Tsunami experience drew the attention of Indonesian policy makers towards the Indian Ocean as a source of vulnerabilities, especially natural disasters. Second, the simultaneous rise of India and Indonesia and their growing strategic ties and shared security concerns may also have given a fresh push to Indonesia to look towards the Indian Ocean. Third, the Indian Ocean, lying to Indonesia's West and a part of its under-explored maritime frontier, appears to be the natural target of any geopolitical expansion in Indonesia's strategic worldview. Indonesia's growing regional profile and its multilateral activism have prompted Jakarta to pay greater attention to this hitherto ignored maritime space. Indonesia's Ministry of Foreign Affairs has incorporated the IOR-ARC (Indian Ocean Rim Association for Regional Cooperation) as a focus area of its regional multilateral diplomacy. Indonesia envisages playing a pro-active role in the IOR-ARC deliberations when it becomes the Chair for two years (2015-2017). Currently, Indonesia is the Vice-Chair of the grouping. Finally, the growing significance of the Indian Ocean in the broader strategic discourse of the Indo-Pacific also seems to have drawn Indonesia's attention. The US 'Pivot to Asia' or Rebalancing strategy has identified the Indo-Pacific as the main arena of great power politics.

Taking these preferences into consideration, one can conservatively identify Indonesia's understanding of the Asia-Pacific as the 'triangular geo-political space between India, Japan and Australia covering South, Northeast, and Southeast Asia, island countries in the Oceania, and Australia and New Zealand.'[9] The region is home to powerful global and continental players (China, India, Indonesia, Japan and the US). It has witnessed the rise of power-based and security-driven alignments, the trend towards integration and community-building, and efforts to create an all-inclusive cooperative architecture under the leadership of ASEAN. Moreover, the long-term strategic interests of regional powers extend beyond their traditional zones of influence and cover both the western Pacific Ocean as well as the Indian Ocean. The region is home to various strategic flash-points, the most culturally and ethnically diverse societies, and faces a whole gamut of both traditional and Non-Traditional Security (NTS) challenges. In other words, the region reflects trends towards both the ascent of the state as well as the state vulnerability.

A Trend Towards Multipolarity

Regional power politics has seen the rise of several power centres possessing both capabilities and ambitions to influence regional strategic discourses. China and India are rising; Japan is normalising; Russia is recovering; and amidst all these, the world's sole superpower, the USA, is returning in the form of what Leon Panetta has called 'rebalancing.'[10] These powers attach considerable importance to their strategic presence in the region, and the evolving multipolarity reflects the interplay of their strategic interests and power projections.

The most important catalyst for the transformation of Asia-Pacific geopolitics in the 21st century is the rise of China, augmenting substantial changes both in regional power politics and processes of cooperation and integration. This system-altering development has prompted both experts and practitioners to examine different aspects of China's rise and its short-term and long-term implications for the region. For example, will the rise of China be a peaceful process? Is the rise of China going to affect ASEAN's community-building process in the region? How does China's growing power place it in the context of its territorial disputes in the region? Moreover, China's rise as an economic power, combined with its large-scale program to modernize its military, raises the question of how this power will be used in the future. Will China try to break ASEAN unity by using its growing power and influence? Can rising China be tamed and convinced to behave within rules of the game as developed in the region?

As the region continues to debate this issue, two trends have come to characterize China's regional outlook as a rising power. First, the rise of China has given a new momentum to regional economic growth and development. Rising China has emerged as the biggest market, an important source of investment, and a large-volume trading partner. While the advanced economies of the West have been facing economic shocks at regular intervals during the last five years (since 2008), China has continued to register a high annual GDP growth rate, rapidly reducing its distance from the largest economy of the world, the USA. In contrast to its position as the sixth largest economy in 2001 (total GDP of US$ 1.10 trillion), China is ranked today as the second largest economy, with some estimates projecting China to be the largest economy by 2020.[11] With enormous material resources at its disposal, China has become indispensable for any meaningful deliberation over the management or restructuring of the global or regional order.

Second, new sets of relationships are emerging at the regional/continental level, marked by parallel trends towards cooperation and confrontation, and a greater understanding alongside growing mistrust. The year of 2010 saw not only the emergence of China as the largest trading partner, but also a sudden escalation of the South China Sea dispute, which involves five ASEAN member-states (Brunei, Indonesia, Malaysia, the Philippines and Vietnam). China is not merely ASEAN's largest trading partner, but also the only major power that has a territorial dispute with the ASEAN countries. The strategic aspects of China's rise have generated uncertainty and regional tension regarding its future steps towards domination and the re-drawing of boundaries. Moreover, the asymmetry in the balance of power between China and Southeast Asia is increasing, rendering the latter more vulnerable to China's growing projections in the region, and less influential in shaping the dynamics of its engagement with the rising power.

The rise of China has been entwined with a sense of fear and an uncertainty as to whether it is a peaceful or conflict-prone process.[12] China shares historical rivalries, territorial disputes, and deep-seated mistrust with many ASEAN countries. China has been viewed as responsible for the rise of communist subversion in countries like Indonesia, Myanmar and the Philippines, and has fought wars with Vietnam. China has shared territorial disputes with two other major powers of the region (India and Japan) and four ASEAN countries (Vietnam, Malaysia, Brunei and the Philippines). Other important players of the region – Australia, Indonesia, Singapore and South Korea – have expressed, if not direct hostility, wariness about the rapid rise of China and its future strategic intentions.[13] A major shock came in December 2013, when Beijing unilaterally designated parts of the East China Sea as its Air Defence Identification Zone, inviting strong protests not only from Japan and South Korea, but also from other countries.

The rise of China has coincided with the rise of India as an important strategic player in the Asia-Pacific during the first decade of the 21st century. With its sustained economic growth, enhanced strategic presence in East Asia, long-standing 'China-threat' theory and a great power posturing, the perception of countries about India has changed from one of an insular South Asian hegemon to an important strategic player with the material capability of altering the balance of power in the region, what C. Raja Mohan characterises as 'a swing state.'[14] India's growing strategic profile can be seen from the nature of its strategic engagements both bilaterally with select Asian players as well as multilaterally. While India and Japan signed the Global Partnership in April 2005, India and the US signed a civil nuclear energy cooperation in July 2005. The Indian entry into the EAS (East Asia Summit) during the same year was an outcome of its growing strategic ties with select ASEAN players, its changing geo-strategic profile in the Asia-Pacific, and its increasingly close relations with two important global players in Asia – Japan and the USA. Highlighting India's growing regional importance, Australia invited India to join the new Asia-Pacific Community in June 2008 and signed an open-ended security cooperation agreement in November 2009. Furthermore, American President Barack Obama, before beginning his Asia trip in November 2010, identified India as a power that has already risen, a widely publicised statement in the Indian media. The increasing strategic involvement of India in the region and its strategic engagement with key regional players are seen as New Delhi's efforts to neutralise China.

The Vladivostok summit of the APEC saw Russia's intent to return to the region as an important pole in the regional structure of power. Instead of hosting the summit in the capital city of Moscow or any other city in the West, the Russian decision to host the summit in the far eastern city of Vladivostok is being viewed as signalling its desire to develop greater strategic and economic linkages with the eastern Asian hemisphere.[15] China replaced Germany as Russia's largest trading partner, adding new momentum to Russia's continuing drift towards the Asia-Pacific.[16]

Highlighting Russia's growing economic relations with the region, Russian President Vladimir Putin declared that Russia's trade relations are shifting from the European Union to the Asia-Pacific.[17] Russian Deputy Prime Minister Igor Shuvalov declared, "Within five years, our foreign trade should balance in favour of Asia and guarantee high growth rates in the Far East. Within 10 years, we want our trade volume with APEC states to be greater than with the European Union."[18] A major stimulus has come from Russia's desire to develop its eastern region.

Its growing desire to enhance its strategic presence in the region led Russia to join the ASEAN cooperative processes. Russia became a member of the ADMM+ (ASEAN Plus Defence Ministerial Meeting) in 2010 and of the EAS in 2011. It is already a member of the ARF. Russia is also an important supply source of defence equipment to many of these countries, including China, India, Indonesia, Malaysia and Vietnam.

Japan has long been a principal power and a dominant economic player in the region. It is one of the largest investors and donors, playing a critical role in the development of the region. Moreover, it has played an active role in strengthening the ASEAN-led regional cooperative processes and viewed them as an important platform for the projection of its strategic interests and importance in the region.

Tokyo remains intricately involved in regional power politics. The country shares territorial disputes with China and South Korea, enjoys a security guarantee from the US as a part of their bilateral security arrangement, and possesses superior military technologies. With the growing salience of the Sino-Japanese rivalry, Tokyo's strategic overtures in the region have intensified. Under the leadership of Prime Minister Shinzo Abe, Japan has indicated that it would pursue strong defence and economic linkages with the countries of the region, especially Southeast Asia.

Regional power politics acquired a sharp edge in 2009 with the US announcement of its enhanced strategic presence in the Asia-Pacific as a part of its 'Pivot to Asia' or 'rebalancing' strategy. The strategy has three important components – consolidation of alliances, building substantial engagement and forging partnerships with other Asian powers such as India, Japan, Indonesia and Vietnam, and intensifying its economic engagement in the region through the TPP (Trans-Pacific Strategic and Economic Partnership). The US re-engagement has been facilitated by its reassessment of a rising China. To quote Kishore Mahbubani, former Singaporean diplomat, 'The U.S. realizes that if they are to retain American influence in this region, they must be able to match what China is doing. If China is improving its ties by leaps and bounds with ASEAN, it is not in America's interest to be left behind.'

The USA augmented its re-entry into the Asia-Pacific by deciding to become a member of the EAS, signing a comprehensive partnership with Indonesia, and sending its naval fleet for 'interaction' with the Vietnamese navy in the South China Sea. President Barack Obama's Asia visit in November 2010 signified America's strategic engagement with the region. In addition to the economic imperatives, Obama's India visit was interpreted as a part of its grand Asian strategy to respond to 'the rise of China on land and sea.'[19]

A Multi-Layered Structure of Regional Rivalries

Indonesia has to grapple not only with the complexities arising from the rise and return of major powers, but also the challenges emanating from the evolving relationship dynamics among these powers. The region is staring at a multi-layered structure of regional rivalries where China, the lone challenger to the US primacy, has entered into multiple levels of rivalries with the countries of the region. Highlighting the possibility of the rise of an anti-China coalition in the region, John Mearsheimer argues that the majority of China's neighbours – India, Japan, Singapore, South Korea, Russia and Vietnam – will join hands against the rising dragon.[20] Though the accuracy of that hypothesis is yet to be tested, the rise of China and its growing assertion has created a sense of wariness in the region against its strategic intent and widened the trust deficit among regional players.

The most high-profile regional rivalry is between the US and China. China's assertion and America's rebalancing have placed the Asia-Pacific within a newly evolving orbit of great power rivalry. China has viewed the US rebalancing as a containment strategy, and the US has responded strongly to the growing Chinese assertions in the South and East China Sea. Various scholars, especially the exponents of the power transition theory, have argued that the Sino-US rivalry is going to escalate in the future, as they would feel threatened by each other's strategic overtures.[21]

In addition to the Sino-US rivalry, the region has also witnessed second-tier and equally destabilising Sino-Indian and Sino-Japanese rivalries, and efforts of these powers to expand their sphere of influence and position themselves on a stronger footing in the prevailing strategic uncertainty. While Sino-Indian equations are experiencing the pressure emanating from each other's growing strategic influence, Sino-Japanese relations have experienced fresh tensions. The region has seen China's growing maritime activities in the Bay of Bengal and Indian Ocean and India's increasing involvement in the Strait of Malacca and South China Sea. Faced with strong nationalistic sentiments in the neighbouring China and its escalatory measures involving the *Senkaku* islands, Japan has adopted tough posturing over the issue of territorial disputes vis-à-vis China's growing assertions. Such a scenario remains inherently unstable and highly vulnerable.

While China faces what Robert Kaplan calls 'a blunt geographic wedge' from India in the Bay of Bengal and Indian Ocean and Japan in the East China Sea and western Pacific, it finds a less formidable challenge to its expansion in its sphere of influence in the Southeast Asian maritime corridors.[22] This realisation has prompted Beijing to consolidate its territorial claims in the South China Sea. The most apt example is the Chinese designation of the South China Sea as falling within its 'core national interest' in August 2010.[23] China's South China Sea foray has led to an escalation of hostility in Southeast Asia and placed the country into another set of hostilities with Vietnam and the Philippines, two other powerful claimants in the South China Sea dispute. Vietnam alleged in June 2011 that the Chinese fishing patrol vessels intruded deep into the former's Exclusive Economic Zones and rammed into the Vietnamese exploration ship, the *Viking 2*.[24] China reportedly attacked a Philippine vessel in March 2011 and Vietnamese vessels in May and June 2011 in the South China Sea.[25]

Era of Strategic Partnerships and Ascent of Complex Diplomacy

The region has witnessed the increasing practice of complex diplomacy as a response to threat perceptions emanating from the crude display of power. There is a growing realisation that analytical templates of foreign relations based on rivalries or friendships alone are 'too simplistic' given the complex nature of their relations, which are marked by rivalry, cooperation, integration, diverse areas of engagement, and interdependence and common stakes in maintaining peace and stability in the region.[26] Moreover, Indonesia has to deal not only with the challenges emerging from the evolving dynamic of major-power rivalries, but also with the complexities associated with Jakarta's bilateral relations (history as well as current dynamic) with each of these players.

The idea of complex diplomacy reflects maturation and sophistication in the modus operandi of strategic behaviour in the region. Moreover, it reflects the simultaneous pursuit of multiple agendas, various levels of objectives and a multiplicity of methods and strategies of engagement.[27] Highlighting the growing sophistication and maturation in the international diplomacy, Gareth Evans states, "with major power relativities shifting, and 'problems without passports' multiplying, diplomacy – and in particular cooperative multilateral diplomacy – has never been more complex, nor more important to get right."[28]

Multi-faceted and open-ended strategic partnerships have come to constitute an important component of complex diplomacy in the Asia-

Pacific. They are essentially framework agreements, highlighting both the intent as well as the content of the strategic engagement involving two partners. They reflect enhanced engagement between the two powers and their stakes in each other. Moreover, these partnerships could be suitably modified and strengthened, reflecting the type of relationship between two partners in a time-specific context. China has signed strategic partnership arguments with ASEAN, Cambodia, India, Indonesia, Malaysia, Myanmar, New Zealand, North Korea, South Korea, and Thailand.[29] Similarly, the US has signed strategic partnership arguments with ASEAN, Australia, India, Indonesia, Japan, Malaysia, the Philippines, Singapore, South Korea, and Vietnam. India has already signed strategic partnership arguments with Australia, Indonesia, Japan, Malaysia, South Korea, Thailand, and Vietnam, with wide-ranging defence and security cooperation agreements. Japan has signed strategic partnership arguments with Australia, India, Indonesia, South Korea, and the US.

Another important component of complex diplomacy is the display of being a responsible regional citizen through active participation in the ASEAN-driven regional cooperative architecture.[30] It has served important purposes – it allows space to create its own strategic constituencies, prevents any multilateral ganging-up against a singular power, and penetrates the agendas and deliberations of the regional cooperation. Highlighting China's responsible institutional citizenry as a part of its larger strategy for dealing with the USA, Aaron Friedberg argues that it allows Beijing 'to ensure that [it] cannot be used as a platform to criticise China or contain its rise,' and also provides Beijing a 'low cost way to reduce regional anxieties about its long-term objectives.'[31]

Parallel Processes of Economic Integration

The Asia-Pacific region has seen the emergence of parallel processes of economic integration. These are the APT (ASEAN Plus Three)-led East Asian Free Trade Agreement under the CMI (Chiang Mai Initiative), the EAS-led CEPEA (Comprehensive Economic Partnership in East Asia), the US-led TPP, and the ASEAN-led RCEP (Regional Comprehensive Economic Partnership).[32] While China has played a lead role in the APT, Japan seems to be the main driving force behind the CEPEA. While the RCEP appears to be ASEAN's compromise formula between the CMI and CEPEA, the TPP, a small power initiative, has grown out of the APEC membership under US patronage.

The CMI took shape in November 2000 when leaders of ten ASEAN countries and three Northeast Asian countries (China, Japan and South Korea) met in Singapore and agreed to examine the feasibility of an East Asian Free Trade Agreement.[33] The main objective of the CMI is to create a single market and an integrated production network. It has also launched two more initiatives – the CMIM (Chiang Mai Initiative Multilateralisation) and ABMI (Asian Bond Market Initiative). While the CMIM aims to provide financial support through currency swap arrangements, the ABMI works towards the development of efficient and liquid bond markets in the region.[34]

The main support for this initiative has come from China. China has shown activism in facilitating financial cooperation under the Chiang Mai Initiative, supporting the efforts towards the East Asian Free Trade Area, and promoting political and security dialogue, all under the APT banner. It was the APT summit in November 2002 at Phnom Penh that brought all the claimants together and led to the signing of a Declaration on the Conduct of Parties in the South China Sea.[35] However, China insisted on creating an exclusive East Asia Community with APT as its main platform.[36]

The second process of economic integration in the region is the CEPEA, which has grown within the EAS. Beijing initially openly supported the idea of setting up the EAS as an exclusive and overarching regional cooperative architecture when the Malaysian leadership tabled it in the APT meeting in 2004. After the inclusion of Australia, India and New Zealand, China has given primacy to the APT, sensing the loss of its privileged position in the EAS. At the broader multilateral level, the EAS has launched a feasibility study to examine the possibility of a Comprehensive Economic Partnership in East Asia (CEPEA), an initiative proposed by Japan. The CEPEA represents half of the global population and two-thirds of the global GDP. Surin Pitsuwan, the Secretary General of ASEAN, has called it 'the world's largest business space in a vibrant and more integrated East Asia' (ASEAN Secretariat 2008). However, the CEPEA is still in its infancy.

Finally, in a major step towards inter-continental economic integration, nine member-countries of the Asia-Pacific Economic Cooperation joined hands on 13 November 2011 in Hawaii to create one of the largest global trade blocs, involving three continents – Asia, South America and North America. This initiative is known as Trans-Pacific Strategic and Economic Partnership (TPP). Such an initiative, it is anticipated, would allow the member countries to benefit from each other's economic growth through mutual exploration of market, innovation, and job-creation.[37] The Singapore

Prime Minister, Lee Hsien Loong, has characterised the initiative as an 'additional safety raft' in a time of global crisis.

The TPP was started in 2005 by four small countries – Brunei, Chile, New Zealand and Singapore – with a combined population of approximately 25 million people. By contrast, the grouping today covers more than one-fourth of the global GDP and one-tenth of global population. Five economies – Australia, Malaysia, Peru, the USA and Vietnam – joined the initiative on 11 November 2011. It took nine rounds of tough negotiations for the initiative to take its current shape. The member-states have agreed to speed up the process of integration and devise a workable solution. Moreover, other big economies, such as Japan, Mexico and Canada, have shown enthusiasm in joining the initiative. If future negotiations are successful, more players may join. With their inclusion the TPP would create an integrated market of 750 million people and an economy of approximately US$25 trillion, or 40 per cent of total global output.

The most important driving force for the TPP has come from the US, which joined the initiative in 2008 for three reasons. First, Washington needed to compete more effectively and proactively with the rising Asian economies, and the idea of select FTAs provided appropriate avenues for the US to capture the emerging markets. Second, it is an effort by the USA to offset the European shock by diversifying its market. Third, it has helped the Obama government to shun the growing liberal criticism of increasing US protectionism in opposition to the liberal principle of free-trade. The exclusion of China, the second largest global economy and one of the most powerful players in the APEC, reflects the growing Sino-US rivalry over the evolving dynamic of their economic relations. The two countries have already been involved in a 'currency war,' with the US labelling China as a 'currency manipulator' and printing more money as a countermove against the Chinese obstinacy.

Power Politics and ASEAN's 'Reverse Enmeshment'

ASEAN in the twenty-first century faces two enormous tasks of managing the growing divergence within ASEAN and its relations with other powers. Intra-ASEAN dynamics are being increasingly shaped by the strategic priorities of individual states based on their own assessments of contemporary developments, as well as their respective bilateral ties with China. Evolving regional politics and intra-ASEAN divergence have put pressure on ASEAN as a regional grouping that is trying to present a uniform and consensus-based approach to regional cooperation.

One of the most important strategies pursued by ASEAN as a regional interlocutor during the twenty-first century is to steer the region towards greater economic integration and community building. After having included all Southeast Asian countries as members, the regional grouping decided at its 9th Summit, held in Bali in 2003, to build an ASEAN community by 2015. The idea has three key components – a Security Community, an Economic Community and a Socio-Cultural Community. The Vientiane Summit of 2004 adopted a Plan of Action to accelerate the process for achieving this goal and accordingly adopted the Cha-am Hua Hin Declaration on the Roadmap for the ASEAN Community (2009–15). The adoption of this ASEAN Charter is an effort towards regulating the preferences and policy options of ASEAN member states.

Such an approach has been based on two considerations – consensus among the member-states to pursue these two objectives, and the need to offset individual vulnerabilities by developing a united response to regional challenges. The continued emphasis on export-led growth and the opening up of economies have pushed ASEAN countries towards greater economic integration. There has been a greater convergence of the ASEAN countries' priorities in terms of economic integration and community building.

It is well understood in the region that instability and insecurity would jeopardise ASEAN's efforts towards regional integration. And a major source of insecurity and instability, as perceived by ASEAN, has come from its relations with China and the relations among major powers. The prospects of an assertive China on the one hand and of Sino-US rivalry, Sino-Japanese or Sino-Indian rivalries on the other, are considered destabilising. Therefore, besides developing common policy responses to regional challenges, ASEAN as a regional interlocutor has made efforts towards managing its relations with China and with other major powers.

In addition to the process of community-building within ASEAN, the grouping has introduced new structures of cooperation, allowed the entry of new stakeholders and expanded its functions. ASEAN formed the EAS in 2005 and ADMM+ in 2010. Russia and the US joined the EAS in 2011. Their main objectives are to identify and address areas of common concern, facilitate cooperation among member states and ensure peace and stability in the region. The introduction of new structures of cooperation and the entry of new members indicate an incorporation of broader political, economic and security agendas in the ASEAN framework and an attempt to provide an overarching cooperative architecture to the challenges facing the region. While the ARF sees the participation of ministries of foreign affairs, the EAS involves the participation of heads of state. Conversely, the ADMM+ entails the participation of ministries associated with defence and security.

ASEAN's Honest Brokerage and Strategy of Enmeshment

ASEAN's approach to regional power politics combines two strategies, namely, 'honest brokerage or indirect balancing and institutional enmeshing of major powers.'[38] Emphasising ASEAN's 'honest brokerage', Surin Pitsuwan, its former Secretary General, argued that 'dialogue partners, such as China and Japan, found ASEAN meetings a congenial place for their own often difficult bilateral conversations.'[39] The idea of 'honest brokerage' has followed the logic of multipolarity, which can provide a level playing field to all major powers, balancing each other out, creating, in the process, a distinct sense of balance and stability in the regional structure of power.[40] Such a conceptualisation has allowed ASEAN to diffuse the heat coming from the Chinese reaction against this perceived 'ganging up' against China. ASEAN has tried to position the US against China and engaged other Asian major powers, especially India and Japan, in the process. The strategy has relied on ASEAN's neutrality in providing a level-playing field to all its member countries.

The main stimuli of 'honest brokerage' have come from ASEAN's realisation of its limited military and non-military material capabilities, and its desire to manage the China threat, bringing stability to the region and retaining ASEAN leadership in the regional cooperative initiatives. ASEAN's model of 'brokering' great power relations turns on the institution providing unique forums for great power dialogue and confidence-building, and for acting as demonstration precincts from which great powers can demonstrate their commitment, benign intentions, and restraint to the region.[41] ASEAN's comparative advantage is that it is universally acceptable as the 'driver' of regionalism in a situation in which the great powers are suspicious of each other.

Second, ASEAN has used its multilateral forums to bind strategic manoeuvrings of major powers with the commitments emanating from the latter's participation in the large number of annual meetings under the aegis of the ASEAN regional grouping. This strategy, characterised variously as 'enmeshment', or double binding,'[42] seeks to institutionalise great power relations in the region, neutralise China's aggressive behaviour, and encourage China to use its power more responsibly. This is a long-term policy initiative that relies on (a) ASEAN setting the rules of the game, (b) the rules of the game being universally acceptable, (c) treating the commitments as inviolable, and (d) raising the stakes for the participating countries in the cooperative processes. Such a strategy, according to Amitav Acharya, 'involves a conscious effort by ASEAN to enmesh both China and the United States in regional interdependence and institutions so as to induce moderation on the part of China and increase the cost to the Chinese of any use of force.'[43]

This two-pronged strategy is based on its assessment of relative power, engaging as well as binding capacities of ASEAN cooperative institutions and persuasive aspects of community-building processes. While the first strategy projects ASEAN as an 'honest broker,' the second strategy facilitates ASEAN's regulatory role in the management of regional relationships. In other words, ASEAN is acting both as a balancing power bloc as well as a network allowing institutionalised dialogue and cooperation. Such a response has been conditioned by the rapid and wide-ranging impact of China's growing material capacity, the declining economic capacities of the West and the rise of other Asian powers. ASEAN's two-pronged response addresses the issues not only of Southeast Asia-China relations, but also the evolving dynamic of (a) US-China relations and its implications for Southeast Asia, and (b) the relationship among three Asian powers – China, India and Japan.

ASEAN's Reverse Enmeshment

ASEAN's combined approach of engaging the US and other Asian powers and enmeshing them has shown vulnerability with respect to two important factors – unity within ASEAN and the level of asymmetry in the power of China and ASEAN. These two factors have strongly impinged on the ability of ASEAN to manage the evolving dynamic of regional power politics, paving the way for what can be called as ASEAN's reverse enmeshment.

Notwithstanding ASEAN's continued projection as a united regional interlocutor, cracks have begun to appear and are growing wider over the strategies to be adopted to deal with the enormous increase in China's power. Three different positions, according to Rizal Sukma, have developed over the emerging East Asian security order; (a) Cambodia, Laos, Malaysia and Myanmar are sympathetic to China; (b) Singapore, Thailand and the Philippines are closer to the US; and (c) Indonesia and Vietnam are neutral players.[44] However, two major corrections have occurred in this three-pronged relationship – Thailand has maintained equidistance from the Sino-US rivalry, and Vietnam has called for a greater US role in the region.

The South China Sea dispute seems to have engaged both the major powers as well as ASEAN member-states, highlighting the different preferences of some of the ASEAN countries. Lisolette Odgaard has identified three issues – the level of American and Chinese involvement in the dispute, the mandate of any dialogue over the issue, and the scope of any Code of Conduct – over which ASEAN has exhibited internal differences.[45] For example, while the Philippines and Vietnam have advocated a united and multilateral ASEAN representation in the South China Sea dispute, Cambodia, Myanmar and Thailand have supported the Chinese demand for bilateral settlement of the dispute, which, given the huge asymmetry of power relations, would favour the Chinese position. Moreover, throughout the years, rising China has come to exercise considerable influence among the policymakers in the capital cities of Kuala Lumpur, Bangkok, Nyapidaw and Vientiane.[46]

Though ASEAN's management of its relationships with major powers is a challenge, the bigger challenge seems to be how to achieve a collective identity and operate with one voice in the face of the aggressive game of power and persuasion being played by China. ASEAN processes have come under enormous strain during the past few years. ASEAN appears to find it difficult to address the challenge of growing major-power rivalries and steer the regional cooperation, given the growing influence of big powers on its decisions and agenda. While the Bali Summit of 2011 witnessed an assertion on the part of the US and its strategic partners, the Phnom Penh summit has seen a growing Chinese influence on the ASEAN process.

The 45th ASEAN Ministerial Meeting held in Phnom Penh, Cambodia (10-12 July 2012) brought the regional grouping into the dock over three critical issues of (a) unity within ASEAN, (b) ASEAN's leadership role in steering the Asia-Pacific towards cooperation and integration, and (c) the grouping's ability to withstand the enormous pressure coming from the phenomenon of great power politics.[47] The meeting failed to adopt a Joint Communique over the issue of whether reference to China and the South China Sea dispute be made in the communiqué. While both the Philippines and Vietnam wanted to include China and the South China Sea, Cambodia, the ASEAN Chair, insisted on no reference to these two words in the communiqué. The end result was that ASEAN failed to present a common position to negotiate with China and exposed its disunity and lack of coordination, and resulting vulnerability to external pressure.

The absence of a Joint Communiqué implied that the grouping no longer had a common agenda for deliberation among its members and, therefore, was not presenting a united voice while engaging its dialogue partners, which also happened to be important global or regional players. The communiqué lays down an agenda, based on consensus, for the year-long deliberation within ASEAN, culminating finally at the summit level meeting that is held at the end of the year. Moreover, the contents of the Joint Communiqué finds a place of prominence in the grouping's deliberations with its dialogue partners. In other words, the agenda adopted here goes into all-important declarations and statements adopted in different ASEAN-driven forums. Even though member-states had differed in the past over important issues, such as human rights, the South China Sea and Myanmar, they always had managed to develop a compromise formula using the ASEAN Way of consultation, compromise and consensus. The Phnom Penh meeting has made a dent in ASEAN's projection of its united image, the efficiency of its much-touted ASEAN Way and its capacity to deal with its dialogue partners as a united regional voice.

The recent display of discord and the failure to fulfill ASEAN's primary responsibility – steering the region towards unity and community-building – has drawn attention towards what is perhaps the second most pertinent question facing the grouping: is ASEAN able to regulate great power relations, or is it being marginalised by the great power politics? Can ASEAN continue to steer the cooperative and integrative agendas of the grouping and retain its leadership role in deciding the agenda of strategic discourse in the Asia-Pacific, or is its agenda and functioning being shaped by the evolving power politics in the region?

Though ASEAN had begun experiencing pressure from the big-power rivalries during the past few years, the 45th AMM (ASEAN Ministerial Meeting) amply demonstrated ASEAN's growing difficulties in dealing with issues involving the great powers and the recent trend towards the grouping's great power entanglement and potential polarisation. Instead of regulating big-power relations in the region, ASEAN is undergoing the process of 'reverse enmeshment' whereby the grouping appears to have fallen victim to great power rivalries in the region, and its cooperative agenda is gradually being replaced by the agenda of big powers.[48] The issue of the unity of

ASEAN and its leadership role in the Asia-Pacific has once again acquired salience in the backdrop of the growing vulnerability of the grouping.

Recent events seem to have also put to rest an important debate going on in the region – has rising China been able to translate its enormous material power into influence in the region, especially over the smaller powers of Southeast Asia? In contrast to the material power that is quantifiable and, therefore, measurable, the idea of influence remains abstract and subjective in nature. The Cambodian adamancy not to reference China and the South China Sea and its insistence on not upsetting China, Phnom Penh's principal benefactor, seems to have proved what statesmen and leaders of the region have been trying to ignore at their own peril. Rising China has made deep inroads in Southeast Asia and exercises considerable influence.

While rising China has added to the weakening of the ASEAN collectivity, the responses of the US-led West and ASEAN member states to the rise of China has been, at best, half-hearted and narrowly construed. At the same time, the US-led 'Pivot to Asia' or 'rebalancing' has not been able to generate enough assurance in the region. Though the grouping has relied on the US as a balancer, the latter's promises seem to have proven to be ephemeral. The absence of President Obama in various summits of ASEAN and APEC in October 2013 made a major dent in the credibility of the US as a balancer in the region. However, the US active role in the disaster management and rehabilitation efforts in the aftermath of Haiyan Typhoon in the Philippines and the flight of the B-52 bombers after the Chinese announcement of ADIZ in the East China Sea are being used to showcase America's continued commitment to the region.

ASEAN has not been able to effectively follow its strategy of honest brokerage as well as enmeshment. It is imperative that ASEAN retains its unity, independence and effectiveness when it is undertaking its most ambitious task of building the three pillars of the ASEAN community. Indonesia, as the most important ASEAN player and informal leader of ASEAN, has to shoulder the responsibility of steering the ASEAN centrality while the grouping accomplishes its two-fold objectives.

Non-Traditional Security Issues Confronting the Region

Indonesia as an archipelagic nation-state has felt more vulnerable to non-traditional sources of threat. The region of Asia-Pacific houses various multi-ethnic and multi-religious societies, such as India, Indonesia, Malaysia,

China. These societies have faced several internal security challenges in various forms, such as terrorism and insurgency. The bomb blast in Bali in October 2002 that killed more than 200 Australians shook the Asia-Pacific, revealing in the process a growth in the pan-regional terror network in the form of *Jemaah Islamiyah*. Since then, Indonesia has faced sustained terror attacks at regular intervals. Various terrorist operations in Jakarta (April 2003, September 2004, July 2009) and Bali (October 2002, September 2005) point towards growing inter-linkages between global vectors of Islamic terrorism and local agents (*Jemaah Islamiyah*),[49] operating in domestic constituencies (Poso, Ambon, Java).

The outbreak of large-scale Muslim-Christian violence and narratives of sufferings of the abstract Islamic '*Ummah*,' in general, and sufferings of Indonesian Muslims, in particular, have offered a conducive socio-political setting for the rise of Islamic radicalism in the country. While the initial phase of radicalization derives from domestic stimuli, the later-phase radicalization during the last decade of 20th century points towards a growing nexus between global processes and players and domestic constituencies. It has been contended that there is a need for a movement that aims to purify the corrupt and corroded, strictly adhere to Islamic principles (known as 'santri-isation'), effectively implement *shariah* law,[50] and declare *Jihad* (holy war) even against the members of other religions. The Indonesian authorities reported two incidents of terrorism during the last six months – one foiled in March 2012 by the police in the Indonesian island province of Bali and another failed attempt in September 2012.[51] The country continues to face insurgency in its far eastern province of West Papua.

Maritime Security, over the years, has come to form an important component of Indonesia's regional diplomacy. The main concerns have emerged in the form of the growing militarisation of the maritime space, the safety of the SLoCs (Sea Lanes of Communications), sea-piracy, the safety of the maritime commons, and the protection of maritime trade. The rising powers have embarked on expanding their strategic influence by modernising their navies and developing mobile military platforms on the seas for greater outreach. This process has added to the existing uncertainty and instability in the region. As the Asia-Pacific has moved towards greater attention, maritime space has become the main trade highway, raising stakes for the countries regarding the safety of the SLoCs and the protection of maritime trade. Over the last twenty years, maritime piracy and maritime terrorism have also drawn the attention of regional stakeholders.

Natural disasters constitute one of the most important NTS challenges facing Indonesia. The Indian Ocean Tsunami of 2004 that affected India, Indonesia, Sri Lanka and Thailand not only highlighted a shared vulnerability of countries cutting across sub-regional boundaries of South and Southeast Asia, but also jolted Indonesia to recognise its stakes in the Indian Ocean. The Indian Ocean Tsunami of 2004 wiped out the entire infrastructure, caused enormous loss of lives and resources, and disrupted the whole process of development in parts of India, Indonesia, Sri Lanka and Thailand. Out of the total economic impact worth US$10 billion, Indonesia alone registered the loss/damage of US$4.5 billion.[52] Similar disasters have occurred in the form of earthquakes in China and Pakistan, Cyclone Nargis in Myanmar and Bangladesh, and Cyclone Gene in Fiji. More than 18 natural disasters took place in Indonesia in 2012 alone.[53] The UNDP (United Nations Development Programme) has identified Indonesia as one of the most disaster-prone countries in the world.[54] As per the 2009 Global Assessment Report on Disaster Risk Reduction, Indonesia was ranked third in terms of human exposure to earthquakes and first in terms of exposure to tsunamis.[55]

The Asia-Pacific has witnessed a sudden spurt of pandemics in the region during the last ten years. The spread of SARS (Severe Acute Respiratory Syndrome) in 2002-03 affected both security and developmental activities in the region. It stalled business activities, created panic among investors and contributed to the flight of capital from the effected countries. The pandemic originated in China in November 2002 and engulfed approximately 30 countries by the end of 2003. Seven Asian countries/regions were among the top ten on the list. Highlighting the severity of impact of these pandemics on the security and development in the region, ABC news reported in 2004, "The SARS virus has now hit nearly every country in Asia, spreading fear, panic, and economic chaos in its wake."[56] To quote the then Prime Minister of Singapore, Goh Chok Tong, "SARS will knock you backward, it may even kill you. But I can tell you SARS can kill the economy, and all of us will be killed by the collapsing economy."[57] Even though Indonesia was not as severely affected as some other East Asian economies, the former suffered to the tune of US$2 billion in 2003.[58] Similarly, the Avian Influenza, popularly known as the Bird Flu, struck Asia in 2003 and continued to cause deaths and panic in different parts of Asia-Pacific. Cambodia, Indonesia and Vietnam reported deaths due to bird flu even in early 2012.

Conclusion

As rising Indonesia readies itself to project its growing power, it has to grapple with changing regional geopolitical realities. These challenges come from both traditional sources, such as the balance of power, as well as non-traditional threats. The evolving great power politics and their multi-layered rivalries carry the danger of derailing peace and stability in the region and, consequently, Indonesia's success story. A key challenge facing Indonesian leadership is determining what ways it can retain the regional great power rivalry at a manageable level and benefit from the positive outcomes of the rise and return of great powers to the region. Moreover, questions surround whether the regional cooperative architecture under the leadership of ASEAN is capable of addressing the key security challenges or will buckle under the pressure of great power politics.

ENDNOTES

1. Simon Dalby, "Critical Geopolitics: Discourse, Difference, and Dissent," in Klaus Dodds (ed.) *Geopolitics,* second volume (New Delhi: Sage Publications, 2009), p. 254.
2. "Ministry of Foreign Affairs – Multilateral Cooperation," *Government of Indonesia*, http://www.kemlu.go.id/Pages/IFP.aspx?P=Regional&l=en (accessed on 09 December 2013).
3. David Camroux, "Asia ... whose Asia? A 'Return to the Future' of a Sino-Indic Asian Community," *The Pacific Review*, vol. 20, no. 4, December 2007, pp. 556–58; Dennis Rumley, "The Geopolitics of Asia-Pacific Regionalism in the twenty-first Century," *The Otemon Journal of Australian Studies*, vol. 31, 2005, p. 7.
4. Ibid, p. 7.
5. Tommy Koh, 'Australia's Asia Pacific Community Proposal: Some Issues for Discussion', Conference on the Asia-Pacific: A Community for the twenty-first Century, Sydney, 3-5 December 2009, http://www.apc2009conference.org/userfiles/Koh.pdf.
6. "Ministry of Foreign Affairs – Multilateral Cooperation," op.cit.,
7. Ibid.
8. Andi Abdussalam, "Indonesia Eager to Become Regional Power through APEC, *The Jakarta Globe,* 05 October 2013, http://www.antaranews.com/en/news/91012/indonesia-eager-to-become-regional-power-through-apec (accessed on 10 December 2013).
9. This book refers in its Conclusion to the Indonesian Foreign Minister, Marty Natalegawa's articulation of Pacific-Indo-Pacific and his definition of the term Indo-Pacific.
10. Leon Panetta, "The US Rebalance towards the Asia-Pacific," *Shangri La Dialogue Plenary Speech*, 02 June 2012, http://www.iiss.org/en/events/shangri%20la%20dialogue/archive/sld12-43d9/first-plenary-session-2749/leon-panetta-d67b (accessed on 15 September 2012).
11. "China Since 1990: Facts and Figures Tell of Rising Prosperity," *People's Daily*, 16 September 2002, http://english.peopledaily.com.cn/200209/16/eng20020916_103251.shtml (accessed on 15 September 2012); "How to gracefully step aside," *The Economist*, 10 January 2011, http://www.economist.com/blogs/freeexchange/2011/01/china (accessed on 15 September 2012).
12. Thomas J. Christensen, "Fostering Stability or Creating a Monster?: The Rise of China and

U.S. Policy toward East Asia," *International Security*, vol. 31, no. 1, Summer 2006, pp. 81-126.

13. "Defending Australia in the Asia-Pacific Century: Force 2030," *Defence White Paper 2009*. Department of Australia, Commonwealth of Australia, http://www.defence.gov.au/whitepaper/docs/defence_white_paper_2009.pdf. (accessed on 14 October 2012); Rizal Sukma, "ASEAN and Major Powers in the New Emerging Regional Order," in Tsunekawa, Jun. (ed.) Regional Order in East Asia : ASEAN and Japan Perspectives, NIDS Joint Research Series, no. 1, 2009, http://www.nids.go.jp/english/publication/joint_research/series1/series1.html (accessed on 13 October 2012); Kuik Cheng-Chwee, "The Essence of Hedging: Malaysia and Singapore's Response to a Rising China," *Contemporary Southeast Asia*, vol. 30, no. 2 (August 2008), pp. 159-185; Evelyn Goh, "Singapore's Reaction to Rising China: Deep Engagement and Strategic Adjustment," RSIS Working Papers, no.67, 2004, http://www.rsis.edu.sg/publications/WorkingPapers/WP67.pdf (accessed on 12 October 2012); Michael G. Gallagher, 'Future Indian-South Korean ties: can Seoul use India to balance China?," Korean Journal of Defense Analysis, vol. 22, no. 1, 2010, pp. 44-46.
14. C. Raja Mohan, "India in East Asia," Australia-India Strategic Lecture Series 2007, Lowy Institute for International Policy, Melbourne, 21 February 2007, http://www.lowyinstitute.org/Publication.asp?pid=548 (accessed on 10 October 2012).
15. "Russia asserts its power in the Asia-Pacific at APEC summit," *The China Post*, 05 September 2012, http://www.chinapost.com.tw/commentary/afp/2012/09/05/353297/Russia-asserts.htm (accessed on 08 October 2012).
16. Barry Deskar, "Russia looks to boost its Asia-Pacific credentials," *Today Online*, 06 September 2012, http://www.todayonline.com/World/EDC120906-0000023/Russia-looks-to-boost-its-Asia-Pacific-credentials (accessed on 08 October 2012).
17. Paul Mozur, Mitsuru Obe and Alexander Kolyandr, "Territorial Spats Overshadow Asian-Pacific Summit," *Wall Street Journal*, 09 September 2012, http://online.wsj.com/article/SB10000872396390444554704577641301712512154.html (accessed on 07 October 2012).
18. Artem Zagorodnov, "Apec summit: Vladivostok talks reveal Russia's eastern trading plans," *The Telegraph*, 01 October 2012, http://www.telegraph.co.uk/sponsored/russianow/business/9578664/apec-summit-vladivostok-russia.html (accessed on 07 October 2012).
19. Robert D. Kaplan, "The Geography of Chinese Power: How Far Can Beijing Reach on Land and at Sea?," *Foreign Affairs*, vol. 89, no. 3, May-June 2010, pp. 22-41.
20. John J. Mearsheimer, "The Rise of China will not be Peaceful at all," *The Australian*, 18 November 2005, http://mearsheimer.uchicago.edu/pdfs/P0014.pdf (accessed on 10 October 2012).
21. Ronald L. Tammen and Jacek Kugler, "Power Transition and China-US Conflicts," *Chinese Journal of International Politics*, vol. 1, no. 1, 2006, pp. 35-55.
22. Robert D. Kaplan, op.cit., p. 26.
23. "A clear Signal of "Core Interests" to the World," *China Daily*, 02 August 2010, http://www.chinadaily.com.cn/usa/2010-08/02/content_11083124.htm (accessed on 12 October 2012).
24. "Vietnam says China Fishing Boat Rams Research Ship," *The Straits Times*, 9 June 2011, http://www.straitstimes.com/BreakingNews/SEAsia/Story/STIStory_678024.html (accessed on 12 October 2012).
25. "China, Vietnam, Philippines press maritime claims," *Reuters*, 07 June 2011, http://in.reuters.com/article/2011/06/07/idINIndia-57541120110607 (accessed on 07 October 2012); "Vietnam accuses China in seas dispute," *BBC News*, 30 May 2011, http://www.bbc.co.uk/news/mobile/world-asia-pacific-13592508 (accessed on 07 October 2012).

26. Peter Drysdale, "China and India as Strategic Partners," *East Asia Forum*, 16 July 2012, http://www.eastasiaforum.org/2012/07/16/china-and-india-as-strategic-partners/ (accessed on 13 October 2012).
27. Andrew F. Cooper, "The G8 as Complex Diplomacy," http://g8heiligendamm.wordpress.com/2007/06/07/the-g8-as-complex-diplomacy/ (accessed on 13 October 2012).
28. Cited in Pauline Kerr and Geoffrey Wiseman (eds.) *Diplomacy in a Globalizing World: Theories and Practice* (New York, Oxford University Press, 2012).
29. LI, Chenyang, "China–Myanmar Comprehensive Strategic Cooperative Partnership: A Regional Threat?," *Journal of Current Southeast Asian Affairs*, vol. 31, no. 1, 2012, pp. 53-72; Su Hao, "Harmonious World: the Conceived International Order in Framework of China's Foreign Affairs," in Masafumi Iida (ed.) *China's Shift: Global Strategy of the Rising Power* (Tokyo, National Institute for Defense Studies, 2009), pp. 29-56.
30. Aaron L. Friedberg, *A Contest for Supremacy: China, America, and the Struggle for Mastery in Asia* (New York, Norton, 2011), pp. 52-54.
31. Ibid, p. 53.
32. Please see chapter 3 for discussion on RCEP.
33. Takashi Terada, "Constructing an 'East Asian' concept and growing regional identity: from EAEC to ASEAN+3," *The Pacific Review*, vol. 16, no. 2, 2003, p. 52.
34. "ASEAN Plus Three Cooperation," *ASEAN Secretariat*, no. 16580, 16 April 2012, http://www.aseansec.org/16580.htm (accessed on 14 October 2012).
35. Michael A. Glosney, "Heading towards a Win-Win Future?: Recent Developments in China's Policy toward Southeast Asia," *Asian Security*, vol. 2, no. 1, 2006, p. 38.
36. Kuik Cheng-Chwee, "Multilateralism in China's ASEAN Policy: Its Evolution, Characteristics, and Aspiration," *Contemporary Southeast Asia*, vol. 27, no. 1, 2005, p. 111; David Camroux, "Towards an Asian Community: the East Asian Summit, Kuala Lumpur," *CERi Sciences Po*, January 2006, http://www.ceri-sciences-po.org (accessed on 14 October 2012); Mohan Malik, "The East Asia Summit," *Australian Journal of International Affairs*, vol. 60, no. 2, June 2006, p. 209.
37. Vibhanshu Shekhar, "TPP: A step towards integrating continents," *Business Standard*, 27 November 2011, http://www.business-standard.com/article/opinion/vibhanshu-shekhar-tpp-a-step-towards-integrating-continents-111112700014_1.html (accessed on 14 October 2012).
38. Amitav Acharya, "Will Asia's Past Be Its Future?" *International Security*, vol. 28, no. 3 (Winter 2003/04), p. 153; Evelyn Goh, "Meeting the China Challenge: The U.S. in Southeast Asian Regional Security Strategies," *East-West Center Policy Studies*, no. 16, 2005, p. 2.
39. Surin Pitsuwan, "Charter is Key for ASEAN Revitalization," East-West Center Press Release, 24 January 2008, http://www.eastwestcenter.org/news-center/east-west-wire/surin-charter-is-key-for-asean-revitalization (accessed on 14 October 2012).
40. Vibhanshu Shekhar, "ASEAN's Response to the Rise of China: Deploying a Hedging Strategy," China Report vol. 48, no. 3, 2012, p. 263.
41. Ibid.
42. Amitav Acharya, op.cit., p. 153.
43. Ibid.
44. Rizal Sukma, op.cit., p. 88.
45. Liselotte Odgaard, "The South China Sea: ASEAN's Security Concerns about China," *Security Dialogue*, vol. 34, no. 4 (March 2003), p. 14.

46. Rizal Sukma, op.cit., p. 88.
47. Vibhanshu Shekhar, "Polarised ASEAN: 'Reverse Enmeshment'," *IPCS Article*, no. 3685, 31 July 2012, http://www.ipcs.org/article/southeast-asia/polarised-asean-reverse-enmeshment-3685.html (accessed on 14 October 2012).
48. Ibid.
49. For details on *Jemaah Islamiyah* see *White Paper: The Jemaah Islamiyah Arrests and the Threat of Terrorism*, Ministry of Home Affairs, Government of Singapore, 7 January 2003, http://www.mha.gov.sg/publication_details.aspx?pageid=35&cid=354; *Indonesia Backgrounder: How the Jemaah Islamiyah Terrorist Network Operates,* International Crisis Group (ICG) Asia Report, no. 43, 11 December 2002; Sidney Jones, "The changing nature of Jemaah Islamiyah," Australian Journal of International Affairs, vol. 59, no. 2, June 2005, pp. 169-178; Zachary Abuza, "Tentacles of Terror: Al Qaeda's Southeast Asian Network," *Contemporary Southeast Asia,* vol. 24, no. 3 (December 2002), pp. 427-65.
50. Shari'a is a collection of Islamic laws. See John L. Esposito, *Unholy War: Terror in the Name of Islam* (New York, Oxford University Press, 2002), p. 53.
51. "Olivia Rondonuwu and Stuart Grudgings, "Bali attack plot shows Indonesia terror threat evolving," *Reuters,* 22 March 2012, http://www.reuters.com/article/2012/03/22/us-indonesia-militants-idUSBRE82L0FS20120322 (accessed on 16 September 2012); "Indonesian police say bomb being prepared for terrorist attack explodes, 2 suspects escape," *The Washington Post,* 09 September 2012, http://www.washingtonpost.com/world/asia_pacific/indonesian-police-say-bomb-being-prepared-for-terrorist-attack-explodes-injuring-5-people/2012/09/09/e0499e6a-fa3a-11e1-a0a1-b07778c66e04_story.html (accessed on 16 September 2012).
52. Loy Rego, "Social and Economic Impact of December 2004 Tsunami," *Asian Disaster Preparedness Center,*http://cmsdata.iucn.org/downloads/social_and_economic_impact_of_december_2004_tsunami_apdc.pdf (accessed on 10 December 2013).
53. "Recent Natural Disasters In Indonesia," www.disaster-report.com/.../recent-natural-disasters-in-indonesia.html (accessed on 10 September 2012).
54. "Indonesia Crisis Prevention and Recovery Update," *United nations Development Programme,* http://www.undp.or.id/programme/cpr/ (accessed on 15 September 2012).
55. Irene Kuntjoro and Sofiah Jamil, "Triple Trouble in Indonesia: Strengthening Jakarta's Disaster Preparedness," *RSIS Commentary,* no. 138/2010, 1 November 2010, www.rsis.edu.sg/publications/Perspective/RSIS1382010.pdf (accessed on 15 September 2012).
56. Mark Litke, "SARS Virus Devastating Asia's Economies," *ABC News*, 19 April 2003, http://abcnews.go.com/Health/story?id=116746&page=1#.Uased5Xkbdk (accessed on 16 September 2012).
57. Ibid.
58. Emma Xiaoqin Fan, "SARS: Economic Impacts and Implications," *ERD Policy Brief,* Asian Development Bank, no. 15, May 2003, http://www.adb.org/sites/default/files/pub/2003/PB015.pdf (accessed on 10 December 2013).

3

INDONESIA AS AN ASIA-PACIFIC POWER

Indonesia no longer remains merely a Southeast Asian player, but rather has emerged as an important voice and a stakeholder in the Asia-Pacific region. Jakarta occupies a place of prominence in the strategic calculations of major global and regional powers. Indonesia is the most powerful ASEAN member, enjoys the leadership role in Southeast Asia, and occupies an enviable position of being one of the most acceptable interlocutors of the region. It is the sixth largest economy in the Asia-Pacific, and oversees critical maritime trade routes. Dewi Fortuna Anwar, a well-known Indonesian expert on international affairs, identifies Indonesia as a 'global swing state,' straddling strategic choke points between the Indian and Pacific Oceans and exercising considerable influence in regional and international affairs.[1] Having performed remarkably as ASEAN Chairman in 2011 and won accolades for hosting one of the best summits in the history of the Asia Pacific Economic Cooperation (APEC) in October 2013, Jakarta expects to play an active role as the Chairman of Indian Ocean Rim Association of Regional Countries (IOR-ARC) for two years (2015-2016). These three cooperative processes position Jakarta as a powerful facilitator of cooperation in the larger geopolitical setting encompassing East Asia, South Pacific and Indian Ocean.

Indonesia's rise has coincided with the growing shift in the gravity of power from the Atlantic to the Asia-Pacific, the emergence of a new regional structure of power politics, the competing processes of regional economic integration, the expansion of the ASEAN cooperative architecture, and the continued existence of a plethora of Non-Traditional Security (NTS) challenges. The region is exhibiting trends towards integration, instability and uncertainty as it grapples with an unstable multipolarity, multi-layered structure of rivalries, and great power politics. These developments have exhibited their own complexities, introducing significant variation in both the content as well as intent of Jakarta's regional diplomacy. While dealing with the changing regional outlook, Indonesia has begun to lay down rules of its long-term strategic engagement in the Asia-Pacific.

This chapter argues that Jakarta's regional diplomacy is no longer merely an ASEAN-driven, Southeast Asia-centric, and inward-oriented diplomacy of a hesitant player. It is pan-Asia-Pacific strategic positioning of a rising power as the country continues to acquire new roles and responsibilities in an expanding geo-political arena of its strategic engagement. Though ASEAN forms the most important focus of its regional diplomacy, Jakarta's stakes and influence transcend ASEAN and encompass the entire Asia-Pacific region. There are five principal objectives of Jakarta's new-evolving regional diplomacy: (a) sustaining a benign and peaceful atmosphere in the Asia-Pacific; (b) projecting Jakarta's new-found confidence and importance in the region; (c) maintaining strategic autonomy amidst power politics; (d) managing the side-effects of big power rivalries on the region and regional cooperative processes; and (e) steering the integrative and community-building processes of ASEAN.

While pursuing these objectives, Jakarta has sought to follow a nuanced strategy of hedging involving (a) stability in the multipolar regional structure of power, (b) balancing itself between the evolving power politics through some sort of equidistant but aggressive engagement, (c) leading proactively the ASEAN process of integration and community-building, and (d) developing a multilateral approach to the NTS challenges. As a part of its regional diplomacy, it is leveraging power politics and accelerating integrative processes in the region. The pursuit of such a strategy has allowed Indonesia to not only steer the ASEAN integrative processes, but also cushion them from the overwhelming pressure emanating from the evolving power politics in the region.

In order to contextualise Indonesia's regional diplomacy in a broader historical context and appreciate its changing outlook, a brief timeline in table form is given in Table 3.1. Five stages can be identified, highlighting elements of both continuity and change in Indonesia's regional diplomacy.

Table 3.1: Timeline of Indonesia's Regional Diplomacy

Eras	National Character	Regional/Systemic Contexts	Geographical Focus	Methods and Strategies
Sukarno	Anti-colonial, anti-western, non-aligned	Cold War Polarisation	Pan-Asian	Assertive Non-alignment Konfrontasi
Suharto	Authoritarian dictatorship	Cold War polarization Chinese subversion	ASEAN-5 focus	Pro-US, anti-China, ASEAN-centric
Post-Suharto Reformasi (1998-2004)	Onset of Democratisation Undergoing a comprehensive Crisis	End of Cold War, Limited US withdrawal, ASEAN Expansion, Economic Crisis	ASEAN-10 Focus	ASEAN-centric, Tentative
Phase of Internal Recovery (2004-2009)	Coalition-based Democratic Regimes Gradual Economic Recovery Stable polity	Rise of China Regional Economic Integration Expansion in the ASEAN functions	ASEAN-centric Gradual expansion towards East Asia (Northeast and Southeast Asia)	ASEAN-centric Economic diplomacy highlighting its larger role in the region beyond ASEAN
Democratic Consolidation & Assertion (2009 Onwards)	Confident Democracy growing economy stable polity	Crisis in the West Return of the US multi-layered structure of rivalries	Pan-Asia-Pacific/East Asian	pro-active and assertive approach rising Power Diplomacy

These stages have been assessed along four reference points – national outlook of the country, regional or systemic contexts, geographical focus, and methods and strategies. These elements offer a broader perspective on Indonesia's regional diplomacy connecting domestic outlook and strategic worldview of the elite with regional and systemic changes.

Indonesia's Expanding Regional Canvas: Southeast Asia to Asia-Pacific

There has been gradual expansion in the geopolitical canvas of Indonesia's regional diplomacy. This expansion is an expression of Jakarta's growing power, realisation among the leadership of the increasing importance of the broader Asia-Pacific in the country's regional diplomacy, the growing inter-connectedness of developments taking place in the sub-regions surrounding Southeast Asia, and its ambition to play a greater role in the region. Indonesian leadership is becoming more and more aware of its stakes and interests in the entire Asia-Pacific, and the impact of regional integrative processes in the form of shared prosperity and vulnerability of member-countries. Indonesia stands much more connected today – economically, politically, as well as strategically – with the countries of the region than it was two decades ago.

The year of 2008-09 gave a new momentum to Indonesia's pan-Asia-Pacific posture. The formation of the Bali Democracy Forum in 2008 is understood as an Indonesian effort to transcend ASEAN. The same year, Indonesia also submitted its request to hold the Chairmanship of the APEC, exhibiting its desire to play an active role in the Asia-Pacific and benefitting from the economic momentum characterising the region. The APEC promises to integrate Indonesia with a bigger market and greater economic dynamism. An important trigger came in 2009 when a group of Indonesian strategic thinkers began questioning their country's somewhat exclusive focus on ASEAN in the face of continued bickering within the grouping over opposition to the ASEAN Charter, the problem of Myanmar and the postponement of ASEAN meetings due to the domestic crisis in Thailand in 2008-09.[2]

The pan-Asia-Pacific focus of Jakarta's regional diplomacy received a major boost during the Bali summit of the APEC in October 2013. For Yudhoyono, it was not only a display of his own charm, but also his country's projection at the larger level of geopolitics of the Asia-Pacific.[3] The APEC Ministers' Joint Statement echoed the Indonesian push in its prescription for maintaining 'regional resilience' and its role as a growth-engine. Indonesia moved its ASEAN chairmanship from 2013 to 2011 in part so it could dedicate its full attention to the Bali Summit of the APEC in 2013. Jakarta used state resources extravagantly to ensure the summit's success. Malaysian prime minister Najib Razak's congratulatory reference to the Bali summit as the "best APEC" meeting highlights a success for Yudhoyono and Indonesia. Indonesian leaders' excitement and extravaganza, their active thrust to the APEC, and the success of Bali summit seem to have also put a lid on the host state's unhappy experience almost fifteen years ago. Indonesia received a severe jolt from the APEC when the latter intervened effectively in the East Timor Crisis in 1998-99 and steered the independence of East Timor. The intervention did not go well with the then leadership of Indonesia.

Jakarta actively campaigned to project the APEC as an important leg of its multilateral diplomacy, along with the G-20 and ASEAN, as a larger geo-strategic space for Indonesia's strategic positioning, and as an active platform to pursue its economic diplomacy. In fact, almost all ministerial remarks on the APEC alluded to Indonesia's long-term interests in the region and the role of the grouping in promoting Jakarta's regional and global profile. Indonesia's Coordinating Economic Minister Hatta Rajasa declared that the Bali Summit of the APEC in October 2013 'strengthened Indonesia's position in 'becoming a regional power, with the promise of being a global power in the future.'[4] The fast-growing Asia Pacific region, which accounts for more than two-thirds of Indonesia's total trade, is an important stimulus for offsetting the country's economic slowdown. President Yudhoyono pushed for more economic integration, better connectivity, and greater market access within the region while inaugurating the Bali summit.

A vast and geographically dispersed country of Indonesia finds itself equally involved in the developments taking place in the Indian Ocean. The Indian Ocean Tsunami of 2004 affected not only Indonesia, but also India, Sri Lanka and Thailand. The idea of stand-alone vulnerability seems to have become a relic of the past and can be pursued at a country's own peril. Indonesia is perhaps the only country that could form the nucleus of the region straddling the Indian Ocean in the West and Pacific in the East. Indonesia's geopolitical location makes it a bridge between the two maritime systems of the Indian and Pacific oceans and positions it to play a critical role in shaping the strategic discourses in the coming years. Indonesia's status as a founding member of the IOR-ARC further justifies its roles in this extremely relevant geo-political landscape of the Indo-Pacific. Indonesia will replace Australia in 2015 as the IOR-ARC Chair for 2015-16. To quote President Yudhoyono,

> There is every likelihood that in the twenty-first century the Indian Ocean will grow in geostrategic importance. We must make sure that the Indian Ocean does not become an area of new strategic contest and rivalry. Indeed, now is the time to cultivate the seeds for long-term cooperation, based on common interests in that part of the world.[5]

Benign Leadership, Pro-active Approach and Regional Mediation

A distinct characteristic of Indonesia's regional demeanour is its activist image manifested in the articulation of its worldviews on various aspects of the prevailing regional strategic atmosphere, its stakes in regional peace and stability, and the region's growing strategic uncertainty and instability. Two considerations have prompted Indonesia's activist regional diplomacy. First, its leadership has come to believe that conflict and instability is detrimental to its national interest at a time when the country is gaining momentum in economic growth and recovery. Second, there is growing realisation that as the largest Southeast Asian power, it should steer the regional power relationships towards peace and stability. Such an approach seems to have received a push from the country's apt assertion of both material and ideational strength. The growing vulnerability of Southeast Asia to the great power politics and growing disunity within ASEAN has prompted Indonesia to assume the role of pro-active leadership.

Indonesian Foreign Minister, Dr. R.M. Marty M. Natalegawa, while speaking at the Indian Council of World Affairs, New Delhi in July 2012, declared that regional peace and stability has contributed substantially to the country's economic growth and better human development indices, and Jakarta's primary objective should be to sustain a benign and peaceful atmosphere in the Asia-Pacific.[6] Underscoring the importance of regional peace and stability, Minister Natalegawa called upon the countries of the region in May 2013 to build an Indo-Pacific Treaty of Friendship and Cooperation. Such a treaty envisages clearer rules of engagement and scopes of dialogue and confidence-building measures in the event of bilateral or multilateral differences or conflicts.

The pro-active leadership of the Yudhoyono-Natalegawa duo seems to have given a major thrust to Jakarta's leadership and mediatory role in the region. They have been on the forefront in articulating Indonesia's priorities and policies on various issues concerning the region. Natalegawa's idea of 'dynamic equilibrium' is being viewed as one of the guidelines shaping Indonesia's foreign policy in the 21st century. He was quick to react against the adverse effect of the American declaration of stationing marines at Darwin in Australia. The sheer frankness of Natalegawa flustered both the American and Australian government, forcing them to open diplomatic channels of clarification and bringing Indonesia within the circle of trust and confidence. Similarly, Indonesia played a critical role in fixing the issue of ASEAN disunity after the latter's failure in reaching a consensus for the first time in the history of ASEAN at the 45th ASEAN Ministerial Meeting in Phnom Penh, Cambodia in July 2012. Both Yudhoyono and Natalegawa showed equal promptness in fixing the Phnom Penh fiasco. On the advice of his President, Minister Natalegawa, assuming the role of a crisis manager, embarked on a shuttle-diplomacy to salvage ASEAN's image and convinced all its member-states to come up with a Joint Statement.

'Rowing between Multiple and Multi-layered Reefs' (*Mendayung Antara Karang Karang*)

Mohammad Hatta, considered to be the father of Indonesian foreign policy, laid out two cardinal principles of Indonesian foreign policy: (a) *bebas dan aktif* (free and independent) foreign policy and (b) *mendayung antara dua karang* (rowing between two reefs). While the first principle promoted Indonesia's independent worldview, the second principle advocated non-alignment during the Cold War era when the global politics was marked by a bi-polar structure of power. Both these policies have, since the 1950s, continued to shape Indonesia's strategic thinking at regional and global levels.

However, regional geopolitics in the 21st century has taken a somewhat different turn towards multipolarity, demanding greater attention and complex diplomacy. The rise of Asian powers and the re-engagement of the USA and Russia have necessitated that any formulation of a regional security order must be based on the principle of multipolarity. Indonesia, while responding to the evolving power politics in the region, has followed a strategy of engaging these powers and redefining its relations with them, navigating through their rivalries, and managing the side-effects of a major-power tussle. This approach has allowed Indonesia to pay equal attention to its crucial strategic partners and its much-needed economic diplomacy that focuses on the rising economies and emerging market of the Global South.

There are three important components of this strategy. First, Indonesia has called for a multi-polar power structure. To quote Minister Natalegawa,

> ...We think the world today is no longer a world of two reefs but it's of multiple reefs. We have so many; it's a very multi-polar world, with different kind of challenges, no longer East and West, no longer about security, political issues; about the environment; about food security, energy security.[7]

Such an arrangement allows space to each of these powers and creates a buffer between these powers for Jakarta's own manoeuvrings. Second, Indonesia has, like other major powers, embarked on partnership diplomacy, developing a wide range of comprehensive and strategic partnerships with key players in the region. Indonesia signed a strategic partnership with China in April 2005, with India in November 2005, with Japan in 2006 and with the US in 2010.

Finally, Indonesia has pursued the strategy of 'equidistant engagement,' or what it calls 'Dynamic Equilibrium' with each of these powers depending on what Jakarta expects from a particular power and what the latter can offer. The policy of equidistant engagement is aimed at developing strong relations with key players of the region, maintaining peace and stability in the region and putting a lid on an escalation of hostility. The Indonesian President's advocacy of the idea of a 'million friends, zero enemies' further testifies to Indonesia's policy of equidistant engagement. Moreover, by pursuing this policy, Indonesia has been able to create a sense of equidistance and separate but common agendas for cooperation with each of these powers. Though rising China continues to be seen as a matter of concern and 'handle with care', Indonesia has embarked on developing greater strategic engagement with China, with a special focus on building defence and security cooperation and greater economic relations. Similarly, Indonesia has developed strong strategic engagement with India, Japan, Russia and the US.

Though Indonesia has viewed the US as the principal security provider and balancer in the region, it has shown no excitement over greater American military presence in the region, as such presence could further escalate hostility and destabilise regional geopolitics. Reacting to the American decision to deploy marines at the Australian port of Darwin, Minister

Natalegawa declared that such a move would create a 'vicious circle of tension and mistrust.'[8] He was referring to two possibilities – the impending Sino-US rivalry and subsequent militarisation and escalation of insecurity in the region. The deployment may be construed by China as its containment and push China towards greater military modernisation and its deployment in the neighbourhood, further militarising China's foreign policy, especially towards Southeast Asia, and triggering an arms race in the region. An unstable strategic atmosphere may not be commensurate with two important objectives of democratic Indonesia – the consolidation of democracy and sustained economic growth. Echoing similar sentiments at the Shangri La dialogue in June 2012, President Yudhoyono stressed on the geopolitics of cooperation rather than rivalry.[9] China remains, perhaps, the most important driver of economic growth in the region, while the US is the most powerful player in the region.

Advocating a Multipolar Regional Order

Regional politics of the Asia-Pacific is defined by an unstable multipolar security order, with each regional power trying to create its own sphere of influence, generating competition and rivalry in the region, and thereby, deepening the prevailing strategic uncertainty. In this multipolar Asia-Pacific, Southeast Asia has emerged as the focal point of strategic competition and Indonesia as a pivotal state. Any major power that wishes to enhance its strategic presence in Southeast Asia cannot do so without developing a strong relationship with Indonesia since it is a resurgent economy, a confident democracy and the most powerful ASEAN player. Indonesia has regained its pre-eminence in the ASEAN-driven multilateral cooperative processes, which offer the main platform for strategic projections of these countries.

Any multipolar regional order would place Indonesia in a pivotal position and enable the country to effectively address three pertinent issues facing regional geopolitics. These issues are greater economic integration, the growing prominence of great power politics, and desperate efforts to institutionalise the integrative processes and great power relations. The regional multipolarity may or may not diffuse the great power tension, but it has the potential to engage other regional players as important stakeholders in the regional project of building peace, stability and prosperity. Indonesia's 'Dynamic equilibrium' takes cognisance of inherent risks in evolving regional geopolitics and calls for a multipolar power structure in the Asia-Pacific that builds on the strengths of each power. The US President Obama's visit to the country in November 2010 signalled the positioning of Indonesia as an important variable in the US strategic calculations in the Asia-Pacific and acknowledged its growing indispensability for any multi-polar power structure emerging within the geopolitics of the Asia-Pacific.

Though Indonesia has developed strong economic linkages with China, the former continues to remain uncertain and suspicious towards Beijing's growing strategic influence in Asia, as well as its strategic agenda and assertive posturing in Southeast Asia. The South China Sea dispute, which puts China at loggerheads with four ASEAN countries – Brunei, Malaysia, the Philippines and Vietnam – continues to undermine China's overall diplomatic standing in Southeast Asia and within ASEAN. Moreover, any alignment with China might disrupt Jakarta's growing strategic engagement with two other Asian giants – India and Japan. At the same time, Indonesia remains wary of the domestic backlash against growing alignment with the US. Though President Obama, during his visit to Indonesia in November 2010, tried to win over the Indonesian Muslim constituency by speaking at the famous Ishtiqlal mosque in Jakarta, his gesture proved to be too little and too conspicuous.

At the same time, an important question facing Indonesian foreign policy today is whether it should take sides in the new-evolving geopolitical equations in the continent or whether it should assert its own strategic ambitions, contributing, in the process, to the rise of a loose multi-polar structure of power along with other major powers. In fact, Indonesia can ill-afford to join any anti-China Asian coalition for two reasons. First it does not look prudent to follow an overt antagonistic foreign policy approach in a globalised and integrated world against a rising global player. Second, Indonesia can not risk undermining its economic relations with China at a time when the country is on the path of economic recovery and the world is still recovering from an economic crisis. China, over the years, has emerged as the one of Indonesia's largest investors and trading partners. The country continues to focus on domestic economic and democratic consolidation to bolster its regional prominence. The region, on the other hand, is undergoing the process of greater economic integration through a web of bilateral and multilateral FTAs, mergers and acquisitions, and assembly-line processes of production. In fact, these powers are moving towards a state of mutual economic interdependence, and either a continental level instability or an individual country-level economic vulnerability can trigger shock-waves across the continent, bringing the entire Asian story to the brink of disaster.

A multi-polar power structure diffuses the concentration of power and therefore diversifies the claims and stakeholders in regional geopolitics. Though regional strategic equations hinge on the nature of relationships between these powers, there exists a considerable degree of uncertainty as to how they are going to relate to each other since they are still rising and consolidating their strategic positions. A disparate and multi-focal structure of power would allow Indonesia to manage the side effects of the major-power rivalries. A multi-polar power structure also frees Indonesia from choosing sides, a problem posed in the case of a bipolar structure of power.

Therefore, highlighting the country's own autonomous and eclectic outlook and its current strategy of equidistance, Jakarta is poised to push the region towards a multi-polar power structure. The evolving structure of multi-polarity offers Jakarta an important opportunity to project its own strategic ambitions and continue its leadership role within Southeast Asia, which is gradually emerging as the main theatre of power politics in the region. It seems that Indonesia's best interest for is viewed of its leaders now lies in a multipolar power structure in Asia.[10]

Pursuit of Partnership Diplomacy

Indonesia has embarked on the process of building strategic partnership as a means of developing multi-faceted engagement with important players and stakeholders in Indonesia's rise. Indonesia has signed strategic partnerships with Australia, China, and India, and comprehensive partnerships with the US, Japan, and Russia. By June 2012, Indonesia had signed such agreements with 14 countries, including all the major powers.[11] The question arises as to what these strategic partnerships entail and what they mean for Indonesia's regional diplomacy.

Strategic partnerships occupy a place of prominence in Indonesia's strategic thinking for several key reasons. They serve fundamental strategic interests, symbolise an enhanced level of multi-dimensional engagement, and reflect either the strategic necessity of cooperation or a shared worldview bringing the two partners together. The speech of President Yudhoyono at the Shangri-La Dialogue in June 2012 identified and highlighted the main aspects of Indonesia's partnership diplomacy. These partnerships, according to President Yudhoyono: (a) represent attempts to redefine and upgrade relations between the partners, (b) reveal positive strategic intention and, (c) in cases where the two parties are involved in a dispute, open up possibilities to alter the dynamics of how the disputes are handled.'[12] He also predicted that 'the number of countries involved in new bilateral, trilateral or regional partnerships will continue to grow significantly,' and their 'overall impact will be a sweeping change to the geopolitical landscape.'[13] The Indonesian Defence Minister, Purnomo Yusgiantoro, highlighted the defence and security connotation of the partnership diplomacy. He stated,

> "Indonesia attaches great importance to developing defence diplomacy and forming strategic security partnership in order to pursue confidence-building with our partners, enhance our military capability and promote defence industry. In doing so, as part of Indonesia's confidence-building measures, we have conducted defence-military official reciprocal visits, dialogues and consultations, information and intelligence sharing, officers training and educational exchanges, as well as joint-military exercises, be it bilaterally or multilaterally."[14]

Redefining Relations with Key Players: Towards Equidistant Engagement

Indonesia's foreign policy has become much more nuanced over the years in contrast to growing confusion and lack of focus that characterized Indonesian diplomacy during the early years of *Reformasi* era. Facing the growing presence of other global players in its vicinity, Jakarta perceived the necessity of developing a balanced response to the evolving major-power rivalries in Asia. Jakarta has embarked on balancing its relations with different major powers with the objective of diversifying its strategic engagement and stakes in its relations. This approach has allowed Indonesia to pay equal attention to its crucial strategic partners and its much-needed economic diplomacy, which focuses on the rising economies and emerging market of the Global South.

The most definitive step taken by Indonesia in this direction is the shift from Suharto's 'China-threat' to an 'engage China' policy. The stimulus for change has come from two sources – a domestic shift in its policy towards China after the departure of Suharto, and a growing desire to benefit from China's economic rise. In an attempt to normalize and strengthen its relationship with a rising China, Indonesia signed a strategic partnership with China in April 2005, and entered into a comprehensive FTA agreement by 2010. Concomitantly, Indonesia has scaled down the level of threat perceptions coming from China's rise. In fact, the growing depth of Indonesia-China relations can be seen at all three important levels of interaction: government-to-government, business-to-business, and people-to-people.

During his meeting with the Chinese President, Hu Jintao, on the sidelines of the APEC meeting in Vladivostok in September 2012, President Yudhoyono agreed to further strengthen Sino-Indonesian strategic partnership in both the areas of economic cooperation and security engagement.[15]

Substantial improvement can be seen in Indonesia's defence and security relations with China. Ever since the two sides began defence and security consultation in 2006, the engagement has expanded in three key directions – development of defence infrastructure, cooperation in the maritime security, and the military training. Following the June 2012 meeting between the Indonesian Defence Minister, Purnomo Yusgiantoro, and the commander of China's Second Artillery Corps, General Jing Zhiyuan in Indonesia, China has offered to supply new coastal radar systems, set up a new missile manufacturing base and train Indonesian air force pilots.[16] The two sides also discussed their plans to hold bilateral naval exercises and strengthen maritime security cooperation. The Indonesian Special Forces (KOPASSUS) and the Chinese People's Liberation Army (PLA) conducted their first joint training, known as 'Sharp Knife 2011' in Bandung in Indonesia in June 2011.[17] The two sides also held their first defence industry cooperation in Jakarta in July 2012.[18]

On a different note, Sino-Indonesian economic relations exhibit a distinct buoyancy. Bilateral trade between the two countries went up from US$16 billion in 2005 to US$66 billion in 2012, prompting the two sides to set a new bilateral trade target of US$80 billion by 2015. As per the reports, China has emerged as Jakarta's second largest trading partner, biggest source of import and second biggest export market.[19] Indonesia's exports to China totalled US$21.65 billion and its imports reached US$29.38 billion, registering an unfavourable balance of trade for Jakarta.[20] A large number of Chinese companies have begun investing in the Indonesian economy ever since the entry into force of the China-ASEAN FTA in January 2010, raising the total Chinese investment to US$2.9 billion. The bulk of the investment has taken place in the infrastructure sector, with the two sides willing to further increase Chinese investment in the critical sectors of energy and transport. In addition to commercial agreements worth US$10 billion, China agreed to offer preferential export buyers credit worth US$1 billion and US$8 billion worth of commercial funding to support infrastructure development and industry during the visit of the Chinese Premier Wen Jiabao to Indonesia in April 2011.[21]

Sino-Indonesian relations gained new traction during the visit of the Chinese President Xi Jinping to Indonesia in October 2013, highlighting a growing level of diplomatic trust between China and Indonesia. The presidents of the two countries, while meeting on the sidelines of APEC, exhibited a new interpersonal chemistry and mutual appreciation. Beijing and Jakarta also agreed to elevate their bilateral relations to a comprehensive strategic partnership and introduce substantive content to their engagement. Xi acknowledged Indonesia as an emerging market with global and regional influence, and Yudhoyono identified the bilateral comprehensive strategic partnership as a historical event. The two countries agreed to strengthen their cooperation in trade, investment and infrastructure, and signed various bilateral agreements, including a currency swap agreement of $16 billion. The two rising powers of the Asia-Pacific have made it clear they are going to engage in both bilateral and multilateral partnerships on a range of levels – economic, security, and political – irrespective of the United States' presence or absence. It is yet to be seen whether President Obama's absence has made a dent in U.S. credibility as a reliable balancer in the region. It has certainly prompted what seems to be a warming-up in the region toward China. And the first signal has come from the informal leader of ASEAN – Indonesia.

Nevertheless, the South China Sea dispute continues to generate anxiety and uncertainty among ASEAN players, including Indonesia. Indonesia has begun developing strategic ties with other important global and Asian players as an important component of Indonesia's 'hedge China' strategy. Indonesia's 'comprehensive partnership' with the US, an idea proposed by President Yudhoyono during his visit to the US in November 2008, can be seen as a step towards that direction. The press release on the US-Indonesia Comprehensive Partnership underscored, "the global significance of enhanced cooperation between the world's second and third largest democracies, the tremendous possibilities for economic and development cooperation, and the importance of fostering exchanges and mutual understanding between two of the world's most diverse nations."[22] Moreover, the Obama administration agreed in July 2010 to resume defence and security ties with the Indonesian Special Forces. The ties had been suspended in 1998 after the reports of their involvement in the large-scale human rights violations in East Timor and other parts of Indonesia.

Japan, another important regional power, continues to play a critical role in Indonesia's regional positioning. The two countries agreed in 2006 to elevate their bilateral relations to the level of a strategic partnership. The growing Sino-Japanese rivalry has prompted Tokyo, especially under the leadership of current Prime Minister, Shinzo Abe, to consolidate Japan's strategic and economic presence in Southeast Asia. Indonesia, as the principal ASEAN player and what President Yudhoyono called a 'long-standing good friend' of Japan, seems to have taken the centre-stage in the latter's policy towards Southeast Asia.[23] Japan has long been the largest trading partner of Indonesia, one of the largest investors in the country and also its largest donor. Japan has been one of the largest buyers of Indonesia's raw materials, whether natural gas, paper products or metal ore, and has played a key role in the development of infrastructure in the country. The total bilateral trade in 2012 stood at US$52.90 billion with its exports (US$30.13 billion) outweighing its imports (US$22.76 billion).[24] The bulk of the trade surplus has come from the Oil and Gas sector.

Indonesia-Japan bilateral relations have been strengthened with regular high-level dialogues including both the summit-level and three ministerial-level dialogues – the Defense Ministers' Dialogue, the Ministerial-level Strategic Dialogue, and the Ministerial Economic Dialogue– taking place annually. President Yudhoyono met with the Japanese Prime Minister Noda in Mexico on the sidelines of the G-20 meeting in June 2012. The two leaders acknowledged the importance of their cooperation for regional peace and stability. Prime Minister Abe's visit to Indonesia in January 2013 and his summit meeting with the Indonesian President added a new momentum in the bilateral relationship. President Yudhoyono, during his visit to Japan in October 2013 on the occasion of 40th anniversary of Japan-ASEAN relations, called for Japan's greater role in maintaining peace and stability in the Asia-Pacific.

Besides consolidating its relations with the United States and Japan, democratic Indonesia has also engaged Russia, another important player in the region. The Indonesia-Russia relationship has gained momentum during the six years since the visit of the Russian President Vladimir Putin to Indonesia in 2007 when the two sides signed a defence deal worth US$3 billion. Russia has expressed support for the Indonesian entry into the BRICS (Brazil, Russia, India, China and South Africa) grouping. The two countries have also agreed to develop their relations into a strategic partnership in the near future.[25] Several high-level bilateral visits have taken place since then. The Presidents of the two countries met on the sidelines of the APEC meeting in Honolulu, USA in November 2011. Trade relations between the two countries more than doubled from roughly US$1 billion in 2007 to US$2.2 billion in 2011. The two countries signed a MoU in December 2011 for the delivery of six more fighter Jets (SU-30MK2) to Indonesia.[26] Russia has also agreed to develop rail infrastructure in the Indonesian province of East Kalimantan.[27]

Similarly, Indonesia has been developing strong strategic engagement with India, another rising Asian power. India and Indonesia signed a strategic partnership in November 2005. Indonesia's strategy of equidistant engagement is very much reflected in the primary objectives of the India-Indonesia Strategic Partnership, which stipulates no domination of any single power in Asia, a stable and peaceful strategic atmosphere and an integrated Asian economy benefitting both the small as well as large economies.

Indonesia has engaged India in different aspects of defence and security cooperation – counter-terrorism, maritime security, joint development of defence infrastructure and training. The important elements of India-Indonesia maritime security cooperation include periodic goodwill visits by each other's navies, bilateral and multilateral naval exercises, and coordinated patrolling along with joint efforts to facilitate the creation of a multilateral maritime security regime, such as ReCAAP (Regional Cooperation for Combating against Armed Robbery and Piracy).

Indonesia has also strengthened its economic ties with India with the former enjoying a favourable balance of trade with the latter. Indonesia has emerged as the largest supplier of palm oil and one of the most important suppliers of coal.

Indonesia's engagement with India received an important thrust during the visit of the Indian Prime Minister, Manmohan Singh to Jakarta in October 2013.

Indonesia Resumes Intellectual Leadership of ASEAN

Indonesia's foreign policy and ASEAN's continued role as a regional interlocutor has been interdependent and mutually reinforcing ever since the latter's inception on 8 August 1967. This interdependence has emerged out of Indonesia's historical role in the making of ASEAN and the place of ASEAN in Indonesia's overall worldview. The major imperative for Indonesia's leadership role in the grouping has come from its continued belief in the critical importance, if not indispensability, of ASEAN in steering cooperation and stability in the region, managing the side-effects of regional rivalries, and keeping Southeast Asia together through a united voice.

Indonesia's multi-faceted contribution to ASEAN's existence, as many have enumerated and highlighted, can be identified in at least five important areas: (a) the provision of an international clout and strength to withstand pressure from major powers, (b) the development of a normative and value-based approach, (c) an unbiased and impartial role in the regional peace-making process, (d) intellectual leadership of the regional cooperative processes, and (e) a much-needed sense of moderation and direction.[28] To quote Rodolfo C. Severino, the former Secretary General of ASEAN, "Indonesia, in its wisdom, allowed itself to wield its already considerable weight in the world in the new context of ASEAN....Indonesia's international influence, prestige and activism, magnified by its new internationalist posture, were to be placed in ASEAN's service – at the United Nations, in the Non-Aligned Movement, in the Group of 77, and in other international forums."[29] Suharto's insular New Order regime focused primarily on regional issues and declared ASEAN as the cornerstone of Indonesia's foreign policy.[30]

Jakarta not only housed the ASEAN secretariat and coordinated its regular functions, but also provided strong international clout and overall guiding principles and *modus vivendi*. The cardinal principles of the ASEAN Way – *Musyawarah* (consensus) and *Mufakat* (consultation) are Indonesia's contribution. Indonesia played an important role in addressing and resolving the Cambodian crisis, initiated the confidence-building measures on the South China Sea dispute during the mid-1990s and called upon the claimant countries to engage in dialogue towards developing the rules of engagement in the disputed area.[31] In fact, the genesis of the resolution of the Cambodian problem in 1991 lies in the Jakarta Informal Meetings, held twice in 1989 and 1990 in Indonesia.[32] Jakarta undertook similar initiatives on the South China Sea, despite being dubbed as 'the busybee,' and held three workshops on the South China Sea in Bali, Bandung and Yogyakarta between 1989 and 1992.[33] Moreover, all ASEAN summits under Indonesian Chairmanship have taken place in Bali and each of these Bali summits has proved to be epochal in ASEAN's existence, whether it be the Bali summit of 1976, 2003 or of 2011.

Indonesia gradually began to be seen as ASEAN's leader and the intellectual force behind ASEAN until the region plunged into crisis and Indonesia came to the verge of its own disintegration. Indonesia became somewhat insular due to its own uncertain democratic transition in the aftermath of the departure of Suharto, one of ASEAN's patriarchs. Indonesia's internal economic crisis and political turbulence during the late 1990s seems to have been coterminous with the loss of direction within ASEAN, what Amitav Acharya calls 'floating without a sense of purpose.'[34] During this period, ASEAN faced its worst crisis of regional and international confidence with strong objections raised against the ASEAN Way and the basic method of ASEAN functioning. ASEAN faced serious limitations in addressing several important challenges – regional economic crisis, the Indonesian crisis, the East Timor crisis, the haze problem, induction of new members, the Myanmar problem, intra-mural bickerings between Malaysia and Singapore, and Malaysia and the Philippines. While the ARF was dubbed as a talk-shop, ASEAN was viewed as an inefficient and powerless regional grouping.

The 21st century has seen a gradual resumption of Indonesia's role in ASEAN as an intellectual leader, a crisis manager and as the anchor of community-building. Indonesia's leadership role in the ASEAN has been an effort to deal with the two-fold challenges of (a) providing leadership to the ASEAN process and convincing the Asian biggies to work together on the ASEAN table, and (b) engaging Asian and global players independently as a regional power. Four events have amplified Indonesia's leadership role during the last ten years.

A Tale of Two Summits: The Bali Summits of 2003 and 2011

Shedding its earlier tendencies towards insularity and uncertainty, democratic Indonesia has, once again, begun to lend its full normative, intellectual and strategic support to the grouping. The first glimpse came during Indonesia's chairmanship of ASEAN for 2003-04, when the grouping took many decisions of considerable regional importance. One such decision was to establish a three-tiered ASEAN Community – the ASEAN Political and Security community, the ASEAN Economic Community, and the ASEAN Socio-Cultural Community.[35] The Bali Concord II proved to be the first major statement by ASEAN towards regional cohesion and community-building as well as the first major initiative from democratic Indonesian leadership towards ASEAN. The Bali Concord II also declared the ARF as the 'primary forum in enhancing political and security cooperation in the Asia-Pacific region, as well as the pivot in building peace and stability in the region.'[36] Indonesia's role came not only in the form of leadership and decision-making but also in providing input in the making of ASEAN

Community. In fact, the idea of the ASEAN Security Community was based on the draft report prepared by the Indonesian Ministry of Foreign Affairs and this report was based on the concept paper developed by a prominent Indonesian scholar, Rizal Sukma.[37]

ASEAN's growing confidence in the Indonesian leadership was apparent during the Indonesian Chairmanship in 2011 when the grouping took a proactive approach towards engaging the major powers and de-escalating hostility in the South China Sea. ASEAN inducted the USA and Russia into the East Asia Summit, reiterated the freedom of navigation in the South China Sea and projected a united and strong voice against any effort towards hostility escalation and destabilising the region. A pro-active Indonesia as an ASEAN chair also displayed its mediatory role in two inter-state disputes – the Thailand-Cambodia dispute and the South China Sea dispute. Indonesia tried to mediate resolution of the Thai-Cambodian dispute and arranged for consultation and dialogue between the two parties on the sidelines of the ASEAN summit in Bali in 2011. Jakarta's mediation effort was also acknowledged by the International Court of Justice when it called upon Cambodia and Thailand to admit Indonesian observers to monitor the ceasefire.[38] In continuation of its earlier efforts to mediate in the South China Sea dispute during the 1990s, the Indonesian leadership took on similar role in 2011. President Yudhoyono, while addressing the 44th ASEAN Ministerial Meeting of Foreign Ministers in July 2011, called upon the involved parties to engage in the resolution of the dialogue, implementation of the Declaration of the Conduct of the Parties (DoC) of 2002, and sustained efforts towards developing a binding Joint Code of Conduct.[39]

While laying out Indonesia's role as an ASEAN Chairman for 2011, Minister Natalegawa insisted, "Indonesia will continue to invest its efforts...[and] attention on the building of a strong ASEAN. Because a strong ASEAN, an ASEAN marked by all the visions that we have in terms of the community, is also in the vital national interest of my own country, Indonesia."[40] In pursuit of its own directives, the Indonesian leadership introduced important concepts into the theme of an "ASEAN Community in a Global Community of Nations" as an ASEAN motto to give a new push to the creation of an ASEAN Community by 2015.[41] During its chairmanship, Indonesia promoted the concept of a 'People-oriented and People-centered ASEAN' and organised ASEAN Civil Society Conference (ACSC)/ASEAN People's Forum (APF) in Jakarta in 2011.[42] The main objectives behind these efforts were the promotion of ASEAN both at the global level and the grass-roots levels.

A pro-active Indonesia has also called for modifications in the foundational principles of the 'ASEAN Way' to adapt to the changing geo-political realities. It befits both the grouping as well as Indonesia that calls for change have come from the same country that provided the main source of normative strength. Indonesia's promotion of democracy and human rights, and political reforms in Myanmar under the Indonesian chairmanship are steps in that direction.

The ASEAN Charter

Democratic Indonesia has played an important role in the formulation and adoption of the ASEAN Charter. The same Singapore summit that saw internal dissent among members and Myanmar's obstinacy also adopted an ASEAN Charter, which entered into force during the special session of the grouping in Bali in the aftermath of the failure of Thailand to hold the summit in 2008. The Charter designated ASEAN as a legal entity, enabling the grouping to receive envoys and designated representatives at its headquarter in Jakarta.[43] Since then, the Indonesian capital city of Jakarta has emerged as the diplomatic capital city, prompting people to compare it to Brussels, the EU headquarters.[44] Rodolfo C. Severino, ASEAN's former Secretary General, identifies three important implications of the ASEAN Charter – ASEAN's move down a rule-based path, the introduction of a sense of responsibility among the member-states towards the success of ASEAN, and a culture of compliance towards the implementation of ASEAN decisions.[45] In fact, the Charter has introduced a gradual drift towards a certain set of formalism or rule-based behaviour in the grouping that has traditionally relied on somewhat informal and norm-based method of engagement. Indonesia's Trade Minister characterised this blueprint as 'a radical change' and 'a milestone' in the history of the grouping.[46]

The adoption of Charter, though in a truncated form, placed human rights on the agenda, enabling ASEAN member states to discuss such issues, which, hitherto, remained a taboo under one of the norms of ASEAN Way, the principle of non-interference, and respect for state sovereignty. The Charter also stipulates the setting up of a human rights body located within the ASEAN Secretariat in Jakarta that would oversee alleged human rights violations in the member-states and recommend appropriate actions to address the situation.

Nevertheless, the setting up of the ASEAN Charter has not been an easy experience for a democratic Indonesia. The non-democratic members raised objections to some of the critical components of the document, especially in the areas of democracy promotion and human rights. Their adamancy seemed to have frustrated the Indonesian leadership, prompting the latter to set up the Bali Democracy Forum in 2008, which can be understood as an Indonesian effort to go beyond the ASEAN limitations. The continued opposition to the ASEAN Charter from a few ASEAN countries, the problem of Myanmar and the postponement of ASEAN meetings due to the domestic crisis in Thailand in 2008 and 2009 seemed to have triggered an Indonesian reaction. Some also argue that the current ASEAN framework is not strong enough to respond to the emerging geo-political complexities facing the continent, nor efficient enough to benefit from the growing Asian economies. As a result, regional powers like Indonesia are being left out of the whole Asian strategic churning. The questioning over ASEAN-centrality has come from one of the most dominant think-tanks of Indonesia – the Jakarta-based Centre for Strategic and International Studies.

Indonesia and ASEAN after the Phnom Penh Fiasco

The inability of ASEAN leaders to bring out, for the first time in the history of ASEAN, a Joint Statement from its 45th Annual ASEAN Ministerial Meeting exposed the disunity and growing influence of power politics over the regional grouping. At the time of crisis, it was the Indonesian President Yudhoyono took the initiative and sent Minister, Natalegawa to five ASEAN capital cities in order to develop a consensus among the member states.[47] It was essentially the effectiveness of the Indonesian leadership of ASEAN and its role as a crisis manager to salvage ASEAN's image that convinced all its member-states to come up with a Joint Statement. As a result of Indonesia's consensus-building role, ASEAN has been able to adopt a six-point formula over the ASEAN's strategy of approaching the South China Sea dispute. These points are:

- the full implementation of the Declaration on the Conduct of Parties in the South China Sea (2002);
- the Guidelines for the Implementation of the Declaration on the Conduct of Parties in the South China Sea (2011);
- the early conclusion of a Regional Code of Conduct in the South China Sea;

- the full respect of the universally recognised principles of the International Law, including the 1982 United Nations Convention on the Law of the Sea (UNCLOS);
- the continued exercise of self-restraint and non-use of force by all parties; and
- the peaceful resolution of disputes, in accordance with the International Law, including the 1982 United Nations Convention on the Law of the Sea (UNCLOS).[48]

Moreover, the Indonesian initiative ensured the commitment from all the ASEAN countries to 'intensify ASEAN consultations in the advancement of the above principles, consistent with the Treaty of Amity and Cooperation in Southeast Asia (1976) and the ASEAN Charter (2008).'[49] The former US Secretary of State Hillary Clinton applauded Indonesia's role in 'unifying ASEAN members and helping to maintain stability in the region' in a joint press conference after meeting with Minister Natalegawa during her visit to Indonesia in October 2012.[50]

Building an Open, Inclusive, and ASEAN-driven Regional Cooperative Architecture

The ASEAN-driven regional cooperative architecture represents the confluence of power politics and cooperative processes. It has not only facilitated greater integration and community-building in the region, but also witnessed major powers jockeying for a greater say in shaping the architecture, setting its agenda and in the final deliberation over issues of regional concern. Both the institution of dialogue partnerships and introduction of ASEAN Plus initiatives – ARF, APT Initiative, EAS, and ADMM Plus – have facilitated the participation of major powers in regional affairs.

The interplay of power and institution has been taking place since the decision to expand the geographical ambit of ASEAN cooperative processes beyond Southeast Asia and use the grouping to engage and manage evolving dynamic of power politics in the region. Two issues have dominated the duel – the geographical canvas and membership of the architecture. These issues have not only divided the ASEAN member-states but also polarised major powers in terms of their roles and contributions to the ASEAN cooperative architecture in the region. One school of thought supports an architecture that is focused, exclusive and caters to the interests of countries belonging to classical East Asia, i.e., the ASEAN+3 countries. It emphasises the value of a focused approach towards addressing the challenges facing these thirteen countries only. The main exponents of this school have been China, Malaysia, and Cambodia. The second line of thought supports an open and inclusive architecture that includes participation from any country that has important stake or role in regional affairs. Such an approach has led to the inclusion of Australia, India, New Zealand, Russia and the USA in the regional architecture, represented by ASEAN+8 processes, such as EAS and ADMM+. The principal advocates of this school of thought have been Japan, Indonesia, and Singapore.

Indonesia has, from the beginning of the debate, advocated the building of an open and inclusive regional architecture with an ASEAN centrality and the involvement of all major players and stakeholders in the regional cooperative processes. Such an approach can be seen in the form of Indonesia supporting the multipolarisation of the Asian balance of power and bringing important global players to the ASEAN table for cooperation. It has sought to use the ASEAN-driven multilateral processes to facilitate greater economic integration with important economies and regions. As an ASEAN member, Indonesia shares FTA agreements with Australia, China, India, Japan, New Zealand, and South Korea. Indonesia seems to have played an instrumental role in introducing these principles not only in the ASEAN+ forums, but also in the basic purposes and modalities of carrying out ASEAN functions as envisaged under the ASEAN Charter. According to Article 1, section 15 of the ASEAN Charter, the basic purpose of ASEAN is "to maintain the centrality and proactive role of ASEAN as the primary driving force in its relations and cooperation with its external partners in a regional architecture that is open, transparent, and inclusive."[51]

Jakarta has always stressed that such an architecture should be comprehensive in terms of the participation of players and the agenda of cooperation and multipolarity. Indonesia has played a crucial role in facilitating the entry of Australia, India, New Zealand, Russia and the USA within the EAS. Another important component of regional security architecture – the ASEAN Plus Defence Ministerial Meeting (ADMM+) – shares a similar membership of 18 countries. Indonesia, at present, would like to see continued engagement and active participation from these 18 member countries in building an effective regional architecture. To quote Minister Natalegawa, "Indonesia will continue its leadership by shaping the agenda and the strategic role of the East Asia Summit...the East Asia Summit should be the main leaders' forum for discussion of strategic issues at both global and regional levels...throughout 2010, Indonesia made concrete and proactive contributions to the discussions on the Regional Architecture Building, in order to maintain the principle of ASEAN as the driving force. The expansion of East Asia Summit membership, through the simultaneous admittance of the United States and Russia is one of the manifestations of these concrete efforts."[52]

Moreover, an open and inclusive architecture must be led by ASEAN. Minister Natalegawa declared, "...for Indonesia, an East Asia Community or Asia-Pacific Community cannot be realized without the ASEAN Community as its main foundation."[53] In its vision of regional security architecture, Indonesia as an ASEAN Chair for the year of 2011 focused on two initiatives – the EAS and building the ASEAN Community. The two forums, in fact, are indispensable for Indonesia's vision of regional architecture.

Indonesia's emphasis on open regionalism and inclusivity can also be seen in the formulation of the ASEAN-driven Regional Comprehensive Economic Partnership (RCEP) as a compromise formula with ASEAN centrality between the APT and EAS processes of integration? The structure and mandate of the RCEP took shape under the chairmanship of Indonesia in 2011 before its final structure was accepted and approved during the 19th ASEAN summit in Bali, Indonesia. The RCEP envisages the participation of not only the APT members but also the EAS members, with its processes and activities regulated by ASEAN. The framework agreement of RCEP outlines its purpose as "to achieve a comprehensive and mutually beneficial economic partnership agreement" that will "involve broader and deeper engagement with significant improvements over existing ASEAN FTAs/CEP with Dialogue Partners."[54] Moreover, the framework agreement also stipulates that any ASEAN FTA partner can negotiate the terms of membership at any stage through its open accession clause.[55]

Addressing NTS through a Multilateral Framework

An important component of the rising Indonesia's regional diplomacy has been efforts for developing regional cooperative institutions towards the management of non-traditional security challenges. The two maritime systems constituting the Asia-Pacific have brought forth another equally important challenge for Indonesia's regional diplomacy in the form of several

NTS issues. Five of them – terrorism, maritime security, natural disasters, climate change and insurgency – have drawn greater attention from the Indonesian leadership. This focus and concern has emanated from Indonesia's growing realisation that though it may not face a direct military threat from any state, its security continues to be jeopardised by the growing spectre of NTS challenges. To quote Indonesia's former Foreign Minister, Ali Alatas, "International peace and security depends as much on social and economic factors as on traditional military factors. We must therefore also address the non-military threats to peace and security such as poverty, under-development, population pressures, environmental degradation, mass migrations, international terrorism and the trade in illegal drugs."[56]

While addressing different types of NTS threats, Indonesia has relied primarily on multilateral initiatives either through ASEAN cooperative framework or through the global initiatives. There are several forums within ASEAN – the ARF, EAS, and ADMM+ – mandated with the tasks of addressing NTS issues. ASEAN has also set up different institutional mechanisms at the regional level to deal with these challenges.

Displaying its deft regional diplomacy and acting as a bridge-builder between the international multilateral agencies and regional challenges, the Indonesian government in collaboration with the UN convened the Fifth Asian Ministerial Conference on Disaster Risk Reduction in October 2012. The key elements of the resulting Yogyakarta Declaration include calls to (a) integrate local disaster risk reduction and climate change adaptation into national development planning; (b) identify accountability measures for effective implementation; (c) political commitment to deliver at all levels; (d) promote awareness, education, public access to information and resilient investments; (e) and allocate resources to build local capacity.[57]

Conclusion

Rising Indonesia is not only trying to strike a balance between major power alignments, but also trying to ensure that ASEAN as a regional cooperative process remains united amidst rivalries and polarisation. While pursuing its two-pronged regional diplomacy, it has tried to position itself as an active player in the regional strategic discourses, including agenda-setting in the regional integrative processes. By doing so, the country has sought to secure a greater bargain for both its strategic positioning and the ASEAN cooperative processes. Such a positioning has enabled Jakarta to project itself as a leader and saviour of the regional grouping by lending its strategic resources to the grouping and by claiming its superior status emanating from its seat at the high table.

Nevertheless, one critical dilemma confronts rising Indonesia's regional diplomacy. Can Jakarta expect to contribute to regional peace and stability by pursuing strategic autonomy and multipolarity, a situation that creates instability and uncertainty in the region? While the stakes are rising, the strategic space for manoeuvrability and diplomacy is shrinking, as evident from China's growing assertions in both the South and East China Sea, the consequent escalation of hostility in East Asia, and the sheer inability of ASEAN to withstand the enormous pressure generated by major power rivalries. Jakarta has to invest in strategic thinking as to what its roles and responsibilities should be in the changing Asia-Pacific, and in what ways it can play the role of crisis manager and contribute to regional stability and prosperity. The time has come for Jakarta to invest in debating what its long-term grand strategy should be – one that would allow it to ride its rise as an autonomous actor in an unstable multipolar Asia-Pacific and also steer regional cooperative processes and community-building in Southeast Asia.

ENDNOTES

1. Dewi Fortuna Anwar, "A Problem of Mixed Messages," *The Asialink Essays 2012,* vol. 4, no. 6, August 2012, p. 2.
2. Rizal Sukma, Indonesia needs a post-ASEAN Foreign Policy, The Jakarta Post, 30 June 2009, http://www.thejakartapost.com/news/2009/06/30/indonesia-needs-a-postasean-foreign-policy.html (accessed on 12 December 2013).
3. Vibhanshu Shekhar, "A Sino-Indonesian Push for APEC,"*CSIS Asia House*, 22 November 22 2013, http://cogitasia.com/a-sino-indonesian-push-for-apec/ (accessed on 12 December 2013).
4. "APEC Strengthens Indonesia's Position as Regional Power," *The Jakarta Post*, 05 October 2013, http://www.thejakartapost.com/news/2013/10/05/apec-strengthens-indonesias-position-regional-power.html (accessed on 10 December 2013).
5. Susilo Bambang Yudhoyono, "An Architecture for Durable Peace in the Asia-Pacific," *Shangri La Dialogue Keynote Address,* 01 June 2012, http://www.iiss.org/en/events/shangri%20la%20dialogue/archive/sld12-43d9/opening-remarks-and-keynote-address-9e17/keynote-address-7244 (accessed on 10January2013).
6. Vibhanshu Shekhar, "Address by H.E. Dr. R. M. Marty M. Natalegawa, Honourable Foreign Minister of Republic of Indonesia," *Indian Council of World Affairs,* 27 July 2012, http://www.icwa.in/crindonesia.html (accessed on 21 October 2012).
7. "A Conversation with Marty Natalegawa, Minister of Foreign Affairs, Republic of Indonesia," *Council on Foreign Relations,* 20 September 2010, http://www.cfr.org/indonesia/conversation-marty-natalegawa-minister-foreign-affairs-republic-indonesia/p22984 (accessed on 03 January 2013).

8. Tom Allard, "Indonesia fears US forces could create 'vicious circle of tension'," *Sydney Morning Herald,* 17 November 2011, http://www.smh.com.au/world/indonesia-fears-us-forces-could-create-vicious-circle-of-tension-20111117-1nk0e.html(accessed on 03 January 2013); John McBeth, "Indonesia's Quiet Welcome of US Troops in Region," *Straits Times,* 18 September 2012.
9. Susilo Bambang Yudhoyono, op.cit.,
10. Indonesian Ambassador's Interaction at New Delhi-based Institute of Peace and Conflict Studies, 2011.
11. Susilo Bambang Yudhoyono, op.cit.,
12. Ibid.
13. Ibid.
14. "Building Security Partnership in Asia," Speech of Purnomo Yusgiantoro, Minister of Defence of the Republic of Indonesia at CSIS seminar, *Centre for Strategic and International Studies,* Washington D.C. 16 May 2013, p. 5, http://csis.org/files/attachments/130516_Purnomo Yusgiantoro_Speech.pdf (accessed on 10 June 2013).
15. "Chinese, Indonesian Presidents Meet on Cooperation," *Xinhuanet,* 08 September 2012, http://news.xinhuanet.com/english/china/2012-09/08/c_131835517.htm (accessed on 20 October 2012).
16. Trefor Moss, "Indonesia Talks Defense With China," *The Diplomat,* 01 August 2012, http://thediplomat.com/flashpoints-blog/2012/08/01/indonesia-talks-defense-with-china/ (accessed on 20 October 2012).
17. Christine Susanna Tjhin, "Indonesia's Relations with China: Productive and Pragmatic, but not yet a Strategic Partnership," *China Report,* vol. 48, no. 3, 2012, p. 307.
18. "China, Indonesia Expand Military Cooperation," *Defence Update,* 29 July 2012, http:/ /defense-update.com/20120729_china-indonesia-military-cooperation.html (accessed on 20 October 2012).
19. Christine Susanna Tjhin, op.cit, p. 310.
20. "Balance of Trade With Trade Partner Country: China," *Ministry of Trade,* Government of Indonesia,http://www.kemendag.go.id/en/economic-profile/indonesia-export-import/ balance-of-trade-with-trade-partner-country?negara=116(accessed on 13 December 2013).
21. Christine Susanna Tjhin, op.cit.,
22. "The U.S.-Indonesia Comprehensive Partnership," Press Release, US Embassy, Jakarta, 28 June 2010, http://jakarta.usembassy.gov/pr_06282010.html(accessed on 20 October 2012).
23. "Japan-Indonesia Summit Meeting (Summary)," Ministry of Foreign Affairs of Japan, 19 June 2012, http://www.mofa.go.jp/region/asia-paci/indonesia/meeting1206_pm.html (accessed on 13 December 2013).
24. "Balance of Trade With Trade Partner Country: Japan," op.cit.,
25. Veeramalla Anjaiah and Yassine Majdi, "Russia's Relations with RI growing in a 'Dynamic Way'," *The Jakarta Post,* 12 June 2009.
26. "Indonesia-Russia Relations Bolstered Through Real Cooperation Agreement," *The President Post,* 26 March 2012, www.thepresidentpost.com/?p=16194 (accessed on 25 October 2012).
27. Ibid.
28. Dewi Fortuna Anwar, *Indonesia in ASEAN: Foreign Policy and Regionalism* (Singapore, ISEAS, 1994), pp. 306-8; Amitav Acharya, *Constructing a Security Community in Southeast Asia: ASEAN and the Problem of a Regional Order* (London, Routledge, 2001); Christopher B. Roberts, *ASEAN Regionalism: Cooperation, Values and Institutionalization* (New York, Routledge, 2012), pp. 117-124.
29. Rodolfo C. Severino, "Indonesia and the Future of ASEAN," *ASEAN Secretariat,* 26 August

1999, no. 3312, http://www.aseansec.org/3312.htm (accessed on 25 October 2012).

30. Dewi Fortuna Anwar, *Indonesia in ASEAN: Foreign Policy and Regionalism* (Singapore, ISEAS, 1994), p. 7.
31. Vibhanshu Shekhar, "Address by H.E. Dr. R. M. Marty M. Natalegawa Honourable Foreign Minister of Republic of Indonesia," op.cit.; Dewi Fortuna Anwar, *Indonesia in ASEAN: Foreign Policy and Regionalism,*op.cit.,
32. Ibid, pp. 306-8.
33. Vibhanshu Shekhar, "Address by H.E. Dr. R. M. Marty M. Natalegawa Honourable Foreign Minister of Republic of Indonesia," op.cit.; Dewi Fortuna Anwar, op.cit. pp. 308-10.
34. Amitav Acharya, op.cit., p. 259.
35. "Declaration of ASEAN Concord II (Bali Concord II)," *ASEAN Secretariat,* no. 15159, http://www.aseansec.org/15159.htm (accessed on 25 October 2012).
36. Ibid.
37. Christopher B. Roberts, op.cit., p. 119.
38. Ehito Kimura, "Indonesia in 2011: A Glass Half-Empty," *Asian Survey*, vol. 52, no. 1, 2012, p. 193.
39. Ibid.
40. Lina Alexandra, "Indonesia Emerging," *The Diplomat,* 11 August 2011, http://thediplomat.com/asean-beat/2011/08/11/indonesia-emerging/ (accessed on 15 August 2012).
41. Ehito Kimura, op.cit., p. 192.
42. Ibid, p. 193.
43. Rodolfo C. Severino, "The Year in ASEAN: the Charter, Trade Agreements, and the Global Economic Crisis," *Southeast Asian Affairs*, vol. 2010, p. 61.
44. "Jakarta is Affirmed to be a Diplomatic Capital City," *ASEAN Secretariat,* 31 May 2012, no. 27026, http://www.aseansec.org/27026.htm (accessed on 27 October 2012).
45. Rodolfo C. Severino, op.cit., pp. 61-62.
46. Wayne Arnold, "Surprise Pressure From Myanmar's Neighbors," The New York Times, 20 November 2007, http://www.nytimes.com/2007/11/20/world/asia/20asean.html?_r=1&oref=slogin (accessed on 25 October 2012).
47. Ismira Lutfia, "Indonesia Leads from the Front on ASEAN," *the Jakarta Globe,* 08 August 2012, http://www.thejakartaglobe.com/home/indonesia-leads-from-the-front-on-asean/536384 (accessed on 28 October 2012).
48. "Statement of ASEAN Foreign Ministers on ASEAN's Six-Point Principles on the South China Sea," Ministry of Foreign Affairs and International Cooperation, Kingdom of Cambodia, 20 July 2012, http://www.mfaic.gov.kh/mofa/default.aspx?id=3206 (accessed on 28 October 2012).
49. Ibid.
50. Ismira Lutfia, op.cit.,
51. Association of Southeast Asian Nations, *The ASEAN Charter* (Jakarta, ASEAN Secretariat, 2008), p. 5.
52. Marty M. Natalegawa, "Annual Press Statement of the Foreign Minister of the Republic of Indonesia," 07 January 2011, http://indonesia.gr/speech-of-the-minister-of-foreign-affairsannual-press-statement-of-the-foreign-minister-of-the-republic-of-indonesia-dr-r-m-marty-m-natalegawa/ (accessed on 24 October 2012).
53. Ibid.
54. "ASEAN Framework for Regional Comprehensive Economic Partnership," *ASEAN*

Secretariat, no. 26744, http://www.aseansec.org/26744.htm (accessed on 25 October 2012).

55. Ibid.
56. Ali Alatas, *A Voice for a Just Peace: A Collection of Speeches by Ali Alatas* (Singapore, ISEAS, 2001), p. 19.
57. S Ganesan, "Call for Global Pact on Disaster Risk Reduction," *The Hindu,* 27 October 2012, http://www.thehindu.com/sci-tech/energy-and-environment/call-for-global-pact-on-disaster-risk-reduction/article4038619.ece (accessed on 29 October 2012).

4

INDONESIA AND THE CHANGING GLOBAL ORDER

Global politics in the 21st century reflects a fundamental transformation taking place in the structure of power, dynamics of relations, patterns of resource sharing, and the nature of challenges. The emerging global structure of power is marked by the shifting gravity of political and economic transactions from the trans-Atlantic region to the Asia-Pacific, a resurgence of Asian civilisational powers (China, India and Indonesia), a relative decline in the power of the West, and an enormous increase in the material capacities and prosperity of the Global South. The acquisition of mineral and energy resources in far and distant countries exemplifies a new-found thirst for resources by the emerging Global South. The rising global demands for affluence and resources have introduced new sets of challenges that no longer affect states or regions alone, but rather the entire mankind, such as climate change and the preservation of the global commons. Moreover, new demands are being placed upon the existing global institutions and agencies to make them more representative, distributive and democratic. On several occasions, the Global South has felt discriminated and exploited by the policies and programmes of the World Bank and IMF, which have often been seen as structurally flawed and insensitive to local concerns. There is growing realization that the Global South is no longer marginalised, but that it is developing, and warrants greater representation in the 21st century global order.

On the other hand, the process of globalisation, which is marked by technological innovation, digitisation of the world and the free flow of information. It has shrunk the distance between people, communities and countries, and led to greater interdependence and integration in terms of production, resource-sharing, and collective vulnerability. The global economic crisis of 2008 exposed globalisation as a 'double edged sword,' bringing poverty and vulnerability to people across the scales of opulence, ranging from the developed world to the underdeveloped world. Amidst prospects of prosperity and vulnerability, economic diplomacy has gained new momentum as an important foreign policy tool, especially from the Global South.

Indonesia's rise and its growing confidence is manifested in its positioning in the changing global order in the 21st century and in its growing desire to contribute to the ongoing debate over managing global challenges. There is a new sense of activism directed towards presenting its normative capital to the international community. This normative activism is derived from (a) the long-held righteousness of its foreign policy enshrined in the principle of strategic autonomy, and (b) the celebration of its recent domestic achievements – a functional democracy, economic development and political stability – by its leadership.[1] The preamble of the 1945 Constitution calls for Indonesia's 'active role in promoting a peaceful and just world order.'[2] Indonesia presents itself in the 21st century as the largest Muslim democracy, one of the fastest growing economies, an emerging power in the Global South, one of the most important members of the Non-Aligned Movement (NAM), a stable multi-ethnic and multicultural polity, a responsible regional power, and a moderate and tolerant civilizational force with a modern outlook. The Indonesian leadership views its current progress as a validation of its nation-state building process and worth international projection and for emulation by many countries in Asia and Africa. The State Guideline on foreign policy (1999-2004) and the Act No. 37, 1999 on Foreign Relations laid emphasis on two critical components of Indonesia's global positioning – 'restore Indonesia's international image and promote international cooperation that helps build and maintain world peace.'[3] While delivering a lecture at Harvard University in 2009, President Yudhoyono laid out nine imperatives to transform the world into a better living place. They are:[4]

- make the 21st century the century of soft power,
- intensify global dialogue and outreach,

- find a solution to political conflicts that drive a wedge between the Western and Muslim worlds,
- strengthen voices of moderation in our communities,
- promote multiculturalism and tolerance,
- make globalisation work for all,
- reform global governance,
- create educational opportunities in both our homes and our classrooms, and
- develop a global conscience.

Reinforcing the country's normative focus, Foreign Minister Natalegawa declared, "Our foreign policy was always carried out on the basis of a principled approach, one that is visionary and yet pragmatic and anticipatory in responding to global and regional developments."[5]

While speaking at the Wilton Park Annual Conference, London in November 2012, President Yudhoyono identified five important aspects of Indonesia's global role. In his words, Indonesia acts as a norm setter, consensus-builder, peacekeeper, bridge-builder, and a voice of the developing world.[6] By seeking its active normative role in the global debate, Indonesia demands greater space and say in the changing global order as it grows in terms of power and influence.

This chapter looks at four critical areas of Indonesia's global posture, which have received attention from its democratic leadership – the promotion of democracy, fundamental reforms in multilateral institutions, the revival of the Non-Aligned Movement and solidarity of the Global South, and representation of the Muslim world in the discourse with the West.

Indonesia as the Third Largest Democracy: Image-building to Identity-building

Post-Suharto Indonesia embarked on the process of developing the country into a stable democracy during the last fifteen years. In addition to consolidating democracy at home, Indonesia has been engaged in showcasing its democratic image to the international community.[7] The following statement of Foreign Minister. Natalegawa sums up Indonesia's new role.

> Ten years ago, political obituaries were written about Indonesia even as a state, and our economy was in a difficult situation. We now enjoy the democratic dividend thanks to our transformation and now we are beginning at the global level to try to play a bit more of a role to put ourselves on radar screens.[8]

Democratic Indonesia's agenda of democracy promotion stands in sharp contrast to the Suharto regime's rejection of democracy during the 1990s and its emphasis on 'Asian Values' that challenged international campaign for promoting liberal democracy and human rights in Asia.[9] It is also argued that "Indonesia blocked the efforts of Thailand and the Philippines during the early 1990s to modify ASEAN policy on democracy and human rights from one of strict non-interference to a more nuanced 'flexible engagement'."[10]

Indonesia's democratic experience has been viewed not only as a case of celebration and an important reference point in the history of the global growth of democracy, but also as a standard case for observation, examination and emulation for the developing, Muslim and multi-ethnic societies, including the countries of West Asia and North Africa. Such countries have experienced sudden stimuli for change and democratization in the aftermath of the Spring revolution, which witnessed massive popular mobilization for the topple of the autocratic and military regimes. A few writings equated the Arab Spring with the Indonesian *Reformasi* and suggested lessons for the former to learn from the latter.[11] Indonesia's moderate Muslim outlook also raised the hope for the spread of democracy in the revolting societies of the Middle East. The Economist ran a special debate on equating the Middle East issue with the Indonesian transition to democracy.[12] In other words, its democratic credentials have earned Indonesia considerable normative capital, which it attempts to market for the country's overall principled global positioning in the 21st century.

The drivers for the projection of Indonesia's democratic credentials seem to have come from its desire to regain its normative capital by eradicating its authoritarian and undemocratic past and projecting its new identity. Indonesia was criticized globally for its authoritarian regime and large-scale human rights violations in its insurgency-infested areas of West Papua and Aceh, apart from the Indonesian military's widely documented brutality in the now-independent country of Timor Leste. Indonesia's image took a beating even within ASEAN in the aftermath of its failure to manage several domestic and regional challenges during the late 1990s, and the country's overall inability to provide leadership to the ASEAN forum in its time of necessity. It is argued that Jakarta's pro-democracy campaign took shape when the country recognized the necessity of projecting 'a positive image to the rest of the world that would restore the faith in it once held by the international community.'[13]

Jakarta's pro-democracy campaign reflects its aspirations to be treated as a successful democracy and as an example to the vast majority of non-democratic countries in the Global South, especially in the Muslim world. The international community, and especially the West, speaks of Indonesia as an example of building a moderate Muslim democracy and has been campaigning to discredit two notions of incompatibility: first, between Islam and democracy, and second, between the Muslim world and democracies of the West. Moreover, the championing of democracy has also facilitated Indonesia's efforts to introduce democracy and human rights as principal issues of concern and debate within ASEAN and to reclaim its elevated standing among the ASEAN countries, the majority of which are non-democratic. It appears that as early as 2003, Indonesia had begun lobbying within ASEAN for it to adopt a democracy and human rights agenda.[14]

Indonesian policy makers have relied principally on the global and regional multilateral institutions to showcase its democratic character – global multilateral forums such as the United Nations and regional forums such ASEAN Cooperative Processes. During the last five years, Indonesia has hosted various multilateral meetings and has been represented at the highest levels in different multilateral global and regional meetings taking place abroad.[15] In this context, Indonesia's efforts at the Bali Democracy Forum (BDF) require closer scrutiny. The BDF was set up by the democratic Indonesia in 2008 as 'an annual, inclusive and open intergovernmental forum on the development of democracy in the Asia-Pacific region.'[16] The BDF website lists its basic objectives as 'establishing and maintaining a forum among Asian countries that promotes political development through dialogue and cooperation in strengthening adherence to democratic values and development of democratic institutions.' Moreover, the forum also allows Indonesia to project its democratic outlook at the regional level.

While discussing the achievement of the half-decade old BDF, the Indonesian President highlighted its three important contributions – the involvement of an increasing number of countries in the BDF deliberations, an increasing shared commitment to democratic policies and values, and a greater push to the democratic momentum building in the countries of the Asia-Pacific.[17] The number of stakeholders in the BDF has gone up from 43 in 2008 at its first annual meeting to 91 after half a decade of life. The growing participation is, according to President Yudhoyono, indicative of the fulfillment of the basic objective of the BDF of sharing experiences and best practices in democracy.[18]

However, the promotion of democracy has not been a smooth ride for newly democratic Indonesia. It has faced constant challenges both the national level and at the ASEAN level. Indonesia has faced strong resistance while pushing for the adoption of democratic values at the ASEAN level. Many of the non-democratic ASEAN member-states have opposed such moves and threatened their withdrawal from membership if pushed further. Myanmar's case is a good example. Myanmar threatened to withdraw from ASEAN if pushed on the issue of democratic reforms, and Yangon's fierce contestation prompted a writer to call it 'a case of one versus nine.'[19] Indonesia's democratic progress has faced two important national challenges in the form of growing Sunni majoritarianism in the country and the violation of minority rights.

Democratic Indonesia as a Global Multilateralist

One of the most definitive expressions of Indonesia's global diplomacy is its projection as a multilateralist in the form of its participation in the global multilateral institutions and its efforts towards promoting their role in addressing global challenges. Indonesia has actively participated in the UN system, including its peacekeeping operations and in the global deliberations over issues of climate change, religious tolerance, global economic recovery and global economic integration. Jakarta has linked the growth and efficacy of global multilateralism with the efficient functioning of the UN system and its global and representative character. Indonesia has advocated for a greater role by the UN leadership in addressing global challenges, the impartial and effective participation of the UN Security Council in building global peace and security, greater engagement and cooperation among the UN members, greater global representation in the UN institutions, and active support for the UN deliberations and negotiations.

Indonesia at the United Nations

The democratic Indonesia has come a long way during the last 13 years. It status has changed from an object of the UN mission in 1999 to an active and confident contributor to the UN processes in 2012. The Indonesian government, in its bid to give a fillip to its engagement with the UN members, opened diplomatic relations with nine UN members in 2011 alone.[20] Moreover, the Indonesian leadership has unequivocally argued for a greater UN role in ending the conflicts in different parts of the world, such as in Libya, Syria and Palestine.[21] Indonesia's active participation in the UN is also evident from its membership of different UN bodies and committees. For example, Indonesia has been a member of the UN Human Rights Council since 2007 and will remain so until 2014.[22] Indonesia's active role in the 65th UN General Assembly for the period of September 2010-September 2011 can be gauged from its different roles: Vice President of the UN's 65th General Assembly Meeting, Chairman of Commission on Population and Development, and a member of both the Governing Council UNEP and Governing Council UN Human Settlements Program (UN-HABITAT).[23] In addition to taking part in the 67th UN General Assembly in September 2012, the Indonesian President co-chaired 'the first and historic meeting of the High-level Panel (HLP) of Eminent Persons to discuss the global development agenda after 2015.'[24]

Post-colonial Indonesia has prioritized its active participation in the UN peacekeeping operations as an attempt to project its normative capital. Indonesian peacekeepers, known as the *Garuda* contingent, have been deployed in different parts of the world. The following table provides a quick glimpse into Indonesia's participation in various UN operations.

Table 4.1: Indonesia's Participation in various UN Operations[25]

Name of the UN operations	Period	Field-Country
ONUC	1961-1963	Republic of Congo
UNEF II	1973–1979	The Middle East
UNIMOG	1988–1990	Iraq
UNTAG	June–December 1989	Namibia
UNIKOM	1991–2003	Kuwait
UNTAC	1992–1993	Cambodia
UNOSOM	1992–1995	Somalia
UNPROFOR & UNMIBH	1993– 2002	Bosnia and Herzegovina
UNAMSIL	1999–2005	Sierra Leone
MONUC – now MONUSCO	March 2001 onwards	Democratic Republic of the Congo

Moreover, the Indonesian contribution today to the UN operations is considered to be entering into a new chapter for two primary reasons: (a) a quantitative and qualitative jump in the country's contribution to the UN peacekeeping operations, and (b) a widening geographical horizon.[26] Indonesia is planning to increase the total strength to 4000 peacekeepers. The contribution of a naval unit to the Indonesian operations in Lebanon attests to the first trend, while the presence of the Garuda contingent in

Haiti, for the first time in the Americas, confirms the second trend.[27] Besides, there is growing desire among the political leadership to project Indonesia as 'a regional hub of the UN peacekeeping operations in Asia.' According to Foreign Minister Natalegawa, "Indonesia has actively contributed to the development of a strategic concept for global peacekeeping missions. In 2011, Indonesia will attempt to be a hub for the peacekeeping network in the region."[28] Indonesia ranked among the top 20 contributors of UN peace-keeping operations in 2010. Its goal is to become one of the top ten contributors to the UN peacekeeping missions.[29]

The UN Secretary General, Ban Ki Moon, during his visit to Indonesia in March 2012, appreciated the country's significant role in the UN peacekeeping operations.[30] Approximately 2000 Indonesian troops are currently engaged in six of the most difficult UN missions – Lebanon, Haiti, Darfur (Sudan), Liberia, South Sudan and the Democratic Republic of Congo.[31] The Indonesian President, at the request of the visiting UN Secretary General, also agreed to contribute three Russian-made Mi-17 transport helicopters to the UN operations in the Democratic Republic of Congo (DRC), where Indonesia had sent its first ever peacekeeping mission in 1957. Moreover, the country's announcement to commit 4000 troops to various UN peacekeeping missions has made it one of the largest contributors to the UN peacekeeping operations.[32] In order to lend a greater credence to its peacekeeping role, the Indonesian government has decided to set up a peacekeeping facility as part of the Indonesian Peace and Security Center in Sentul, Bogor, which will be the largest international facility in Southeast Asia for the UN peacekeeping purposes.[33] The Indonesian government decided in June 2012 to send one battalion of troops to the UN peacekeeping operations in Darfur, South Sudan.

Indonesia is also willing to play a pro-active role in the UN-led debates on global disarmament after its ratification of the Comprehensive Test Ban Treaty in 2011.[34] Such an approach reflects Indonesia's long-standing viewpoint and cardinal principles of the country's foreign policy. The final communique of the Bandung Conference of 1955 called upon all the member states to 'cooperate especially through the United nations in bringing about the reduction of armaments and the elimination of nuclear weapons under effective international control.'[35] While speaking at Ambon in Maluku in June 2009 on the occasion of the 34th World Peace Day, the Indonesian President declared, "Indonesia will support the UN efforts for nuclear disarmament including a ban on nuclear development anywhere around the world. Indonesia will [provide its] support and continue to do so until nuclear disarmament is realised in the future."[36]

Indonesia and the UN Climate Change Negotiations

The issue of Climate Change is another important global challenge that has seen Indonesia's active participation as a responsible stakeholder at the multilateral level. It remains an open secret that without the involvement of large Green House Gas (GHG)-emitting countries, the global negotiations over addressing the issue of climate change cannot be productive and results-oriented. Indonesia, as one of the most bio-diverse countries in the world and the third largest GHG-emitting country, remains extremely vulnerable to climate change, and therefore is an important stakeholder in the multilateral negotiations over climate change under UN auspices.[37]

Indonesia hosted the 13th Conference of the Parties to the United Nations Framework Convention on Climate Change (UNFCCC), also known as the Third Meeting of the Parties to the Kyoto Protocol in Bali in December 2007. The conference adopted a Bali Road Map that also includes a Bali Action Plan (BAP), which launched a 'new, comprehensive process to enable the full, effective and sustained implementation of the Convention through long-term cooperative action, now, up to and beyond 2012.'[38] The BAP set the target of COP 15 (15th Conference of the Parties) at Copenhagen in 2010 for an agreed outcome on various issues of commitments for their operationalisation. The UNFCCC meet in Bali is believed to have not only successfully projected Indonesia's role as an active and powerful contributor to the climate change negotiations, but also created greater awareness among the common Indonesians by introducing climate change as an important agenda at the domestic level.[39]

Since then, Indonesia has played a pro-active role in supporting the climate change negotiations taking place under the auspices of the UN. Former US Vice-President Al Gore, while testifying before the Senate Foreign Relations Committee in January 2009, identified Indonesia as a constructive force in the climate negotiations.[40] Indonesia has played an active and supportive role in the negotiations over the REDD (Reducing Emissions from Deforestation and Forest Degradation in Developing Countries) and the establishment of the adaptation committee.[41]After much dilly-dallying, it finally approved in December 2012the Rimba Raya rainforest conservation project 'that sets aside an area roughly the size of Singapore and rewards investors with tradable carbon credits in the first of its kind to win formal backing in the country.'[42] The Rimba Raya conservation project is an important component of the UN-led REDD scheme.[43]

Building an Equitable and Representative UN Order in the 21st Century

In addition to greater role of the global multilateral institutions, rising Indonesia has been advocating fundamental reforms in several international institutions – the UN, the World Bank, the IMF and the WTO. These institutions in their current shapes do not reflect the changing reality of the 21st century and growing aspirations and roles of the developing world. Jakarta considers the existing international order to be outdated, moribund, ineffective, triumphalist, reflective of World War II reality and skewed in favour of the advanced West and the developed world. These institutions no longer represent the vast majority of countries and the growing power of the emerging Global South. It believes that '[the UN's] democratic intentions are diluted by the workings of an embedded oligarchy.'[44] In other words, the rules of engagement need to be changed to make these institutions representative, efficient, harmonized, coordinated, and in tune with the changing times.[45] Jakarta's energy and advocacy for the restructuring of international institutions has revolved around the idea of greater global visibility, finding its rightful place in these institutions amidst its emerging profile and the country's growing advocacy for equitable global order and greater cooperation among the developing world.

Indonesian leaders have brought to the table tangible suggestions for discussions regarding the restructuring of the UN system. In 1992, then Indonesian Foreign Minister, Ali Alatas, was chosen as one of the Commissioners of the Commission of Global Governance that was constituted under the Secretary Generalship of Boutros Boutros-Ghali. The Commission laid out various suggestions, such as a standing UN army, the end of the UNSC veto, and a system of global taxation.[46] Since then, Indonesia has actively participated in various working groups and deliberations both within and outside the UN mandate for reforms within the UN. Foreign Minister Natalegawa, while speaking at the 66th UN General Assembly, declared that the only way through which the United Nations can remain relevant and multilateralism can flourish is for it to be able to 'address new and emerging challenges,' identify new opportunities, and offer 'full support for, and reform of the United Nations.'[47] Indonesia has also used other international organisations and forums to advocate the

UN reforms and project its normative credentials, such as its membership of the G-77 and China. Indonesia has shown its intent to enter into the African market and join other emerging powers' clubs, such as BRICS (Brazil, Russia, India, China and South Africa) and IBSA (India, Brazil and South Africa). The G-77 grouping under the chairmanship of Indonesia in 1998 emphasised UN reforms and set up 'an expert group that would help articulate the vision of the South on the future role of the UN.'[48]

The reform of the UN Security Council has drawn the maximum attention in the global debates over UN reforms. Indonesia produced a concept paper in September 1995 entitled 'Criteria for Permanent Membership in the Security Council.'[49] While highlighting the failure of the UNSC in ending violent conflicts in different parts of the world, President Yudhoyono declared in 2012, "World peace should not be determined by only one country among the five veto holders within the Security Council. I suggest that the council be reviewed because it is no longer relevant to the current world situation."[50] Indonesia wants a Security Council that is 'transparent, democratic, representative, and effective in fulfilling its immense responsibility to maintain international peace and security in an even-handed and just manner.'[51] Moreover, it has projected its own candidature as a potential permanent member of an expanded and reformed UN Security Council. Former Australian Prime Minister John Howard supported the Indonesian candidature as a permanent member on the UN Security Council without a veto along with India, Japan, Brazil and Germany for two reasons: its contribution to the global peace and security, and its status as the world's largest Muslim nation.[52]

The democratization of the international financial institutions and greater representation of the global South in these institutions have been additional important campaign areas. This campaign has its genesis in the manner in which these institutions have interacted with the non-developed world in a time of economic crisis. The critical issues – the quota system, the process of decision-making, and the nature of participation of the developing and under-developed economies in the IMF and World Bank – have come under attack from the emerging economies of the Global South, including Indonesia. Moreover, the global economic crisis of 2008 and its genesis in the developed economies of the West have exposed the prevailing bias in the global financial architecture towards the developed world, a ruthlessly exploitative and unsparing approach towards the developing world, an urgent necessity for a greater role of the developing world in the decision-making process, and the need for a re-allocation of the quota-system. While receiving a contribution of US$1 billion from Indonesia as a part of the European bailout package, the IMF chief, Christine Lagarde, declared, "To enhance the global effectiveness of the Fund, dynamic emerging market countries like Indonesia need to have a greater say. In this context, I welcomed Indonesia's support for the IMF's quota and representation reforms."[53] The Indonesian contribution is part of a commitment made in the G-20 meeting in June 2012 to support the IMF, which needs $430 billion to help countries facing financial difficulties.[54]

Indonesia considers itself a victim of a discriminatory mandate and the policies of the international institutions. Many believe that the recommendations of the World Bank and IMF created social and political unrest in the country in the wake of the economic crisis that took place during the late 1990s. The image of a humbled and weak Suharto, the then Indonesian President, signing the US$40 billion bail-out package with then IMF chief, Michael Camdasus overseeing the signing ceremony continues to reverberate in the minds and hearts of common Indonesians.[55] The arrangement, symobilisng the victory of the Washington Consensus, had led to the fall of the Indonesian *Rupiah* and the large-scale retrenchment of Indonesian workers, and pushed the country towards a comprehensive political, economic and social crisis.

Indonesia and the G-20: Deliberating the Global Economic Order

Rising Indonesia represents an underlying paradox that characterizes a developing society – rapid economic growth amidst all-pervasive poverty. According to the report of the World Economic Forum, released in June 2011, Indonesia has emerged as the third fastest growing G-20 economy.[56] Developing economies including Indonesia have proved to be the main driver of global economic recovery and a critical support-base for the world in a time of need. Notwithstanding its rapid economic growth during the last five years, Indonesia continues to remain the second poorest member-state (after India) of the G-20 in terms of per capita income.[57] Therefore, the Indonesian representation in the G-20 deliberations highlights both confidence as well as insecurity, and an assertion of demand for greater democratization of the global economic order along with the projection of its own national interests.

Established in 1999 as an informal grouping of nations, the G-20 has gained significance in the aftermath of 2008 economic crisis that swept the advanced West but spared the emerging economies of the developing world. The G-20, since then, has focused on (a) developing ways and means for global economic recovery, (b) reforms in the international financial institutions, including greater representation of the developing world in the IMF and World Bank, (c) international monetary reform including greater integration of finances and curbing of excessive volatility, and (d) pursuing an agreed development agenda. The members of G-20 are Argentina, Australia, Brazil, Canada, China, European Union, France, Germany, India, Indonesia, Italy, Japan, Mexico, Russia, Saudi Arab, South Africa, South Korea, Turkey, UK, and USA.

Indonesia's role in the G-20 forum has revolved around 'promoting the interests of developing countries, maintaining an inclusive and sustainable global economic system, and encouraging the achievement of a consensus while acting as a bridge builder.'[58] In addition to maintaining the grouping's democratic and problem-solving character, Jakarta seeks to utilise its membership to promote and project the country's growing prosperity as it transitions from 'being a low income country to a middle income country, and a beneficiary country to a beneficiary and concurrently a donor country.'[59] The initial years of Indonesia's participation did not draw much attention due to, as identified by one writer (a) the poor capability of the negotiators, (b) a lack of home work in terms of agenda-building, (c) a limited national budget, and (d) a somewhat stand-alone approach.[60]

Membership in the G-20 has not only elevated Indonesia to an important position in the global hierarchy of nations, but also provided an extremely powerful avenue for the projection of its international image. Indonesia is not only aware of this mutually reinforcing relationship, but also tried to utilize it effectively, as evident from its expressions about the significance of the G-20 membership. Moreover, there has been growing activism during the last few years among the Indonesian leadership towards utilization of the G-20 forum for its global projection as it appears more prepared and innovative while participating in the G-20 deliberations. Indonesia co-chaired with France the Working Group-4 in 2008 to discuss reforms in the Multilateral Development Banks and called for the cleaning up of the infected assets of the financial system and greater market access for developing countries.[61] The Pittsburgh summit of the G-20 in 2010 saw increasing appreciation from among the member-states for Indonesia's success-story of transforming direct fuel subsidy into direct subsidy or the BLT (Extended unconditional cash transfer) program.[62]

In contrast to its previous appearances, Indonesia's performance in the last G-20 summit, held in Los Cabosin in June 2012, has been viewed by some as: (a) focused, due to its concentration on three issues – its 'middle-way' approach to balancing austerity and job creation, financial inclusion and infrastructure investment; (b) strategic, since it refrained from discussing controversial issues such as green growth; and (c) effective, given general appreciation given by the grouping to its two critical proposals – a global financing initiative on infrastructure facilities, and a framework to help develop the pipeline of bankable projects to boost infrastructure development in developing and emerging economies.[63] Moreover, these proposals found space in the final communiqué in the form of the G-20 Finance Ministers' and Central Bank Governors' Agenda, and was 'well received by other developing countries.'[64] As an ASEAN Chair in 2011, Indonesia mobilized ASEAN resources towards greater ASEAN representation in the G-20 meetings.[65] It becomes amply clear that rising Indonesia is more confident, innovative and forthcoming in its participation in the G-20 deliberations, while putting forth the interests and concerns of the developing world.

Reviving Non-Alignment and Solidarity of the Global South: Towards Bandung II

The Bandung summit of April 1955 of the Afro-Asian Conference occupies an important position in the conceptualization of the foreign policy of the post-colonial Indonesia. It symbolizes Indonesia's assertion of (a) a strong and collective voice of the countries of Asia and Africa, (b) a non-partisan view of the global *bodypolitik*, (c) a free and independent (*bebas dan Aktif*) foreign policy, (d) a shared worldview and cooperation among the developing countries, (e) the steering of the post-colonial developing world towards peace and prosperity by walking the path of non-alignment, and (f) the relevance and necessity of a non-aligned foreign policy. The principle of Non-Alignment has come to shape the basic tenets of Indonesian foreign policy, ever since its encapsulation by Mohammad Hatta in 1948 and in his two subsequent writings.[66]

The idea of non-alignment emerged as a strategic response for the post-colonial nation-states to survive in an atmosphere of insecurity marked by polarisation and bloc politics. Together they not only offered a critique of the emerging Cold War scenario, but also developed an alternative front that could represent the erstwhile colonies of Asia and Africa and guide the process of development in these two countries. Sukarno's advocacy of non-alignment found its full expression during the first Asian-African Conference, held in Bandung, Indonesia in April 1955, where leaders refused to take part in the Cold War vulnerabilities and welcomed the pursuit of an independent and alternative security perspective for the new-born republics of Asia and Africa. The Bandung summit augmented an assertion of the above-mentioned trends, which finally took a concrete shape in 1961 at the Belgrade Conference in the form of Non-Aligned Movement (NAM). Indonesia's first President, Mohammad Sukarno was one of the principal architects of what can be termed as 'Bandung Worldview.' Though the Indonesian leadership continued to advocate for greater role of the NAM in the global politics and greater collaboration among the developing South, the movement gradually began to sidestep. Indonesia as Suharto drew the country closer to the United States of America. Indonesia served as the Chair of NAM for three years (1992-95) immediately after the end of the Cold War era.

The democratic Indonesia has made a renewed effort to project the country's long-standing solidarity with the NAM. Indonesia hosted an Asia-Africa Summit in May 2005 to commemorate fifty years of the NAM.[67] The summit adopted a Joint Declaration on the New Asian-African Strategic Partnership (NAASP) that was aimed to be an expression of Indonesia's intent to be an important part of the Afro-Asian solidarity. Moreover, the NAASP Declaration called for close cooperation among the member-states and laid down important objectives of the partnership in the 21st century. It highlighted the need to "(a) continuously strengthen the process of nation and state-building, as well as social integration; (b) actively pursue a common view and collective action to ensure the equitable sharing of the benefits of globalization; (c) support and strengthen multilateralism in order to address global issues, including reforming multilateral institutions; (d) support the creation of a viable and sovereign Palestinian state, in accordance with relevant United Nations resolutions; and (e) facilitate dialogue among civilizations to promote a culture of peace, tolerance and respect for religious, cultural, language and racial diversities as well as gender equality."[68] Moreover, the NAASP laid out a 'framework to build a bridge between Asia and Africa covering three broad areas of partnership, namely political solidarity, economic cooperation, and socio-cultural relations' based on nine principles.[69] As a result of Indonesian advocacy, the G-77 and China agreed during the Second South Summit at Doha in 2005 to adopt a clause regarding the NAASP as recognition of the importance of regional and inter-regional cooperation in improving South-South Cooperation.[70]

In an expression of its continued pursuit of the NAM and its solidarity with the developing world, the Indonesian leadership also convened a commemorative meeting of the Non-Aligned Movement in Bali in May 2011. While hosting the XVI Ministerial Conference and Commemorative Meeting to celebrate the fifty years of the NAM, the President Yudhoyono called upon the member-states to develop the movement into 'a greater force for peace, justice and prosperity in the 21st century.'[71] He also declared that even though the NAM today has the power of numbers (118 member-states), the platform needs to convert its power into influence, and called upon the member states to work in that direction.[72] The meeting not only discussed the progress made on the eight-point Sharm El Sheikh Plan of Action to revive the NAM that was adopted in July 2009 but also adopted 'an outcome document outlining their vision of the NAM for the next fifty years, and a commemorative declaration marking the fiftieth anniversary of the NAM's establishment.'[73]

Indonesia's Focus on Economic Diplomacy and the Emerging Market

Three major trends highlight the global politics of the 21st century. First, economic diplomacy has emerged as, perhaps, the most important component of a country's foreign policy. Second, the gravity of economic exchanges has shifted from the trans-Atlantic world to the Asia-Pacific region, prompting scholars to characterise the 21st century as the Asian century. Third, a somewhat concomitant but equally powerful trend is the rise of the Global South, marked by economic growth and prosperity, as one of the most important players in sustaining the global economic recovery. Both the advanced and emerging worlds seem to be taking note of these trends.

Following this pattern, Indonesia has begun to revitalise its economic diplomacy in the developing world with the objectives of strengthening its international image, becoming an important and integrated part in the global economics, and securing greater access to the emerging market. An important focus of Indonesia's advocacy of its solidarity with the Global South, especially on matters related to global economic issues and its global positioning, is the country's active participation in the South-South cooperation through its memberships in different forums such as G-77, G-20.[74] While taking part in the Second South Summit of G-77 and China, held in Doha in 2005, the Indonesian leadership proposed to conduct a workshop/training in three areas – Small and Medium Enterprise, Microfinance, and

Information Technology. As a follow-up of these commitments, Indonesia submitted its report on Small and Medium Enterprise and Microfinance training activities taking place in Indonesia at the 12th IFCC (Inter-governmental Follow up and Coordination Committee on Economic Cooperation among Developing Countries) in Ivory Coast in June 2008.[75] While taking part in the Annual Meeting of Foreign Ministers of the G-77 and China on the sidelines of the UNGA (United Nations General Assembly) session in New York in September 2011, the Indonesian leadership called for greater unity, effective leadership and innovative strategies to address current global challenges, especially in the areas of global economic recovery, climate change and international monetary and financial stability.[76] Moreover, Jakarta advocated the leadership role of the UN in addressing the issue of global economic governance and called upon the G-77 and China to push the global economic agenda.[77] Jakarta has also pursued its economic diplomacy through its membership of the G-20 that has emerged as the most important forum for deliberation over global economic recovery and growth.

However, the membership alone does not make Indonesia an important player. The country has to possess the requisite economic clout in the form of its projection as an attractive investment destination, an important player in the manufacturing sector and a big market. A rising Indonesia can project its image at the global level and exert international influence only when the country is economically strong and its economic growth is sustained over a longer period of time.

Taking these trends into consideration, the Indonesian government has taken three initiatives. First, the government has sought to enhance the capacity and resources of its diplomatic missions. On 15 February 2012, the Indonesian government, in an unprecedented move, called upon its diplomatic missions to push for economic diplomacy as an important tenet of its foreign policy, with a particular emphasis on economic diplomacy in the emerging markets of the Global South. The government conducted a week-long programme during the last week of February 2012 in which more than 100 senior and mid-ranking officials based at home and in its different diplomatic missions abroad participated. The high-ranking training team included the President Yudhoyono, Foreign Minister Natalegawa, Deputy Finance Minister Mahendra Siregar, and the Coordinating Economic Minister, Hatta Rajasa. The political leadership has rightly understood that its diplomatic missions across the world can be the most appropriate and effective vehiclefor pursuing economic diplomacy.

The Indonesian leadership has called upon its envoys to focus on innovation and implementation. Besides, the heads of diplomatic missions should be well-versed in economic issues and submit annual reports directly to the President. Both the political leadership and diplomatic community received a shot in the arm with the results of 2011. According to the Indonesian News Agency, *Antara*, approximately 60 per cent of the agreements signed by the Indonesian diplomatic missions in the year of 2011 were related to economic issues. This effort resonates with the broader foreign policy guidelines, laid out by Foreign Minister Natalegawa in his annual press statement released in January 2011. It identified economic diplomacy and developing people-to-people contacts as priority areas.

Second, in its effort to introduce vitality and efficiency of its diplomatic missions, the government has bestowed greater responsibility on the diplomatic missions in those countries, which are economically powerful and growing, and share greater engagement with Indonesia. Fourteen countries have been identified, out of which eight countries represent the emerging market in the Global South. The crisis in its traditional market in the West has prompted the Indonesian economic planners to look for an alternative market. The emerging economies of the Global South, the most buoyant economic zone today, have offered an important alternative to Indonesia. Many of these are rising economies and important global or regional players, and can act as an anchor in projecting Indonesia's global image. For example, South Africa offers Indonesia an important foothold in engaging the African continent, and Brazil can provide a similar platform for Jakarta's engagement with the Latin American economies.

Finally, Indonesia has decided to reach out to the wider international community. In its effort to do so, the leadership has decided to open up several new diplomatic missions in different parts of the world. The annual press statement of 2011 aimed at opening more than 20 diplomatic missions abroad to be able to pursue economic diplomacy more effectively.

While these efforts may help Indonesia to attract greater investment from the emerging economies and exploit a wider market, a lot depends on efficiency in the domestic sector – how Indonesia manages its domestic economic issues and how competitive its manufacturing capacities can become. Indonesia can sustain its high economic growth (around 6 per cent in time of global economic crisis) in the long run, provided it upgrades its manufacturing base to international level of competitiveness. For example, issues of corruption, limited investment in the Research and Development, lack of coordination between national and local administration, and the availability of resources can act as important impediments in Indonesia's economic diplomacy.

On February 15, 2012, the Indonesian President announced a week-long training for its diplomats on Indonesia's economic diplomacy. The training, which took place during the last week of February 2012, hosted nearly 100 senior and mid-ranking officials based in its different diplomatic missions abroad. The training team included President Yudhoyono, Foreign Minister Natalegawa, Deputy Finance Minister Siregar, and Coordinating Economic Minister Rajasa.

The main objectives of the training were to apprise the officials about the changing global economic scenario and show them how to strengthen economic diplomacy in the country's foreign policy initiatives. There is a growing realization among the policy makers that Indonesia's economic growth, which has been more than 6 per cent in time of global economic crisis, can be sustained in the long run provided its manufacturing base is strengthened and upgraded to the international level of competitiveness. Such an enterprise would require large-scale foreign direct investment and capture of the emerging market.

The move is in consonance with what Foreign Minister Natalegawa laid out in his annual press statement released in January 2011.[78] The country has shown a trend towards economic diplomacy since 2010 when the economy began to recover while still feeling handicapped with the impending economic slowdowns in the advanced economies of the West.[79] In a bid to strengthen the country's economic diplomacy, the Indonesian government decided in 2011 to open diplomatic missions in 21 countries.[80]

Indonesia as the Largest Muslim Democracy: Bridging the Muslim World and West

While 9/11 awakened Indonesia as a Muslim country to a new set of discourses regarding the growing radicalization of Islam, the Bali Bomb Blast made Muslim-majority Indonesia an active stakeholder in the global discourse on radical Islam. Indonesia felt the heat of a new wave of domestic radicalization – spurred by large-scale ethno-communal violence in the outer islands during the late 1990s and early years of 21st century, the growing Arabisation of Javanese Islam, and a greater politico-legal-juridical role for *Sharia* in the socio-political life of the provinces. At the same time, the process of democratisation has unleashed majoritarian tendencies, which has prompted some of the political parties to advocate for radical Islamic behaviour in order to attract the majority Muslim electorate.

Jakarta responded to these trends by projecting itself as the largest Muslim democracy in order to win over the global Muslim constituencies and offer a powerful and alternative discourse confronting the relations between the world and the second largest religion. The leadership justified its bridge-building role on three bases – the largest Muslim democracy in the world, the country with the largest Muslim population and as a moderate multicultural society having experienced the threat of terrorism during the last ten years.

Three trends can be identified in Indonesia's facilitating role between the Muslim world and West – its moderate Muslim democratic society, its role as a bridge-builder and its expression of solidarity with the Muslim world. Highlighting Indonesia's bridge-building role between Islam and the West, the then Indonesian Ambassador to the United States, Dino Patti Djalal, characterized the Indonesia-US partnership as a 'constructive 21st century partnership between the West and the Islamic world.'[81] At the same time, democratic Indonesia has tried to express unequivocally its leadership role for the cause of Islam. Expressing its solidarity with the Muslim world, Indonesia has shown its continued support for the cause of Palestine. Indonesia continues to have no diplomatic relations with Israel. In this regard, Indonesia has participated actively in the Organisation of Islamic Conference and campaigned for peace and stability in the Middle East. The Megawati government of Indonesia had openly criticized the US interventions in Afghanistan and Iraq.[82] On 26 September 2012, the Indonesian President Yudhoyono, while addressing the UN General Assembly, called for greater global sensitisation about Islamic values and an international codification to prevent insult to the global religions. He suggested a greater UN role in facilitating inter-civilization engagement and greater global sensitization about the religious issues. Proposing the case for a global anti-blasphemy law under the aegis of the UN, Yudhoyono declared:

> I seized the opportunity to stress this point at the UN General Assembly. I called for the promotion of a universal culture of mutual tolerance and mutual appreciation. We are deeply disturbed by the fact that defamation of religions persists. We have seen yet another one in the film "Innocence of Muslims" that has caused an international uproar....Hence, I also called for the establishment of an international

> instrument that stipulates norms, rules, and responsibilities with regard to this very issue.[83]

These pronouncements and prescriptions highlight Indonesia's growing desire to present its international image as a bridge between the Muslim world and West, and its willingness to facilitate 'sanitised and sensitised' dialogue between the two worlds. The potential of Indonesia's mediation again came onto the main stage when the world witnessed violent protests against an obscenely mediocre film, called *Innocence of Muslims*, produced in the US in 2012. The Indonesian President during his speech at the UN called for an 'adoption of a legally binding instrument to ban blasphemy against religious symbols and to promote dialogue between different faiths, civilizations and cultures.'

The international community seems to have responded positively to Indonesia's bridge-building role. The US President, Barrack Obama, while giving his speech at Istiqlal mosque in Jakarta in November 2010, called upon Indonesia to play a greater role in facilitating dialogue between the West and Muslim world and building trust. Similarly, the International Conference on Cultural Diplomacy in the European Union, held in Brussels on December 2011, identified Indonesia as a bridge between Islam and the West and a model of compatibility between Islam and democracy. These positive overtures have further emboldened Indonesian leadership's campaign of its bridge-building outlook.

Conclusion

As rising Indonesia reconnects itself with the global order, it has begun engaging in debates about introducing fundamental transformations in the prevailing global order. Its leadership believes that the country's best interests lie in a representative, democratic, benign, and stable global order. It must be stated at the outset, however, that changes sought or reforms suggested by Indonesia in the international order are not radical, but rather reflective of ongoing debates in the global politics and, therefore, mainstream in nature. In other words, the rising Indonesia reflects the character of a rising power that tends to look at the global politics from a normative prism, and supports incremental changes or corrections in the existing international order rather than fundamental transformation of the system.

Indonesia's global exercise has also exposed its three important limitations – a lack of institutional capacity and resources to innovate, the drift of the

Indonesian democracy towards majoritarianism and a growing strategic uncertainty and economic volatility at the global level. Though Indonesia took an important initiative in reviving the Bandung Spirit, it has remained somewhat lukewarm and directionless in taking the step further towards promoting the Indonesian profile within the NAM. Notwithstanding global acceptability of its moderate Islamic outlook, the democratic leadership has found it difficult to project the vast reservoir of soft power in the form of its liberal outlook and its outlook as the confluence of various civilizations and the production of a unique syncretic culture.

ENDNOTES

1. Ann Merie Murphy, "Democratization and Indonesian Foreign Policy: Implications for the United States," *Asia Policy*, no. 13 (January 2012), pp. 84-85.
2. Dewi Fortuna Anwar, "Key Aspects of Indonesia's Foreign Policy" in *Trends in Southeast Asia Series*, no. 9 (Singapore, ISEAS, 2003), p. 2.
3. Ibid, p. 2; "Indonesia's Foreign Policy," *Embassy of the Republic of Indonesia in Ottawa, Canada,*http://www.indonesia-ottawa.org/discover-indonesia/foreign-policy/ (accessed on 25 December 2012).
4. Susilo Bambang Yudhoyono, "The Confluence of Civilisations," *Common Ground News Service,* 13 October 2009, http://www.commongroundnews.org/article.php?id=26530&lan=en&sp=0
5. "RI's Foreign Policy Consistently Promoting Positive Change," *Antara*, January 4, 2012.
6. Susilo Bambang Yudhoyono, "Indonesia's Role as Regional and Global Actor," *The Wilton Park Annual Address*, London, 2 November 2012, http://www.presidenri.go.id/index.php/eng/pidato/2012/11/02/2001.html (accessed on 12 December 2012).
7. Bantarto Bandoro, "Democracy and Indonesian Diplomacy Beyond 2009," *Jurnal Diplomasi,* vol. 1, no. 1 (June 2009), p. 36.
8. Eric Bellman and Martin Vaughan, "Indonesia Seeks Larger Role in Asean," *Wall Street Journal,* 9 May 2011, http://online.wsj.com/article/SB10001424052748703864204576310613441920214.html (accessed on 29 August 2012).
9. Rizal Sukma, "Indonesia Finds a New Voice," *Journal of Democracy*, vol. 22, no. 4,(October 2011),p. 110; "Indonesia: Defending Democracy – A Global Survey of Foreign Policy Trends 1992-2002," *Democracy Coalition Project,*http://www.demcoalition.org/pdf/Indonesia.pdf (accessed on 01 December 2012).
10. "Indonesia: Defending Democracy, ibid,
11. Ehito Kimura, "Indonesia in 2011: A Glass Half-Empty," *Asian Survey,* vol. 52, no. 1, p. 186; Thomas Carothers, "The New Republic: A Lesson for Egypt In Indonesia," *National Public Radio,* 03 February 2011, http://www.npr.org/2011/02/03/133461179/the-new-republic-a-lesson-for-egypt-in-indonesia (accessed on 20 December 2012); Joshua Kurlantzik, "Is Egypt the Next Indonesia?," *Council on Foreign Relations,* 07 February 2011, http://blogs.cfr.org/asia/2011/02/07/is-egypt-the-next-indonesia/ (accessed on 20 December 2012); Robin Bush, "Indonesia: An Example for Egypt, or a Democracy in Retreat?," *The Asia Foundation,* 16 February 2011, http://asiafoundation.org/in-asia/2011/02/16/indonesia-an-example-for-egypt-or-a-democracy-in-retreat/ (accessed on 20 December 2012).

12. "The Indonesian example: Remember 1998," *The Economist,* 07 February 2011, http://www.economist.com/blogs/asiaview/2011/02/indonesian_example (accessed on 20 December 2012).
13. Rizal Sukma, op.cit., p. 112.
14. Ibid, p. 110.
15. Bantarto Bandoro, op.cit., p. 37.
16. "What is the Bali Democracy Forum," *Bali Democracy Forum,* Department of Foreign Affairs,
17. "Opening Statement by the President of Republic of Indonesia at the Bali Democracy Forum V," *Presidential Secretariat,* 8 November 2012, http://www.presidenri.go.id/index.php/eng/pidato/2012/11/08/1999.html (accessed on 10 December 2012).
18. Ibid.
19. Rizal Sukma, op.cit., p. 119; Meidyatama Suryodiningrat, "ASEAN 9, Human Rights 1," *The Jakarta Post,* 24 July 2009, http://www.thejakartapost.com/news/2009/07/24/asean-9-human-rights-1.html
20. "Indonesia enjoys relations with almost all UN member states: FM," *People's Daily Online,* 04 January 2012, http://english.peopledaily.com.cn/90777/7695887.html (accessed on 16 December 2012).
21. "Indonesia, Countries urge UN to Implement cease fire in Libya," *People's Daily Online,* 28 March 2011, http://english.peopledaily.com.cn/90001/90777/90855/7333132.html (accessed on 16 December 2012).
22. "RI Electedd to UN Human Rights Council for Third Time," *Antara,* 21 May 2011, http://www.antaranews.com/en/news/71746/ri-elected-to-un-human-rights-council-for-third-time (accessed on 16 December 2012).
23. Ibid,
24. Andre Omer Siregar, "SBY's strong message, sense of optimism at the UN," *The Jakarta Post,* 05 October 2012, http://www.thejakartapost.com/news/2012/10/05/sby-s-strong-message-sense-optimism-un.html (accessed on 16 December 2012).
25. Yayan G.H. Mulyana, "Peacekeeping operations and Indonesian Foreign Policy," *The Jakarta Post,* 03 January 2012, http://www.thejakartapost.com/news/2012/01/03/peacekeeping-operations-and-indonesian-foreign-policy.html (accessed on 15 December 2012).
26. Ibid.
27. Ibid.
28. "Indonesia wants to advance peacekeeping role in 2011," *The Jakarta Post,* 08 January 2011, http://www.thejakartapost.com/news/2011/01/08/indonesia-wants-advance-peacekeeping-role-2011.html (accessed on 15 December 2012).
29. Ibid.
30. "On regional tour, Ban salutes Indonesia's commitment to UN peacekeeping," *UN News Centre,* 20 March 2012, http://www.un.org/apps/news/story.asp?NewsID=41589&Cr=Indonesia&Cr1#.UMwig6V33dk (accessed on 15 December 2012); "Indonesia to Send 4,000 Troops, Helicopters to UN Peacekeeping Missions," *The Jakarta Globe,* 20 March 2012, http://www.thejakartaglobe.com/home/indonesia-to-send-4000-troops-helicopters-to-un-peacekeeping-missions/506100 (accessed on 15 December 2012).
31. Ibid.
32. "Indonesia to Send 4,000 Troops, Helicopters to UN Peacekeeping Missions,"op.cit.,
33. Nani Afrida, "Indonesia to send peacekeeping battalion to Darfur," *The Jakarta Post,* 08 June 2012, http://www.thejakartapost.com/news/2012/06/08/indonesia-send-peacekeeping-battalion-darfur.html (accessed on 15 December 2012).

34. "Indonesia wants to advance peacekeeping role in 2011,"op.cit.,
35. "Full Text of final Communique of the Bandung Conference, April 18-24 1955," quoted in Ide Anak Agung Gde Agung, *Twenty Years of Indonesian Foreign Policy 1945-65,* Appendices 13, p. 583 (The Hague, Mouton, 1973).
36. "President: Indonesia supports nuclear disarmament," *Antara News,* 25 November 2009, http://www.antaranews.com/en/news/1259137727/president-indonesia-supports-nuclear-disarmament (accessed on 16 December 2012).
37. Agus P. Sari (ed.), *Indonesia and Climate Change: Current Status and Policies* (Jakarta, Peace, 2007), p. 9.
38. "Bali Climate Change Conference – December 2007," *United Nations Framework Convention on Climate Change,*http://unfccc.int/meetings/bali_dec_2007/meeting/6319.php (accessed on 16 December 2012).
39. Frank Jotzo, "Indonesia a key player in climate deal?," *East Asia Forum,* 08 February 2009, http://www.eastasiaforum.org/2009/02/08/indonesia-a-key-player-in-climate-deal/ (accessed on 16 December 2012).
40. Ibid,
41. Fitrian Ardiyansyah, "Durban climate talks bring mixed results for Indonesia," *East Asia Forum,* 20 December 2011, http://www.eastasiaforum.org/2011/12/20/durban-climate-talks-bring-mixed-results-for-indonesia/ (accessed on 16 December 2012).
42. David Fogarty, "Indonesia Approves Landmark Forest Protection Project, *Jakarta Globe,* 05 December 2012, http://www.thejakartaglobe.com/home/indonesia-approves-landmark-forest-protection-project/559941 (accessed on 16 December 2012).
43. Ibid,
44. "Indonesia and the United Nations: Working Together for Peace and Development," *Permanent Mission of the Republic of Indonesia to the United Nations* (New York, 2005), p. 356.
45. Ibid, pp. 353-356.
46. Ibid, p. 356.
47. "Indonesia Calls for UN Reform," *Antara,* 27 September 2011, http://www.antaranews.com/en/news/76041/indonesia-calls-for-un-reform (accessed on 16 December 2012).
48. "Indonesia and the United Nations: Working Together for Peace and Development," op.cit., p. 356.
49. Quoted in Bardo Fassbender, *UN Security Council Reform and the Right of Veto: A Constitutional Perspective* (Netherlands, Martinus Nijhoff Publishers, 1998), p. 251.
50. Bagus BT Saragih and Yohanna Ririhena, "Composition in UNSC no longer Relevant," *The Jakarta Post,* 01 October 2012, http://www.thejakartapost.com/news/2012/10/01/composition-unsc-no-longer-relevant.html (accessed on 15 December 2012).
51. Statement by H.E. Mrs. Adiyatiwidi A. Adiwoso, Deputy Permanent Representative of the Republic of Indonesia to the United Nations at the Meeting of the Open-ended Working Group on the Question of Equitable Representation on and Increase in the Membership of the Security Council and Other Matters related to the Security Council, New York, 2 September 2008, http://www.indonesiamission-ny.org/NewStatements/ps090208.htm (accessed on 15 December 2012).
52. "Indonesia and the United Nations: Working Together for Peace and Development," op.cit., p. 382.
53. "IMF Managing Director Visits Indonesia, Meets President Susilo Bambang Yudhoyono," *IMF Press Release,* no. 12/254, 10 July 2012, http://www.imf.org/external/np/sec/pr/2012/pr12254.htm (accessed on 17 December 2012).

54. Arientha Primanita, Francezka Nangoy and Tito Summa Siahaan, "Indonesia's Pledge of $1 Billion to IMF Marks an Era Of Financial Independence: SBY," *Jakarta Globe,* 11 July 2012, http://www.thejakartaglobe.com/news/indonesias-pledge-of-1-billion-to-imf-marks-an-era-of-financial-independence-sby/529871 (accessed on 17 December 2012).
55. Peter Alford, "Fifteen years after Humiliation, Indonesia turns the tables on IMF," *The Australian,* 11 July 2012, http://www.theaustralian.com.au/news/world/fifteen-years-after-humiliation-indonesia-turns-the-tables-on-imf/story-e6frg6so-1226422907171 (accessed on 17 December 2012).
56. "Indonesia's Economic Competitiveness Improving: WER Report," *Asia Pulse,* 08 June 2011.
57. Zamroni Salim, "Indonesia in the G20: Benefits And Challenges Amidst National Interests and Priorities," in Wilhelm Hofmeister (ed.), *G20: Perceptions and Perspectives for Global Governance* (Singapore, Konrad Adenauer Stiftung, 2011), p. 97.
58. "Ministry of Foreign Affairs – Multilateral Cooperation," *Government of Indonesia,*http://www.kemlu.go.id/Pages/IFPDisplay.aspx?Name=MultilateralCooperation&IDP=11&P=Multilateral&l=en (accessed on 17 December 2012).
59. Ibid.
60. Zamroni Salim, op.cit, p. 98.
61. Ibid, p. 103.
62. "Ministry of Foreign Affairs – Multilateral Cooperation," op.cit.,
63. Maria Monica Wiharja, "Indonesia and the G20: a door left half open," *East Asia Forum,* 29 June 2012, http://www.eastasiaforum.org/2012/06/29/indonesia-and-the-g20-a-door-left-half-open/ (accessed on 17 December 2012).
64. Ibid.
65. Winfried Weck, "ASEAN and G20 – Indonesia 's Foreign Policy Perspectives," *Konrad Adenauer Stiftung International Reports,* no. 2, 2011, http://www.kas.de/wf/doc/kas_21871-1522-2-30.pdf?110209123433 (accessed on 17 December 2012).
66. Mohammad Hatta, "Indonesia's Foreign Policy," *Foreign Affairs; an American Quarterly Review,* vol. 31, no. 1 (1952-53), pp. 441-452; Ide Anak Agung Gde Agung, op.cit.,
67. "Background Notes: Indonesia," *State Department Press Release,* Government of the United States of America, 03 November 2010, http://www.state.gov/r/pa/ei/bgn/2748.htm#foreign (accessed on 23 December 2012).
68. "Declaration on the New Asian-African Strategic Partnership," http://www.kbri-canberra.org.au/lains/Hasil%20KTT%20AA%202005.pdf (accessed on 26 December 2012).
69. Ibid,
70. The South Summit is the highest level of meeting involving the member states of G-77 and China. So far only two summits have taken place – Havana in April 2000 and Doha in June 2005. "Ministry of Foreign Affairs – Multilateral Cooperation," op.cit.,
71. Abdul Khalik and Desy Nurhayati, "RI Wants NAM to play Greater Role on World Stage," *The Jakarta Post,* 26 May 2011, http://www.thejakartapost.com/print/325293 (accessed on 13 September 2011).
72. Ibid,
73. "Non-Aligned Movement (NAM)," *Nuclear Threat Initiative,* http://www.nti.org/treaties-and-regimes/non-aligned-movement-nam/ (accessed on 26 December 2012).
74. "South-South Cooperation of Republic of Indonesia," Coordination Team on South-South Cooperation, Government of Indonesia, http://www.ssc-indonesia.org/

75. "Ministry of Foreign Affairs – Multilateral Cooperation," op.cit.,
76. "Indonesia Calls for G-77 Countries and China to Push Agenda of Global Economy," Embassy of The Republic of Indonesia in Seoul – South Korea, 24 September 2011, http://www.kemlu.go.id/seoul/Pages/News.aspx?IDP=5169&l=en (accessed on 26 December 2012).
77. Ibid,
78. Annual Press Statement of the Foreign Minister of the Republic of Indonesia Dr. R.M. Marty M. Natalegawa 2011.http://www.indonesiavancouver.org/speeches-a-statements/582-annual-press-statement-of-the-foreign-minister-of-the-republic-of-indonesia-dr-rm-marty-m-natalegawa-2011 (accessed on 04 March 2012).
79. Erwida Maulia, "Economy remains priority for RI diplomacy in 2012," *The Jakarta Post*, 05 January 2012, http://www.thejakartapost.com/news/2012/01/05/economy-remains-priority-ri-diplomacy-2012.html-0 (accessed on 04 March 2012); Ferry Akbar Pasaribu, "Scientific and economic diplomacy a pressing agenda," *The Jakarta* Post, 24 February 2012, http://www.thejakartapost.com/news/2012/02/24/scientific-and-economic-diplomacy-a-pressing-agenda.html (accessed on 4 March 2012).
80. "RI to open 21 diplomatic relations in 2011," *Antara News,* 8 January 2011, http://www.antaranews.com/en/news/66764/ri-to-open-21-diplomatic-relations-in-2011.
81. "Indonesia-U.S. Relations: A Comprehensive Partnership," *Metropolitan Corporate Counsel,* vol. 19, no. 3, 28 February 2011, p. 45, 48, http://www.metrocorpcounsel.com/pdf/2011/March/45.pdf(accessed on 18 December 2012).
82. Kai He, "Indonesia's foreign policy after Soeharto: international pressure, democratization, and policy change," *International Relations of the Asia-Pacific*, vol. 8, no. 1, 2008, p. 66.
83. Susilo Bambang Yudhoyono, "Indonesia's Role as Regional and Global Actor," op.cit.,

5

India and Indonesia: Developing a Common Bilateral, Regional and Global Agenda

Two somewhat interrelated developments have transformed the way India and Indonesia perceive and engage with each other, and in the process, changed the whole gamut of their bilateral relations. These developments relate to the changing outlook of both agencies as well as the structure of power in the 21st century Asia-Pacific. While the agential change refers to the rise of Asian powers, including India and Indonesia, the structural-level change points towards the resurgence of Asia as the fulcrum of global strategic and economic transactions. In other words, not only has the outlook of India and Indonesia changed, but also the atmosphere in which they are coexisting and pursuing their foreign policy. They have, in addition to influencing the bilateral and regional dynamics of India-Indonesia engagement, offered the two countries an important opportunity to contribute to the evolving strategic discourses on (a) what shape global politics should take during the 21st century and (b) the ways in which a resurgent Asia and its players could contribute to the evolving debate.

Outside South Asia, probably no other country shares as much history, culture and politics with India as does Indonesia. They share a relationship built over a millennium, and their bond remains strong and intact. India and Indonesia enjoy strong strategic relations, marked by growing economic engagement, wide-ranging defence and security cooperation, and the highest level of inter-governmental exchanges. Befitting the relationship, President Yudhoyono was welcomed as the special guest on India's Republic Day on 26 January 2011, a welcome received by only one other Indonesian – Mohammad Sukarno, the first President of Indonesia and a close friend of Jawaharlal Nehru.

Since its signing in November 2005, the India-Indonesia strategic partnership has envisaged greater engagement in both conventional bilateral areas and issues of regional and global importance between the two important Asian and global players. The strategic partnership signifies an important component of the transformed strategic outlook of Asia. The partnership aims to consolidate bilateral relations, strengthen ASEAN cooperative processes, moderate hostile tendencies in Asia, work together towards building stable Asian geopolitics, and represent continental Asia in global multilateral initiatives.

The partnership received a major boost during the visit of Indian Prime Minister Manmohan Singh to Indonesia in October 2013. The content of their Joint Statement highlighted the intent of the two rising powers to go beyond the bilateral context of cooperation towards a pan-Indo-Pacific orientation. Both the Indian Ocean and the G-20 were added as important regional and global agendas for bilateral cooperation. The contours of India-Indonesia relations today are not confined to the template of bilateralism alone, but rather incorporate the ASEAN-centric, Asia-centric, and global frameworks of strategic engagement.

In the backdrop of these developments, this chapter seeks to highlight various dimensions of the India-Indonesia strategic engagement that have evolved during the last twenty years ever since the end of the Cold War era and subsequent announcement of India's Look East Policy. It examines the impact that the changing politico-strategic landscape in Asia has brought upon the bilateral relationship and the ways in which the countries intend to influence the continental strategic landscape and prevailing discourses in the region. The following discussion also makes an effort to identify issues of global significance on which the two countries either have decided to work together or could develop a shared understanding given their common economic, political, cultural, and strategic stakes.

Three arguments are put forth here. First, as the largest and the most powerful country in Southeast Asia and an important strategic player in Asia, Indonesia has emerged during the last two decades as an important partner in India's continental and global strategic projections. The evolution of the India-Indonesia strategic partnership is a cumulative outcome of (a) changing geo-political realities of Asia during the Post-Cold War era and the first decade of twenty-first century; (b) multi-pronged strategies of engagement pursued by India under the Look East Policy since 1992; (c) the dynamism of greater economic integration and multilateral cooperation; and (d) a shared understanding of prevailing security discourses in the region.

Second, the Look East policy has proved to be a 'lynchpin' in New Delhi's strong strategic relations with Jakarta. While the discourse of Nehru-Sukarno Asianism has provided an easy reference point to reminisce about their past relationship, the integrative discourse of the Look East Policy and shared threat perceptions have offered a pragmatic outlook and comprehensive framework to translate the relationship into a strategic partnership.

Finally, the two rising powers and millennia-old civilisational entities have, almost subconsciously, developed somewhat similar sets of principles and grand rules of international behaviour in the 21st century. These elements can broadly be clubbed under a common 'Delhi-Jakarta Paradigm.'

Legacy of Nehru-Sukarno Asianism

The fundamentals of India-Indonesia relations have been formed by their shared colonial experiences and anti-colonial struggles, as well as the shared world-views of their founding fathers – Jawaharlal Nehru and Sukarno. Together they offered an ideational critique of the emerging Cold War scenario. They also developed an alternative worldview that could represent the erstwhile colonies of Asia and Africa and guide the process of development in these two continents. The two leaders called for (a) a strong and collective voice of Asia, (b) Asian deliberation over intra-continental problems, (c) Asia's rightful position in the global politics, and (d) a path towards peace and prosperity through non-alignment. While inaugurating the Asian Relations Conference in 1947 in New Delhi, Nehru proclaimed, "a change is coming over the scene and now Asia is again finding itself. We live in a tremendous age of transition and already the next stage takes shape when Asia takes its rightful place with other continents."[1] Their closeness was manifested in Nehru's strong reaction against the Second Police Action by the Dutch Colonial authority in Indonesia in December 1948, leading to the New Delhi Resolution (passed by Australia and 14 countries of Asia and Africa) in January 1949 and the tabling of the Indonesian issue in the

UN Security Council.[2] The New Delhi Resolution is considered to be the first diplomatic action taken by an independent India.[3]

The evolving camaraderie between India and Indonesia could also be seen in their diplomatic efforts during the early 1950s to resolve the issues of Indochina and the Korean Peninsula. They argued that any resolution should not simply be imposed upon the newly independent countries. Reflecting upon the objectives of Nehru-Sukarno Asianism, then Sri Lankan Prime Minister Sir John Kotelawala declared, "five nations, with populations totalling more than 500,000,000 people, were to make it clear that the only scheme to ensure peace in Asia would be one formulated by or approved by the leaders of Free Asian countries."[4] The growing understanding among the leaders of India, Indonesia, Sri Lanka, and Burma seems to have unsettled the US and European powers, forcing the latter to accord self-determination and greater national participation in the deliberations over continental matters.[5] The participation of India and Indonesia in the Geneva conference of 1954 was a result of growing Asian solidarity.

Nehru-Sukarno Asianism found its full expression during the first Asian-African Conference, held in Bandung, Indonesia in April 1955. The Indian leadership, which had expressed its willingness to hold such a conference, finally agreed when Ali Sastroamijoyo, then Indonesian Prime Minister, made a personal appeal to Nehru during a visit to New Delhi in 1954. The high watermark of the bilateral chemistry between the governments of the two countries lies in the explanations as to why Nehru gave his consent. Nicholas Tarling attributes Nehru's consent to his effort to bolster the domestic image of the democratic Indonesian government, which was scheduled to hold general elections in 1955.[6]

Nehru-Sukarno Asianism began to lose shine during the 1960s due to (a) growing ideological differences between the two leaders and their departure from the scene of international politics, (b) the growing insularity of India and Indonesia from international and Asian multilateral political discourses, and (c) the de facto alignment of India and Indonesia along with the antagonistic Cold War power configurations. A rift began to emerge during the late 1950s and early 60s between the two leaders regarding the nature and future directions of the Non-Aligned Movement, Sukarno's policy of 'Crush Malaysia' and Indonesia's relationship with China.[7] Sukarno began to drift towards China while Nehru experienced tension in India's relationship with China over the issue of Tibet and the shared land boundary, resulting into the Sino-Indian war of 1962.

The significance of India's Bandung spirit in its relations with Indonesia and Southeast Asian countries was reflected in the first definitive statement on India's Look East Policy by then Indian Prime Minister, P.V. Narasimha Rao. In his 1994 statement, he relied on Nehru's advocacy of 'a no more submissive and dynamic Asia' at the Bandung conference in 1955.[8] In fact, current ministerial speeches about India-ASEAN relations and the Look East Policy often reference the shared worldviews of Nehru-Sukarno Asianism. Moreover, the resurgence of the 'Asian Century' discourse and the expansion of the geographical canvas of the Look East Policy and the level of India's East Asian engagement have prompted a few scholars and policy makers to characterise the Look East Policy as a revived form of Nehruvian Asianism.[9] As India and Indonesia emerge as pivotal states in the overall Asian strategic calculations, the tone and tenor of Asianism, though it takes a different form from that of the Nehru-Sukarno Asianism of Bandung, is growing louder and more substantive. The India-Indonesia Strategic Partnership of November 2005, which has sought to lend a strategic dimension to their bilateral relations in a changing strategic Asian landscape, draws ideational values and strength from Nehru-Sukarno Asianism.[10]

Mutual Perceptions of India and Indonesia: Continuity and Change

During the six decades of post-colonial India-Indonesia relations, their perceptions about each other have undergone substantial change. The relationship ebbed during the pre-Bandung era before plummeting to indifference and ideological difference during the post-Bandung and Suharto era. While the idea of Afro-Asian solidarity played a key role in shaping foreign relations during the pre-Bandung Sukarno era, Sukarno's relations with China and Pakistan shaped Indonesia's perception towards India during the post-Bandung Sukarno era. India and Indonesia, influenced by a personality clash between Nehru and Sukarno, were engaged in a diplomatic tiff over holding the second NAM summit. India attempted to check Indonesia's projection of its leadership role in Asia and Africa.

Though the departure of Nehru and Sukarno ended the tussle between the two countries during the Suharto era, the countries' divergent priorities did not provide a suitable atmosphere for growth in bilateral relations. By the early 1970s, both India and Indonesia had shrunk into their respective regions, with India joining hands with the communist Vietnam and USSR and Indonesia focusing on ASEAN and its relations with the US. The relationship remained marked by indifference and apprehension, if not an outward leadership rivalry of the Sukarno era.

India-Indonesia relations latched on to a much larger regional discourse of strategic engagement during the post-Cold War era – India's Look East policy. In fact, the two important components of the Look East policy – enhanced economic cooperation and wide-ranging strategic engagement – have figured prominently in India's relations with Indonesia. Indonesia views India as an important strategic player in East Asia and the Indian Ocean, a country with a similar China-threat theory, a maritime neighbour, an ever-expanding market, and a benign and reliable power in the region. On the other hand, India views Indonesia as a launching pad for India's Look East policy, an important supply source of energy and raw materials, and a reliable power in East Asia with its centuries-old cultural and historical linkages.

The rise of India and Indonesia during the 21st century and their shared perspectives have further pushed the two countries towards each other. Both India and Indonesia have begun to appreciate each other's rising profile. Indonesia has increasingly begun to view India as (a) an emerging Asian and global player, (b) an important driver of Asian and Indonesian growth, and (c) an active supporter of ASEAN-driven multilateral cooperative processes. On the other hand, Indonesia has factored prominently in India's Look East policy thanks to the former's crucial strategic support to the Look East policy. There is a growing realisation among the Indian foreign policy makers about the growing importance of Indonesia as a strategic player. Rising Indonesia appeals to India in many ways – as an important maritime neighbour, as an important ASEAN player, as the largest Muslim democracy in the world, as an emerging Asian power, as a natural resource-rich country with a sustained economic rise, as an increasingly important player in the world, and as a country with a shared history and understanding of security and vulnerabilities. Tables 5.1 and 5.2 outline perceptions of India and Indonesia towards each other during the last six decades.

Bilateral Dynamics of India-Indonesia Relations: Look East Policy as the Lynchpin

India-ASEAN engagement and India-Indonesia relations have, over the years, mutually reinforced each other, given Indonesia's strong influence on ASEAN decision-making. Indonesia has played a pivotal role in facilitating India's participation in the ASEAN-driven multilateral cooperative processes, which have proved to be one of the most dynamic and successful

Table 5.1: India's Perception about Indonesia

	Pre-Bandung	Post-Bandung		Look East/Post-Suharto Era
		Sukarno Era	Suharto Era	
Political	A democratic system *Pancasila* as the basis of state philosophy Shared Colonial experience Sukarno as leader of Indonesia Democratic politics	Guided Democracy/ Semi Authoritarian	Military rule Non-democratic Secular character	Presidential form of government Secular bodypolitik Islam as an important political force
Economic	- Mixed economic model - Planning-based economy - Richest economy in Southeast Asia	Similar pattern, mixed economic model	Developmental State Export-oriented economy West-centric economy	Resource-rich (fossil-fuel) A growing economy
Strategic	- Indonesia as "India's main ally in the latter's bid for leadership in Asia"[11] - signed the Treaty of Friendship in March 1951 - Shared views on major aspects of foreign policy/opposed US imperialism	- Nehru-Sukarno rift - Indonesia drifts towards China - Friendship falls victim to the personality clash - supported Pakistan in 1965	- Aligns with USA - Anti-China - Leader of ASEAN and against communist Indochina	- A strategic partner - A lynch-pin state in India's Look East policy.
Global	- "Most suitable partner," according to Nehru in promoting the NAM movement - Advocate of NAM - Sukarno's *Pancasila*	- Getting closer to China - Supporting Pakistan - Personality Clash with Nehru	- Pro-US - Anti-China - Leader of ASEAN and against communist Indochina	- Indonesia as an important strategic partner in the Asia-Pacific - Can be a reliable partner in an uncertain Asia
Socio-cultural	- moderate Muslim-society - Cultural similarities - Images of Bali and Borobudur	- Moderate Muslim society - Images of Bali, Borobudur	- Moderate Muslim society - Images of Bali and Borobudur	- terrorism in Indonesia - radical elements within Indonesian Islam/Islamic Parties

Table 5.1 (Contd.)

	Pre-Bandung	**Post-Bandung**		**Look East/Post-Suharto Era**
		Sukarno Era	Suharto Era	
Stimuli of Engagement	- Cultural-historical linkages - Shared colonial Experiences and freedom movements - Shared world-view on the prevailing politics - Shared educational background of founding fathers	Phase of Drifting Apart	Disengagement continues	Lynchpin state for Look East policy An important supply source of energy and raw-materials, A reliable power in East Asia

Table 5.2: Indonesia's Perception about India

	Sukarno Era	Suharto Era	Democratic Era
Domestic Politics	Former British colony Democratic political system Mahatma Gandhi and Jawaharlal Nehru as leaders of India	Democratic political system	Strong democratic system A stable polity Multi-party system
Economy	A vast economy One of the most advanced British Colonies in Asia	A closed and state-controlled economy marked by 'hindu-growth rate'	An emerging economic powerhouse Growing domestic demand Strong in IT sector
International outlook	An erstwhile British colony An ardent advocate of NAM An important Asian player	An ally of USSR Supporter of Communist Vietnam Supported Heng Samrin regime in Cambodia An Enemy of China	- An emerging power - A comfortable and reliable player to work with to influence the global politics - An important player in Asia
Socio-cultural	A Hindu society Cultural similarity Taj Mahal	A Hindu society Cultural similarity Taj Mahal and Muslim Population	A Hindu society with large number of Muslim population Muslim Intellectual Tradition Taj Mahal
Stimuli for engagement	Idea of Asian-African Solidarity and Non-Aligned Movement Evolving Cold War Bloc Politics	China-threat Theory	End of the Cold War, Onset of the Look East policy, India's economic reforms, Country with a similar China-threat theory, Maritime neighbour,

components of India's Look East Policy. As a result, India has relied on the Indonesian support for its Look East Policy and focused on cultivating a strong bilateral partnership that has expanded considerably in terms of both the content and scale of cooperation during the last twenty years.

Over the years, a distinct complementarity has developed in the realm of bilateral engagement and integration. The idea of 'outward investment' as suggested by the Joint Statement of January 2011 during the visit of President Yudhoyono to India, further highlight common economic interests of India and Indonesia. For example, Indonesia is rich in the fossil-fuel resources and India's energy needs are growing. Similarly, being maritime states, both India and Indonesia share similar sets of maritime security threats. India and Indonesia are maritime neighbours. Indonesia straddles over the Strait of Malacca, a key transit point for global trade and Indonesia's Aceh province is not even 80 kms away from India's Andaman and Nicobar Islands. It is in the interest of both India and Indonesia that the Strait of Malacca remains free from the domination of any power.

India and Indonesia have consolidated their bilateral strategic ties by engaging and expanding the avenues of cooperation, such as in the realm of trade and investment, defence industry, energy, investment, science and technology, sourcing the raw materials, and space research collaborations. They have already signed a framework agreement of strategic partnership in November 2005, a defence cooperation agreement in 2006, developed a Plan of Action in June 2007 for an effective implementation of the partnership, Joint Statement eliciting a vision for the India-Indonesia New Strategic Partnership in January 2011, and Joint Statement highlighting five initiatives for strengthening the India-Indonesia Strategic Partnership in October 2013. According to the Indonesian Ambassador to India, Rizali Indrakesuma, the two countries signed more than 34 MoUs/agreements between 2005 and 2011.[12] New Delhi and Jakarta, bereft of any major sore point in their relations, attempted to add more meat and speed to their strategic partnership during the visit of the Indian Prime Minister, Manmohan Singh to Indonesia in October 2013. The two countries identified five focus areas to strengthen their bilateral ties: strategic engagement, defence and security cooperation, comprehensive economic partnership, cultural and people-to-people linkages, and cooperation in responding to common challenges.

Economic Engagement: High Trade Volume and Integration

The growing bilateral economic engagement can be gauged from the fact that despite the global meltdown, the bilateral trade increased from US$9.22 billion in 2008-09 to US$21.44 billion in 2011-12, registering more than 100 per cent growth in four years. While the export went up from US$2.55 billion in 2008-09 to US$6.67 billion in 2011-12, the import volume increased from US$6.66 billion in 2008-09 to US$14.76 billion in 2011-12, highlighting corresponding increase in India's trade deficit. Indonesia has emerged as India's second largest trading partner and an important supply source for the raw materials, whereas India has emerged as the main market for Indonesia's palm oil export. Three commodities – palm/vegetable oil (crude and processed), coal and petro products constitute the bulk of India's imports from Indonesia. The bilateral economic engagement has expanded from mere trade relations to include cooperation in the corporate management, investment, financial sectors, and economic integration. India and Indonesia have set the bilateral trade target of US$25 billion by 2015.

In order to facilitate the bilateral economic cooperation, the two countries have signed various agreements, declarations and MoUs. While participating in the G-15 meeting in Jamaica in February 1999, India and Indonesia signed an Agreement for the Promotion and Protection of Investments that came into force in January 2004. The India-Indonesia Joint Commission Meeting (JCM), held in Yogyakarta in September 2003, mandated the promotion of bilateral economic and commercial relations and the setting up of an India-Indonesia Expert Working Group to identify avenues to expand their economic relations. The Joint Study Group that was constituted in November 2005 to conduct a feasibility study of entering into a Comprehensive Economic Cooperation Agreement (CECA) submitted its report in October 2009 highlighting the comparative advantages the two countries could have from CECA and potential areas of trade creation. Besides bilateral agreements, India-Indonesia economic linkages have received a major impetus from the signing of India-ASEAN Comprehensive Economic Cooperation Agreement in August 2009. The agreement confined till now to the FTA in goods entered into force since January 2010, considerably lifting the tariff and non-tariff restrictions imposed on the traffic of goods between India and Indonesia.

India's Thrust on Energy and Raw Materials

The fast-changing outlook of India-Indonesia economic relations reflects two trends – growing Indian demand for energy (primarily coal and

Liquified Natural Gas) and raw-materials and consequent Indian investment in Indonesia. Both the public and Private Sector companies of India are queuing in Indonesia to secure their supplies either unilaterally or through joint ventures. The new trend reflects India's growing energy needs, aggressive international procurement strategy of the Indian corporate sector and greater degree of transnational operations of the Indian Companies. India is studying the possibility of procuring natural gas from Indonesia through an under-sea pipeline from Aceh to the Nicobar Islands. Addressing a joint meeting sponsored by the New-Delhi based business forums – the FICCI (Federation of Indian Chambers of Commerce and Industry) and CII (Confederation of Indian Industry), the then Indonesian President Ms. Megawati Sukarnoputri, during her visit to India in 2002, had expressed her country's willingness to supply oil and gas to India. The Spice Energy, an Indian company, entered into an agreement with the Indonesian Pertamina for the annual supply of Liquified Natural Gas (LNG) for its proposed Haldia Import and Regassification Facility to be set up by 2011.

Apart from the energy supplies, Indonesia has, of late, also emerged as an important supply source of raw-materials and an important market. India's big corporate houses, such as Tata Steel and the Arcelor Mittal have entered into the Indonesian Steel market both to procure raw materials as well as market their steel products. The Tata Power has entered into an agreement with a Singapore-based Company – Mercator Lines, which will transship 3.2 million tonnes of coal from Indonesia in the next four years to India. The National Aluminium Company (NALCO) has decided to enter into a joint venture with strategic equity partners (either Indonesian or a multinational) to tap the local market. Similarly, the Indonesian subsidiary of India's ESSAR group has set up an advanced service centre near Jakarta to market various steel products. The Jindal Stainless Steel Company has entered into a joint venture agreement with the Indonesian mining company, ANTAM to develop a nickel smelting and stainless steel plant in Southeast Sulawesi in Indonesia.

Indian Investment in Indonesia: Joint Ventures, Mergers and Acquisitions

The Indian FDI was US$78.1 million across 58 projects in 2012 and US$57.1 million in 59 projects for the period of January-June 2013.[13] The business sectors of India and Indonesia signed 18 MoUs on FDI worth US$15 billion during the visit of the President Yudhoyono to India in January 2011.[14] The search for raw materials among the corporate biggies and the public sector companies have led to a spurt in Indian investment into the country and large-scale mergers and acquisitions between the Indian and Indonesian companies. India's top level corporate names – Tata, Reliance, Essar, and large Public Sector companies like NTPC (National Thermal Power Corporation) have either acquired Indonesian coal mining companies, mining rights for the coal supplies or entered into joint ventures with the local Indonesian companies. The largest coal mining company of India, the Coal India Limited is planning to acquire several mines in Indonesia.[15] An Indonesian newspaper reported in April 2010 that the state-owned Aluminium Company of India, NALCO, has received approval from the Indonesian government to invest US$ 337 million every year for four years to set up a 500,000 metric tons (tonnes) smelter and a 1,250MW coal-fired power plant in East Kalimantan in the next 48 months.[16] Moreover, the Reliance Power Ltd, has acquired three coalmines in the South Sumatra province in Indonesia, investing approximately US$1 billion. The coal supplies will be transshipped to the company's 4,000-MW Ultra Mega Power Project at Krishnapatnam in Andhra Pradesh, and to the 4,000-MW Shahapur power project in Maharashtra, which has a thermal power component of 1,200 MW.[17] The K S Oils Limited of India has bought 20,500 hactares of palm plantation in Indonesia to transport 80,000 tonnes of edible oil from Indonesia to the manufacturing and refining plants in India.[18] These investments are being done in the areas of heavy machinery, steel plants, service centres and power generations, which are not only going to generate large-scale local employment but also develop the local infrastructure, especially in the power sector. In fact, the trends reflect towards an aggressive investment and market policy of India's public sector and the Private Sector.

In order to facilitate their investment and market entry, the Indian companies have adopted the policy of large-scale acquisitions of the local companies. The Arcelor Mittal has been working towards buying the state-owned Indonesian company, PT Krakatau Steel and has also shown interest in buying stakes in the Aneka Tambang (Antam) company of Indonesia. In 2007, the Tata Power agreed to spend around US$1.1 billion and also bought a 30 percent stake in an Indonesian coal mining company belonging to the PT Bumi Resources group. The Surana Industries of Chennai has acquired a 49 percent stake in PT Agate Resources Indonesia and the Star Emmsons Resource has bought Bara Energy Makmur of Indonesia, which owns two coal blocks in the country.[19]

The presence of Indian financial sector in Indonesia further buttresses such a trend. Spurred by the decisions of large number of Indian companies of investment and acquisitions, the Indian banking sector has also decided to expand its operations in Indonesia. Two Indian banks – State Bank of India and Bank of India – are already operating in Indonesia by acquiring majority stakes in the local banks.[20] Several other Indian banks, such as the ICICI and Canara Banks are making their entry either by acquiring stakes in the local banks or opening fresh operating branches.

Policing together the Maritime Neighbourhood

The last two decades have witnessed growing significance of maritime governance in India-Indonesia security engagement, involving several inter-connected security challenges – piracy, maritime terrorism, safety of Sea Lanes of Communications (SLoCs), and trafficking in drugs and arms. India's geographical proximity to Indonesia and the Strait of Malacca and the strategic importance of uninhibited free passage of communication in the Strait have brought forth the strategic necessity of developing close ties with Indonesia. A large part of the Malacca Strait falls under the territorial water of Indonesia and India's Andaman and Nicobar Islands are only 80 nautical miles away from Aceh, the northern tip of Indonesia. Moreover, the disturbances in the busiest and trouble-prone Strait of Malacca can pose a serious challenge to the maritime security of both India and Indonesia. The London-based Lloyd's Agency declared the Straits of Malacca as a 'war zone' in 2005 and the Indonesian waters reported frequent occurrences of maritime piracy. These developments further highlighted the limited capacity of the littoral states and the necessity of collaborating with the likeminded countries in building maritime capability in the region.

India has been increasing its maritime profile in the Asia-Pacific during the last ten years, as evident from the expansion of its Far Eastern Naval base in the Andaman and Nicobar Island groups, humanitarian operations during the natural disasters in Indonesia and Myanmar, and spate of naval exercises as far as off the Japanese coast. Identifying the Strait of Malacca as its 'legitimate area of interest,' India's 2004 maritime doctrine espouses India's maritime pre-eminence in the Indian Ocean.[21] In other words, the rationale for India-Indonesia maritime cooperation lies with the strategies of policing the maritime spaces in and around the Strait of Malacca. India has shown its expertise in maintaining maritime surveillance, large-scale operations in the event of natural disasters, anti-piracy operations and other areas of maritime governance. Much of the bilateral naval engagement has occurred through joint exercises, regular goodwill visits, naval escorts, coordinated patrols, quick relief operations and joint efforts to facilitate the setting up of multilateral maritime security regime, such as ReCAAP (Regional Cooperation for Combating against Armed Robbery and Piracy). The Indian activism in offering quick relief operations using its naval resources, as evident from Indian assistance to Tsunami-struck Indonesia and the Cyclone-devastated Myanmar has lent greater credence to its benign-image building. A key component of the benign posturing has been what G S Khurana calls 'carrying the neighbourhood along' policy, whereby India has been trying to share the maritime concerns of its neighbouring countries.[22]

The two countries, since 1996, have conducted joint naval exercises, which can enhance the quick response capability of the naval forces against sea-piracy and maritime terrorism. The feedback gained from these exercises can help the navies in further upgrading their logistical maneuverability and swift operations against sea-pirates and terrorists or in time of humanitarian crisis. Since 1997, the bilateral SAREX (Search and Rescue Operations) has been converted into a multilateral maritime operation comprising of India, Indonesia, Malaysia and Singapore. Indian naval ships have been paying goodwill visits to the Indonesian ports. Indonesia, along with Singapore, Thailand and Malaysia has been taking part in the biennial gathering of ships known as MILAN hosted by India since 1995. In the aftermath of Tsunami, India launched the Operation Ghambir in January 2005 and sent emergency medical and food supplies to Indonesia. The Indonesian President, Susilo Bambang Yudhoyono during his visit to India in November 2005 and the Vice President Dr. Jusuf Kalla, during his visit in January 2007, expressed their country's gratitude for India's assistance in Tsunami relief operations.

Another important component of bilateral cooperation towards promoting maritime governance is 'coordinated patrolling (CORPAT),' whereby, the navies of two countries patrol in their respective territorial waters along 300 nautical miles of international maritime border shared by India and Indonesia. The primary objective of the CORPAT is to combat sea-piracy, trafficking in drugs, arms and human beings, and poaching into each other's waters. The two countries have been engaged in the coordinated patrolling since 2003 after the signing of the Memorandum of Understanding between the two navies. The navies of two countries conducted 15th coordinated patrolling in March 2010, which began around the Andaman-

Nicobar islands in India and Weh Island in Indonesia.[23] The coordinated patrol was undertaken after a tip-off by the Singapore navy of a possible terrorist attack in and around the Strait of Malacca. Two similar patrols 'along the international maritime border at the mouth of the Malacca Strait' occurred in 2009.[24] The Indonesian News Agency, *Antara*, had reported in March 2009 of the extension of Indonesia invitation to India to help the littoral states in maintaining security in the Malacca Strait.[25]

Towards Capacity Building: Defence Cooperation and Procurement of Military Hardware

India-Indonesia defence cooperation has expanded considerably ever since the signing of a Bilateral Agreement on Cooperative Activities in the Field of Defence in 2001 and its ratification in December 2006. The two countries convened the first meeting of the Joint Defence Cooperation Committee in June 2007 to further consolidate and widen the areas of bilateral defence, away from symbolic training of defence personnel towards more meaningful areas such as joint production of military equipment and their maintenance. Given Indonesia's defence requirement and the similarity of the operating system of the military hardware, India is viewing Indonesia as a big market and potential clientele of Indian military hardware which can be used also on Russian operating system. India had proposed a draft Memorandum of Understanding on Defence Cooperation in 1995 with the focus on supplies, technologies, joint production and joint projects. India has also taken initiatives towards strengthening the military capability of other littoral countries, such as Malaysia and Singapore. As per the 2006 defence agreement, the two countries are going to jointly produce military hardware and India will also help in the maintenance of the hardware, which Indonesia purchases from Russia. The agreement indicates primarily a three-pronged cooperation in the field of (a) joint production of military hardware, (b) maintenance of military hardware bought from a similar source, such as Russia, and (c) purchase of Indian military hardware. To quote the then Indonesian Defence Minister Juwono Sudarsono,

> "We already have many offers of cooperation in the defence sector, such as the possibility of joint production, the possibility of maintenance of similar defence equipment, especially that coming from Russia, because they also have experience in this."[26]

India has been supplying defence equipments, especially for the Indonesian navy and the latter has shown its interest in importing items such as batteries for torpedoes, engines for Parchim Class Corvettes, repair facilities for type 209 submarines and so on. India has been a major buyer of Russian military hardware and has secured production and maintenance rights of these. The two countries are also deliberating over the equipments, which they want to jointly produce, the purchase of the BrahMos for the Indonesian navy and the servicing of the Sukhoi Jet fighters that Indonesia has bought from Russia.[27] The Indonesian government has expressed its interest in benefitting 'from India's expertise in the production of radars, electronic equipment and artillery weapons.'[28] India has, for many years, provided training to the different sections of the Indonesian military under the ITEC-I programme.

Building Cultural and People-to-People Linkages

Though the changing geopolitical reality of Asia and the rise of India and Indonesia have led to strong strategic ties, the strength of the relationship has flowed also from the two countries' long standing civilisational, cultural and people-to-people linkages. These attributes have acted as important cultural resources in broad-basing the inter-governmental exchanges to reach a wider popular and cultural audience. Over the years, the number of Indians in Indonesia has increased, with people settled primarily in Jakarta, Indonesia's capital city. At the same time, the number of Indonesian students or tourists coming to India has shown a gradual increase. While Bali has emerged as an important tourist destination for Indians, the Taj Mahal and Indian educational institutions are gradually drawing the attention of more and more Indonesians. Furthermore, Indian cinema and celebrities are very popular in Indonesia and are looked upon as icons.

India and Indonesia signed six Memorandums of Understanding (MoUs) in October 2013 during the visit of Prime Minister Singh to Indonesia. These MoUs covered greater collaboration between institutions of the two countries in the areas of health, natural disasters, drug-trafficking, intelligence training, and research.

However, the two countries have yet to optimally capitalise on their historical and cultural linkages, which could provide a strong foundation to speed up the process of engagement between the people of the two countries. The Indian diaspora remains small in Indonesia, and it does not carry much political weight. Besides, academic exchanges have remained insignificant. The number of Indonesian students in India is small, and reasons for not choosing to study in India include procedural complexities and the extremely low amount of available scholarships. Any people-to-people connectivity is predicated upon a certain level of physical connectivity between the two countries. Two major issues remain – the absence of any direct flight by any Indonesian airlines to India, and a stricter visa regime. Also, there is limited scope for education and learning about India and South Asia in Indonesia and about Indonesia and Southeast Asia in India.

India and Indonesia in a Resurgent Asia

As the 21st century unfolds, Asia has emerged as a continent of important actors rather than a mere object of study determined by the strategic priorities of players outside the continent. Such a shift has occurred from two major developments – the rise of Asian powers and a growing shift in the epicentre of global economics from the trans-Atlantic to Asia. Today three of the four largest economies of the world (GDP in Purchasing Power Parity) come from Asia – China, Japan and India – and Asian economies have been at the forefront of reviving global economic prospects. The participation of 6 Asian countries (the ASEAN Chair, China, India, Indonesia, Japan and South Korea) in the G-20 grouping, which has taken over the G-7 as the main body to discuss the global economic scenario, further signifies the growing importance of Asia in world politics.

Nevertheless, the resurgent Asia is far from a region of peace, stability and certainty. The emerging structures of relationships in Asia are marked by long-standing hostility and existing unpredictability about the behaviour of these Asian powers towards one-another. The same set of players that has been steering the process of cooperation, integration and community-building in Asia has exhibited tendencies towards mutual antagonism and mistrust. Though China has emerged as the central axis of strategic discourses in Asia, due primarily to an enormous swell in the former's economic influence, it is not certain whether the rise of China is going to be a peaceful process or not. Moreover, important Asian players, such as India and Japan, have experienced long-standing hostility with China, which, in turn, can set in motion a great power rivalry and new power alignments in the continent. In other words, the avenues for cooperation in Asia are embedded with the elements of strategic rivalries and deep-seated animosity. Reflecting on the responsibilities of emerging powers in an uncertain and leaderless Asia, Amitav Acharya states:

> ... [the] Asian security is not a function of who occupies the White House. The emerging powers of Asia must also bear responsibility for

> maintaining order if the one that America built collapses. Asia is clearly in the midst of a power drift. Uncertainties about the future of American military power will persist, given legitimate doubts over whether rebalancing will work or will suffice in arresting the expansion of Chinese military power...Today, the US is less able to provide leadership while emerging power China is neither a ready nor acceptable alternative. There has been much said about an Asian Century, but the key Asian powers are too busy competing with each other to offer even a semblance of regional or global leadership....[29]

As Asia finds itself at the fulcrum of global actions and strategies, both India and Indonesia have emerged as important stakeholders, grappling with the challenge of how to balance continental geo-politics between a juxtaposition of conflict and integration. An unstable Asia can derail the prospect of continued growth stories, economic integration and efforts towards community building in the eastern Asian hemisphere. Two decades of renewed camaraderie and shared experiences have convinced both India and Indonesia of the necessity of combined efforts for a stable Asian order. Their growing emphasis on and stakes in ASEAN cooperative processes can introduce greater vitality into the grouping and also help to sustain its continued relevance amidst uncertainty and rivalries.

The rise of Asian powers along with the re-engagement of the USA and Russia has pushed the continental power structure towards multipolarity. The underlying principles of strategic autonomy and regional leadership enshrined in India's Look East Policy and Indonesia's 'dynamic equilibrium' policy somewhat necessitate a multipolar Asian order and a security architecture that is inclusive, draws on strength of each players in building a stable regional strategic atmosphere and pushes the players towards mutually beneficial and cooperation-driven rather than conflict-driven relations. India-Indonesia relations have latched on to a much larger discourse of strategic engagement during the 21st century – they are both committed to building a stable, developed, peaceful and powerful Asia. This vision was once shared by the founding fathers of these two countries – Nehru and Sukarno – and enshrined under the Bandung Spirit.[30]

Notwithstanding the larger geo-political imperative of India-Indonesia relations, domestic stimuli have contributed significantly, in at least two ways, to the strengthening of bilateral relations. A major thrust to the Look East discourse came from a paradigmatic shift in India's domestic economic priorities from state regulation to market regulation and the subsequent augmentation of the liberalisation discourse within Indian economic planning during the early 1990s. The liberalising and globalising nature of the Look East Policy drew the attention of Indonesia towards the Indian market and facilitated cooperation among business houses, a trend seen in the form of mergers and acquisitions of companies from the two countries during the early years of twenty-first century. Moreover, the democratisation of Indonesian politics after the downfall of Suharto has not only offered an important strategic space for joint projections as democracies, but also strengthened linkages between the civil societies and institutions, thereby, further broad-basing the canvas of bilateral cooperation.

Shared Strategic Vulnerability, Shared Security

India-Indonesia security engagement has acquired significance during the last twenty years in the strategic calculations of both the countries as well as in the geo-political equations of East Asia. Much of the significance emanates from the rising profile of India and Indonesia in Asian geopolitics, the nature of their defence cooperation, and their geographical location overseeing the traffic entering and exiting the Strait of Malacca and the Indian Ocean. While Indonesia is the largest military power in Southeast Asia, India is its powerful maritime neighbour. The security engagement between the two neighbours and largest Asian democracies can contribute to a formidable partnership, ensure the safety and security of the Sea Lanes of Communications (SLoCs), and effectively combat non-traditional security challenges in the Strait of Malacca and the Indian Ocean. Both India and Indonesia stand to gain from a stable regional order. Moreover, the dependence of these two economies on the sea in terms of their sea-borne foreign trade and the growing trans-national nature of security threats has rendered the territorial waters of these two countries vulnerable.

Much of the bilateral security engagement has emerged out of (a) the idea of 'shared vulnerability', (b) India's growing naval outreach and benign image, (c) India's growing image as a technologically sophisticated military power, and (d) Indonesia's desire to diversify the sources of its defence supplies. The idea of 'shared vulnerability' emanates from their similar societal characteristics, the developing nature of their economies, their inefficient politico-administrative agencies, and the maritime nature of their nation-states. In addition to these internal characteristics, the geographical contiguity of these two countries and their shared maritime border have made the two countries further recognize their common vulnerability from sea-borne threats. A similar shared experience is the growing Islamic terror networks in these two countries. The two countries signed a MoU on Combating International Terrorism in July 2004 that led to the setting up of a Joint Working Group (JWG). The JWG held its first meeting in New Delhi in February 2005 and agreed to strengthen bilateral cooperation in combating terrorism and other acts of transnational crime and maritime security through exchange of information and intelligence, capacity building and mutual legal cooperation.[31]

While the rise of Asian powers – China, India and Indonesia – has repositioned Asia in the world, a new debate has ensued about the evolving structure of power within continental geopolitics – how to pursue regional stability and cooperation amidst growing capabilities and ambition of the member-states. Regional geopolitics has been rattled by a few pronouncements of fundamental strategic consequence during the past three years – the Chinese designation of the South China Sea as an area of 'core national interest, the US rebalancing strategy, and China's declaration of Air Defence Identification Zone (ADIZ). They not only augment the emergence of new power configurations in the region, but also further confound the prevailing strategic uncertainty and instability in the region. Though the US has been viewed as a positive and stabilising force, rising China, generally viewed as a traditional source of instability and rivalry, has been gaining influence in the region and winning more friends, if not allies, in the region. There has been a growing realisation among the policy makers of both India and Indonesia that great power rivalries are not going to be conducive to the regional stability and their sustained economic growth.

Strengthening ASEAN-driven Security Architecture

The simultaneous rise of India and Indonesia to the upper echelon of the global hierarchy of power offers an important opportunity to the two countries to develop a more meaningful agenda for engagement in the ASEAN-driven cooperative forums – the ASEAN Regional Forum (ARF), East Asia Summit (EAS), and ASEAN Plus Defence Ministerial Meeting (ADMM+). These forums have not only provided effective avenues for India's wider strategic positioning in the Asia-Pacific, but also broadened its canvas for strategic manoeuvrings from South Asia to the Asia-Pacific. India would require continued Indonesian support in these forums to make effective use of this opportunity. There is a growing necessity for India and Indonesia to work together in facilitating their continued relevance by supporting consensus-building in the deliberations, implementation of the agendas, introducing new agendas of cooperation and exhibiting activism in the discussions over the issues facing the Asia-Pacific. These forums aim to create an inclusive regional security architecture, and both India and Indonesia share those objectives.

Both India and Indonesia attach considerable importance to these forums and have worked towards strengthening them. Indonesia played an instrumental role in securing for India the full-dialogue partnership of ASEAN in 1995 and membership of the ARF in 1996. The early stages of India-Indonesia multilateral engagement as a part of the Look East Policy remained confined to India-ASEAN networks of cooperation, including interaction in the ASEAN Post-Ministerial Conferences and in the ARF. While ASEAN occupied centre-stage in Indonesia's foreign policy, India's Look East discourse focused initially on ASEAN-driven multilateralism. It was the statement of none other than then Indonesian Foreign Minister, Ali Alatas, during the Manila meeting of the ARF that evenly distributed the onus for India's nuclear tests in 1998 on both India as well as the discriminatory and faulty policies of the global non-proliferation regimes.[32] The two countries, in these cooperative frameworks, engaged bilaterally, developed a shared understanding about the prevailing politico-strategic landscape in the Asia-Pacific, and worked together to strengthen these institutions. Together they pushed forth the non-traditional security agenda during the track-I and track-II meetings of the ARF. The two countries have also been working towards developing a common understanding over the issues of climate change, disaster management, regional security and governance.

India became a summit-level partner of ASEAN in 2001 and a member of the newly-floated EAS in 2005, thanks to crucial diplomatic support from Indonesia on both occasions. The significance of Indonesia in India's Look East discourse can be gauged from the fact that these two developments mark the onset of the second phase of the Look East Policy, the arrival of India in East Asia as an important player, and India's positioning as an integral part of the East Asia community-building process. Besides membership, Indonesia has also contributed to India's sustained participation in the East Asian community-building process by supporting and sustaining the existence and relevance of the EAS. While China, Malaysia and Thailand seem to favour the ASEAN+3 process, Indonesia, along with Singapore, Vietnam and Japan, has favoured the EAS as the overarching community-building process in East Asia. Viewed from this perspective, Indonesia has played a significant role in the actual expansion in the geographical canvas of the Look East Policy from ASEAN-centrism to Asia-centrism, India's comprehensive engagement and economic integration with ASEAN, and the projection of India's strategic profile in the Asia-Pacific. On each occasion, the Indonesian diplomatic support emanated from a shared understanding of the changing politico-strategic landscape of Asia and the urgent necessity of working together towards peace and stability in the continent. While the ARF has offered an avenue for joint discussion over non-traditional security issues, the EAS has facilitated joint deliberation at the highest level over the issues of economic integration, developing ways and means to overcome the 2008 global economic crisis, and creating a common approach to issues of energy security and climate change.

While the early outlook of India-Indonesia engagement remained ASEAN-centric, it reacquired the pan-Asian character by the early 21st century as the discourses of the 'Asian Century' became louder, a point highlighted by the India-Indonesia Strategic Partnership. The emerging powers of Asia – China, India and Indonesia – have been speaking for and articulating the interests of developing countries, primarily when negotiating with the developed world. Therefore, the resurgence of Asia has also coincided with an overall growth in the standing of the developing countries, which have been demanding equitable representation in global multilateral bodies and safeguarding their economic interests. Besides sharing common stakes in the East Asian processes of cooperation and economic integration, India and Indonesia have also lobbied for the interests of the developing countries in the global deliberations.[33] Reflective of their past Nehru-Sukarno Asianism, the India-Indonesia Strategic Partnership calls for efforts to go beyond bilateral cooperation and work together towards structural reforms in the global multilateral institutions to facilitate equitable representation of the developing countries from Asia and Africa. The active participation of India and Indonesia in setting up the New Asia-Africa Strategic Partnership (NAASP) in April 2005 reinforces the two countries' desire to 'rekindle the Bandung Spirit.'[34]

A somewhat related issue is what India and Indonesia can discuss together in these forums. While the issues have already been making rounds in the discussions, India needs to proactively participate. There is a need to make its presence felt in these forums by offering proposals, areas of cooperation and new agendas. New Delhi's offer at the EAS has occurred only in the sector of capacity-building. India should come up with its own proposals on the ideas of balanced growth, environmental issues, international terrorism, social sector, food security, maritime security, energy security including alternative sources of bio-fuels, greater economic integration and peace and stability in the region. The idea of a benign presence does not and should not restrict India's active participation in these forums.

A Shared Understanding of the World: Towards the Delhi-Jakarta Paradigm

As India and Indonesia rise together at the end of the first decade of the 21st century, their outlook tells us a somewhat similar story. They are emerging powers, ethnically most diverse societies in the world, the largest Asian democracies, and countries with the largest Muslim population. They have registered a high level of sustained economic growth and maintained global growth momentum amidst crisis. Their emergence as successful and stable democracies has broken many myths of governance and politics in Asia. Moreover, their participation in global politics have seen their advocacy of common guiding principles – democratisation of international order, greater representation of Asia in the global discourse, multilateral thrust to address common problems, and concerted global focus on development of the underdeveloped and poor. These principles and practices carry both a normative and pragmatic outlook and can broadly be clubbed under a common 'Delhi-Jakarta Paradigm.'[35]

India and Indonesia have proven that democracy as a form of governance, though somewhat imperfect, can be ideated and practiced in the multi-ethnic, Muslim, Asian, and erstwhile authoritarian polities. Moreover, Asian societies can indigenise and give a completely native accent to the democratic political discourse based on principles germane to human relations. Also the rise of democratic India and Indonesia have challenged the notions of an 'Asian way' that suggests that (a) development is more important than the form of governance; (b) democracy and development can not coexist harmoniously in multi-ethnic Asian societies; and (c) authoritarianism is a political necessity. The combined experiences of India and Indonesia in the 21st century suggest that democracy and development can co-exist in the Asian multi-ethnic societies. Democracy can be practiced even in the absence of a high level of per capita income or any vague notion of political stability, and democracies can achieve a high level of economic growth. These polities need not take the authoritarian path and justify large-scale human-rights violations being committed in the name of stability and development.

While speaking at Harvard University in September 2009, the Indonesian president called for devising new methods and strategies for dialogue between the West and Muslim world and between civilizations. As democracies and with the largest Muslim populations of the world, both India and Indonesia are better placed to facilitate worldwide moderate and harmonious civilisational dialogue between the West and East, and between the West and Muslim World. Notwithstanding their common experience of terrorism and the radicalisation of Islam, India and Indonesia represent a moderate outlook of Islam. Both countries have felt the necessity to work together to challenge the process of radicalisation with a discourse that is inclusive, harmonious and peaceful.

The rise of India and Indonesia (along with China) has changed the way the world looks at Asia, necessitating greater Asian representation in the prevailing international order. Both the powers are important stakeholders in and claimants for the structural reforms in the global institutions that were formed in a particular setting in the aftermath of the World War II and represented the world-views and interests of the victorious West (European and other Anglo-Celtic societies). These institutions in the changing geopolitical realities of 21st century need to be more democratic and representative. Not long ago, on their way to stability and development, the democratic leaderships of both India and Indonesia felt strong-armed by the structurally flawed and insensitive policies of the World Bank and IMF in the aftermath of the economic crises.

There is a growing realisation among the two rising powers that they need to work together towards fundamental reforms in the UN and equitable representation and rights in the global financial institutions. As developing societies with extremely diverse levels of social and economic developments, ample opportunities exist for the two countries to discuss and learn from each other's experiences in the accomplishment of the Millennium Development Goals.

At the same time, their growing ambitions need not create differences between New Delhi and Jakarta. Both India and Indonesia would be keen to have permanent membership in a reformed and expanded UN Security Council (UNSC). Notwithstanding their common call for reforms in the UN, they have remained silent on supporting each other's candidature for permanent membership of the UNSC. Indonesia, under the presidency of Abdurrahman Wahid, had supported India's candidature for the permanent membership of the UNSC when he visited India in February 2000.

India and Indonesia also represent the rise of the Global South. As G-20 members, they have agreed to ensure greater representation of the interests of Asia and developing countries. They also share the G-77, G-33, and G-15 platforms along with other developing countries, pushing forth the agendas and interests of the developing world in WTO negotiations, reforms of the UN, or deliberations over climate change solutions. It was in this context of greater participation and democratisation of international institutions that President Yudhoyono, while speaking at Global Economic Forum in January 2011, called upon Asian nations to be the 'change makers.'[36] India and Indonesia are members of the G-20 platform that discusses 'key economic and financial policy issues among systemically significant economies.'[37] They are also the two poorest member-states of the grouping. Though their growth has lifted a large number of people out of poverty, the task of development remains far from complete in both countries. They must engage with each other and the world about increasing the pace of the developmental agenda and the realisation of millennium development goals.

Conclusion

India-Indonesia relations have seen comprehensive expansion in terms of both the content as well as context of cooperation. There is a growing understanding between the two powers that they can work together to usher the continent towards peace, stability, and greater cooperation. The contours of India-Indonesia relations, today, are not confined to the template of bilateralism alone, but rather incorporate the ASEAN-centric, Asia-centric, and global frameworks of strategic engagement. As they rise together, they have been experiencing critical challenges at the regional and global level. The regional uncertainty and instability remains of paramount concern. The rise of China and consequent escalation of hostility in the South and East China Seas require concerted regional and global attention and greater India-Indonesia strategic dialogue about finding ways to minimise tension and hostility. Nevertheless, their common agenda is not confined to strategic aspects alone. A critical challenge lies in overcoming their own institutional and implementational inertia that characterise their foreign policies. Though four major documents – the India-Indonesia Strategic Partnership of 2005, the Plan of Action Mechanism adopted in 2007, the Joint Statement of January 2011, and the Joint Statement of October 2013 – have identified a wide range of areas for cooperation, it is time that they are implemented at a faster pace.

ENDNOTES

1. Cited in I K Gujaral, "Lands of the Asian Miracle," *The Hindu*, 10 August 1996.
2. D. Kimche, "The Afro-Asian Movement: Ideology and Foreign Policy of the Third World," (New York: Halsted Press, 1973), p. 33, cited in Pang Yang Huei, "The Four Faces of Bandung: Detainees, Soldiers, Revolutionaries and Statesmen," *Journal of Contemporary Asia*, vol. 39, no.1 (February 2009), p. 68.
3. Ibid.
4. Ibid, p. 69.
5. Nicholas Tarling, "'Ah-Ah': Britain and the Bandung Conference of 1955," *Journal of Southeast Asian Studies,* vol. 23, no. 1 (March 1992), pp. 75-79.
6. Ibid, p. 78.
7. Ganganath Jha, "A Brief Survey of India-Indonesia Relations," *Contemporary Southeast Asia,* vol. 17, no. 4 (March 1996), p. 390.
8. P.V. Narasimha Rao, "India and the Asia-Pacific: Forging a New Relationship," Singapore Lecture, *Strategic Digest* (October 1994), p. 1412.
9. Christophe Jaffrelot, "India's Look East Policy: an Asianist Strategy in Perspective," *India Review,* vol. 2, no.2 (April 2003), pp. 35-68; Prakash Nanda, *Rediscovering India: Evolution of India's Look East Policy* (New Delhi: Lancer Publishers & Distributors, 2003).
10. "Joint Declaration between the Republic of India and the Republic of Indonesia," Ministry of External Affairs, Government of India, 23 November 2005, no. 7067, http://mea.gov.in/bilateral-documents.htm?dtl/7067/Joint+Declaration+between+the+Republic+of+India+and+the+Republic+of+Indonesia(accessed on 13 March 2013).
11. Ide Anak Agung Gde Agung, "Twenty Years of Indonesian Foreign Policy (1945-65)," (The Hague: Mouton, 1968), p. 510.
12. Rizali Indrakesuma, "Indonesia-India relations: Some updates," *The Jakarta Post,* 11 October 2013, http://www.thejakartapost.com/news/2013/10/11/indonesia-india-relations-some-updates.html (accessed on 22 December 2013).
13. Ina Parlina, "Indonesia, India take further steps to strengthen relationship," *The Jakarta Post,* 12 October 2013, http://www.thejakartapost.com/news/2013/10/12/indonesia-india-take-further-steps-strengthen-relationship.html (accessed on 22 December 2013).
14. Rizali Indrakesuma, op.cit., n.12.
15. Shutapa Paul, "CIL Plans to Invest in Overseas Coalmines," Livemint,31 January 2010, http://www.livemint.com/Companies/KsJg6c5qQYDM9N9wrzjWxI/CIL-plans-to-invest-in-overseas-coal-mines.html (accessed on 05 May 2013).
16. "India's Nalco To Invest Big In Indonesia's Aluminium Project," *Borneo Post Online,* 13 April 2010, http://www.theborneopost.com/2010/04/13/nalco-to-invest-big-in-indonesia's-aluminium-project/ (accessed on 05 May 2013).
17. "Reliance Power buys 3 coal mines in Indonesia," *The Financial Express,* 03 May 2008.
18. "KS Oils buys palm plantation in Indonesia," *The Hindu Business Line,* 27 March 2010.
19. "Surana buys 49% in Indonesian coal mine," *The Hindu Business Line,* 10 January 2008.
20. "List of subsidiaries of Indian Banks abroad as on November 30, 2007," *Reserve Bank of India,* Government of India, http://fi.ge.pgstatic.net/attachments/36129_a3ee88e975ca420087e4965de2a45783.pdf (accessed on 10 May 2013).
21. Rahul Bedi, "A new Doctrine for the Navy," *Frontline,* vol. 21, no. 14 (03-16 July 2004), http://www.frontline.in/static/html/fl2114/stories/20040716002104600.htm (accessed on 10 May 2013).
22. India has also taken initiatives towards strengthening the military capability of other littoral

countries, such as Malaysia and Singapore. Gurpreet S. Khurana, "Maritime Security in the Indian Ocean: Convergence Plus Cooperation Equals Resonance," *Strategic Analysis,* vol. 28, no 3 (July-September 2004), p. 418.

23. "Indonesia, Indian Navies Conduct Joint Patrols in Malacca Strait," *BBC Monitoring Asia Pacific – Political,* 12 March 2010.
24. Veeramalla Anjaiah, "Relations between RI and India reach 'historic high' in 2009," *The Jakarta Post,* http://www.thejakartapost.com/news/2010/01/04/relations-between-ri-and-india-reach-'historic-high'-2009.html (accessed on 18 May 2013).
25. "RI Invites India to help Maintain Malacca Strait Security," *Antara News Agency,* 05 March 2009.
26. "Indonesia, India consider joint production of military equipment," *Agence France Presse,* 26 November 2006.
27. "RI, India Increase Mily Cooperation," *Antara News Agency,* 09 February 2009.
28. "India, Indonesia Mull Joint Defense Hardware Production," *India Defence Online,* 15 June 2007.
29. Amitav Acharya, "What Obama's second term means for Asia," *East Asia Forum,* 11 November 2012, http://www.eastasiaforum.org/2012/11/11/what-obamas-second-term-means-for-asia/ (accessed on 11 November 2012).
30. Vibhanshu Shekhar, "India and Indonesia: Reliable Partners in an Uncertain Asia," *Asia-Pacific Review,* vol. 17, no. 2, 2010, pp. 76-98.
31. "First Meeting of India-Indonesia Joint Working Group on Counter-Terrorism," Ministry of External Affairs, Government of India, no. 5792, 25 February 2005,http://www.mea.gov.in/press-releases.htm?dtl/5792/First+Meeting+of+IndiaIndonesia+Joint+Working+Group+on+CounterTerrorism (accessed on 10 May 2013).
32. Sudhir Devare, *India and Southeast Asia: Towards Security Convergence* (Singapore, ISEAS, 2006), p. 77.
33. "Joint Declaration between the Republic of India and the Republic of Indonesia," op. cit.,
34. "Statement by Mr. Biren Nanda, Ambassador of India to Indonesia and Head of Delegation at New Asia-Africa Strategic Partnership Ministerial Conference on Capacity Building for Palestine at Jakarta," Ministry of External Affairs, Government of India, no. 14080, 14 July 2008, http://meaindia.nic.in/speech/2008/07/14ss01.htm (accessed on 06 May 2010).
35. Vibhanshu Shekhar, "SBY's visit and the Delhi-Jakarta Paradigm," *The Jakarta Post,* May 09 2011.
36. Susilo Bambang Yudhoyono, "Keynote Speech at World Economic Forum 2011," 27 January 2011, http://www.presidenri.go.id/index.php/eng/pidato/2011/01/27/1572.html (accessed on 13 May 2013).
37. "Meeting of the G-20 Finance Ministers and Central Bank Governors," G-20 Communique, Berlin, 15-16 December, 1999.

6

SPOILERS IN THE INDONESIAN SUCCESS STORY

Any growth story has both drivers as well as spoilers. Powers rise and fall back to stagnation and oblivion. Indonesia is no exception. While its growth drivers have elevated Indonesia to a place of regional and global prominence, they have shown trends challenging the long-term sustainability of Indonesia's success story. These spoilers, if unchecked, may cast a shadow over the country's international image, arrest its momentum and erode its long-term prospects. The continued success depends on the leadership's management of key challenges confronting the country's national landscape.

While certain domestic processes have received the credit for the rise and growth, some other domestic factors have proved to be impediments. In fact, domestic responsibilities often receive greater attention in case of the decline of a power. Such potential spoilers in the case of Indonesia are, to name a few, a stressful economic situation, the indecisiveness of the ruling political elite in addressing issues of modernising its out-dated, under-equipped and under-staffed military, the nature and functioning of the coalition-based government, Indonesia's radical turn and the rise of Sunni majoritarian, and issues associated with governance. These 'processes from within' pose challenges of both short-term and long-term significance. Rising Indonesia may not climb very far if it does not put its house in order.

Various scholars have expressed a similar opinion. Since domestic politics has always considerably influenced Indonesia's foreign policy direction, it is suggested that the country's "desire to play a bigger global role – as a functioning democracy, as a moderate Muslim country, and as a 'bridge builder' and 'problem solver,' – remains subject to the limits imposed by persistent domestic weaknesses."[1] Australia's former Foreign Minister Gareth Evans identifies three important domestic challenges confronting Indonesia's otherwise smooth rise – a shaky anti-corruption drive, religious freedom under duress, and continuing general governmental weakness.[2] Others point out that major handicaps facing Indonesia today are a 'poor and in some areas declining infrastructure, a legal regime very little trusted by its citizens to provide equal justice to all, and a corrupt and cumbrous bureaucracy.'[3] What is more worrisome is their long and continuing existence and the lack of political will and consensus within the country as to how these challenges should be dealt with.

However, it would not be fair to lay all the blame on domestic spoilers alone. Systemic trends are also posing a challenge to Indonesia's success story. One worry is the possibility of a brake on regional growth momentum. The World Bank Executive Director and Indonesia's former Economic Minister, Mulyani Indrawati, drew the country's attention towards external vulnerabilities when she admitted, "the Indonesian economy has weakened due to external factors. It has been a challenge to safeguard the domestic economy from the impact of the US quantitative easing policy."[4] The announcement by the US Federal Reserve Bank that it would taper its stimulus package sent shockwaves across the Asia-Pacific, causing stress for the regional economies and their currencies, including Indonesia's. The Indonesian *Rupiah* registered a major slide in the months of August and September 2013, prompting the government to embark on a policy of capital control. New government initiatives have led to a capital outflow, further reducing the possibility of large-scale investment in key sectors of the Indonesian economy. Moreover, the sluggish global demand has put a lot of pressure on the domestic sector of the Indonesian economy. The UN Report, *The Economic and Social Survey of Asia and the Pacific*, highlighted the slowdown in the Asia-Pacific economies and attributed this to 'the impact of persistent weaknesses and uncertainties in the developed economies.'[5] Overall, three large Asian economies – China, India and Indonesia – experienced a slowdown in the second half of 2013, prompting international financial agencies to revise growth prospects for the region as a whole.[6] These challenges are a reflection of systemic pressure, and thus there is not much the Indonesian leadership can do about it apart from responding to them in a prudent manner and with a long-term policy framework.

Increasing Domestic Pressure on the Indonesian Economy

It is argued that Indonesia's rise has been 'an unambiguous economic success story,' leading to high living standards, reduced poverty, and political stability.[7] Following this argument, the biggest challenge confronting the Indonesian leadership is sustaining its economic growth that has come under pressure. Some view this as a sign of the country falling into a 'middle-income trap.'[8] The Indonesian growth story has revolved around two domestic catalysts – the rise of the middle class and the consumption boom. These developments have given a new fillip to Indonesia's economic growth and are credited with saving the national economy from the adverse impacts of the economic crisis emanating from the developed West. The role of internal demands in the country's growth trajectory appears much more critical in light of the fact that the crisis-ridden advanced economies of the West have been traditional markets for Indonesian businesses. At the same time, due to its democratic consolidation and market-friendly atmosphere, the country has emerged as one of the most favoured destinations for investment from different parts of the world.

Nevertheless, the Euphoria and excitement about Indonesia's growth story has lately begun to create a sense of scepticism among experts, practitioners and businesses about the long-term viability and sustainability of the consumption-driven and commodities boom-based current growth model.[9] The national economy has shown signs of a possible slowdown in the coming years. The McKinsey Global Institute's report of 2012 has identified three important bottlenecks that could slow Indonesia's economic recovery – a limited productivity imperative, growing economic inequality across the archipelago, and infrastructural and resource constraints.[10] The increasing reliance on exports of raw commodities (such as the export of coal and gas to India and China) and import of consumer goods can not only undermine the country's local manufacturing industry, but also derail the Indonesia economic planners' dream of converting Indonesia into a manufacturing hub in the region.[11] The Indonesian manufacturing sector is reported to have lagged behind all other important sectors of the economy.[12]

A somewhat related challenge is the inadequate infrastructure that is unable to support the demands of Indonesia's growing economy and sustained high-level growth rate. Though the demand for electricity, faster road and rail networks, education infrastructure, and air transport has gone up during the last ten years, the progress in these sectors has remained limited. Road transport has worsened over the years in the major cities of Java with the growing number of vehicles on the road and limited expansion in road capacities.[13] Jakarta's traffic jams, known as *Machet*, have their own stories to tell. Port infrastructure has suffered from similar limitations and many of them are today 'dilapidated, crumbling and notoriously slow.'[14] Moreover, infrastructure development projects have often suffered from limited funding, delayed implementation, corruption and a complex land acquisition process.[15] The only major addition to the existing transport network in Jakarta has come in the form of dedicated lanes for buses. Moreover, the rural areas in Java and other islands have experienced reduced road connectivity.[16] The coal exporters from Kalimantan reportedly prefer to export coal directly to China rather than sending them to Jakarta 'due to high cost of transportation.'[17] Perhaps Bali is the only exception where the growing demand of tourism has prompted the government to ensure an adequate transport network.

In the medium and long run, the infrastructural inadequacy may not only prompt foreign investors to look to other competitive markets in the region, but also slow down the economic growth of the country.[18] The condition of Indonesian infrastructure ranks even below that of Malaysia, the Philippines and Thailand.[19] The Indonesian government launched the Master Plan for the Acceleration and Expansion of Indonesia's Economic Development (MP3EI) in 2012 with the objective of making the country one of the ten biggest economies by 2025.[20] The country is going to invest approximately US$240 billion in the next five years 'to boost the country's infrastructure and improve connectivity and the movement of goods throughout the archipelago.'[21]

A bigger problem that is waiting to explode is the growing socio-economic inequality across the archipelago at various levels. Indonesia ranks 124th out of 187 countries at the UN Human Development Index, reflecting the need for substantial progress in the areas of health, education and income. This situation is much more precarious in the outer islands. Life expectancy is lower and the infant mortality rate is higher in the outer islands compared to Java.[22] The outer islands have experienced higher levels of poverty, illiteracy, and a lack of education.[23] As a result, their contribution to the national economy has remained much less than that of the islands of Java and Sumatra.[24]

The ongoing economic boom does not seem to have uplifted the majority of Indonesians, especially outside of Jakarta.[25] If anything, the boom seems to have had an adverse impact on the social distribution of wealth. It has been observed that Indonesia's Gini Index has been steadily going up, from 0.37 in 2009 to 0.41 in 2011.[26] The increase in the Gini index has also coincided with the country's economic growth. As per one estimate, half of the Indonesian population is below the poverty line based on the World Bank criteria of US$2/day.[27] While 7 out of 33 provinces were above the national average of per capita income (GDP) in 2002, there were only 5 provinces left above the national average in 2010.[28] Indonesian provinces experienced worsening income inequality in 2011 in comparison with the figure of 2007 and 2009, with resource-rich provinces exhibiting the greatest inequality.[29]

As the level of income inequality in Indonesia grows, fewer segments of society will actually be able to contribute to and benefit from the country's economic growth. As a result, more and more people, especially the poor, will be left out of the development process. Such a situation may be short-lived and unsustainable in the long-term, making the Indonesian economy more and more vulnerable to even smaller economic shocks and market volatility. In their IMF report, two economists – Andrew Berg and Jonathan Ostry – concluded that 'longer growth spells are robustly associated with more equality in the income distribution.'[30] This is especially true in the context of the emerging Asian economies where, according to them, the duration of the growth process may double if income inequality is reduced by half.[31] Moreover, any prospect of Indonesia getting out of the middle-income trap would require comprehensive contributions from different segments of society given growing external and internal challenges facing the Indonesian economy.

The impact of growing income inequality on the Indonesian economy and development can also negatively impact the social fabric of the country. The rising socio-economic disparities might interfere with the existing and dominant ethnic and political faultlines in the outer islands. Their convergence may destabilise the socio-political relationships in the outer islands, which witnessed devastation, violence and political chaos not so long ago. The Indonesian political leadership faces an important challenge to address these concerns.

Cracks in Indonesia's Muslim Democracy Model: Towards Radicalisation

One of the most important challenges to the rise of Indonesia comes from the growing radicalisation that undermines Jakarta's credentials as a model

Muslim democracy and cuts into its growing global popularity and rising power status. The process of radicalisation has troubled the Indonesian leadership since the beginning of the country's democratic transition in the aftermath of the departure of Suharto, who ruled Indonesia with an iron fist and maintained the state's moderate identity.

The process of radicalisation during the last fifteen years can be seen in two different stages marked by different goals, modus operandi and focus areas. During these two stages, state and the law-enforcement agencies also seem to have exhibited different characters. While the first phase saw Christian minorities serving as the main target, the second phase has seen the targeting of non-Sunni Muslims. While the outer islands were the main theatre of change during the first stage, the island of Java seems to have emerged as the focus area of radical forces during the second phase. In other words, the radicals perceived threats coming primarily from non-Muslims and the state during the first phase. During the second phase, they have begun to view non-Sunni Muslims and nominal believers (the *Abangans*) of Java as the main threat. The first stage was marked by ethno-communal violence and terrorist operations, in reaction to which the government adopted a zero-tolerance policy. On the other hand, the second stage has seen frequent sectarian attacks against non-Sunni Muslims, with the state gradually caving in to the radical pressure.

The First Phase (1998-2007): Radicalisation against the State and Minorities

The first phase of radicalisation occurred during the formative years of post-Suharto Indonesia's experiments with democracy. Three major elements of radicalisation were seen during this phase: a large-scale outbreak of ethno-communal violence in the outer islands, the rise of Islamic paramilitaries and the emergence of local and regional Al-Qaeda-linked terror networks. As post-Suharto Indonesia was celebrating the resurgence of democracy in the country, it was simultaneously witnessing the horror stories of ethno-communal violence on its various islands. As a result of this violence during the late 1990s, more than 10,000 people died and approximately 100,000 families were displaced. Many houses, religious structures and places of public utility were burnt down, and economic activities in the conflict areas came to a standstill. Although the geography of these conflicts indicates their widespread distribution, the most extensive devastation occurred on three islands – Kalimantan, Sulawesi and Maluku.

Out of the process of radicalisation arose several Islamic paramilitary organizations. These organisations include the *Front Pembela Islam* (FPI)[32] or Islamic Defenders Front, the Yogyakarta-based *Laskar Jihad*, and the much smaller but still national *Laskar Mujahidin* of the Council of Islamic Fighters or *Majelis Mujahidin Indonesia*. These militias were mobilizing nominal and devout Muslims by capitalizing on the discourse of 'victimization,' and projecting non-Muslims as enemies and the state as anti-Islamic. While the *Laskar Jihad* claimed to protect Muslims from being victimized by the Christians in Maluku and Central Sulawesi, the FPI aimed to eliminate the impurities allegedly creeping into the Indonesian social and individual space – banning bars, discotheques, and nightclubs, enforcing dress codes and so on.[33] Noorhaidi Hasan identifies three reasons for the rise of radical Islamic paramilitaries in Indonesia: (a) the dispersal of state capacity across various regional and national centres, (b) the tendency among the political elite to reach out to 'uncivil forces' in society, and (c) the rise of factional politics within the Indonesian army.[34]

Another important trend that proved to be the hallmark of the radicalisation of Indonesian Islam was the rise of terror networks, led by Jemaah Islamiyah. It represented a multi-faceted narrative, weaving together local, regional and global stories of Islamic radicalism. While the 9/11 attack awakened Indonesia as a Muslim country to a new set of discourses regarding the growing radicalization of Islam, the Bali bomb blast made Indonesia an active participant in the global discourse on radical Islam. Democratic Indonesia had to choose between the growing domestic support for the radical Islam against the West and its role as a good international Samaritan to counter radical Islamic tendencies both within as well as outside the country. Various terrorist operations in Jakarta (April 2003, September 2004 and July 2009) and Bali (October 2002 and September 2005) point towards growing inter-linkages between global vectors of Islamic terrorism and local agents such as Jemaah Islamiyah),[35] operating in domestic constituencies (Poso, Ambon and Java).

Major drivers for the radicalisation during this phase came from a weak and vulnerable state, a discredited military with vested interests, an untrained and partisan police, under-developed institutional checks and balances and the negative fallout from twin virtues of governance – democratisation and decentralisation. The process of democratisation introduced majoritarianism into electoral and political processes, prompting political parties and groups to mobilise the majority Muslim population. The decentralisation and regional redistricting not only brought out vested interests, but also set in motion a scramble for power in the provinces. The mutually reinforcing relationship between the state capacity for governance and politico-economic crisis gave a fillip to the criminal elements and the manipulation of mass sentiments. Apart from structural limitations, the inefficiency of the security agencies in managing the conflict and maintaining law and order also emanated from their vested interests, a hallmark of the New Order regime.

The Second Phase (2008 onwards): Towards Sunni Majoritarianism

In the past few years, Indonesia's social spectrum has witnessed a new trend in the process of radicalisation with more frequent attacks on non-Sunni Muslims, more intense debates on purifying Indonesian Islam with an emphasis on an outward observation of Islamic outlook, and the growing advocacy of the Arab-variant of Islam. Moreover, the state – with its indifference, inaction, juridico-legal support for stricter observance of Sunni Islam, partisanship amongst the law-enforcement agencies, and majoritarian politics of many of the political parties – has been seen as facilitator of the process. The new sectarian trend can best be understood as a growing Sunni majoritarianism within the country's national political and social life. The following elements testify to such a trend.

First, the non-Sunni Muslims and nominal Muslims of Java have been major targets of the radicals. As per the reports of the Human Rights Watch (HRW), more than 200 attacks have taken place against the minorities every year since 2010.[36] The Ahmadiya Muslim community has been banned from publicly professing its religion by the decree of 2008 and their religious places have been attacked on several occasions during the last five years. Ahmadiyas Muslims were attacked and killed by the radical militias on two occasions in western Java in February and August 2011.[37] The Shia community has also been targeted during the last few years, including an attack on a community in the Sampang district of Madura in August 2012.[38] Similarly, atheists have not been spared and many of them seem to have gone underground.[39]

The process of radicalisation seems to have also acquired a juridico-legal character. The HRW report identified 156 statutes, regulations, decrees and by-laws enacted by 2010 that restrict religious freedom, many of them justified under article 28J (2), the constitutional provision ensuring freedom of religion.[40] Moreover, Indonesia has witnessed the greater application of

Sharia law in social, legal and cultural affairs. There have been more than 60 cases of implementation of *Sharia* laws throughout the country, with roughly half of 33 provinces reporting to have implemented different sets of *Sharia* laws.[41] Even the districts and regencies, have begun to implement *Sharia* laws, as made possible by manipulating the Laws no. 22 and 25 of 1999 on decentralisation.[42] Since 2005, governments at both the national and provincial level have also resorted to more frequent application of the Anti-Blasphemy Law of 1965.[43] Moreover, the decrees on houses of worship of 1969 and of 2006 have rendered difficult the construction of the religious places of worship for the minorities.

Two explanations for traditionally moderate Indonesia's drift towards Sunni majoritarianism stand prominent. The most important factor is the majoritarian outlook of the national politico-electoral processes emanating from the lack of political will and the compulsion of coalition politics. Bahtiar Effendy, a prominent scholar on Indonesian Islam, writes, "Had the state been strong enough and functioned the way it's supposed to function, I don't think that this so-called radicalism would escalate."[44] The HRW report of 2013 mentions, "Despite occasional positive rhetoric, however, President Yudhoyono has responded weakly to growing intolerance and acts of violence against religious minorities, has not insisted firmly that national laws be enforced, and has often been unwilling to use his powers as president to see that the laws be enforced."[45] The defamatory statements from the Minister for Religious Affairs, Suryadharma Ali of the United Development Party (PPP), against Shias and Ahmediyas since 2011 seems a repetition of what Hamza Haz, his predecessor and the then Vice-President of Indonesia, was spouting during the presidency of Megawati Sukarnoputri.

While the state has taken effective actions against both the Islamic terror networks as well as the radical Jihadi groups, it has trodden softly when it comes to socio-religious life of the country. The best example of this paradox came when the Indonesian parliament passed the anti-pornography bill in October 2008 and the same day, the Indonesian court sentenced Habib Rizieq Shihab to 18 months of rigorous imprisonment for inciting violence at a religious tolerance rally.[46] It is feared that the contents of the bill, such as the involvement of civil society in the enforcement of its provisions, might allow greater social and political space to the religious vigilantes or militia groups such as the FPI (Islam Defenders' Front) to enforce the Arabic version of Islam.[47] The provincial legislatures of West Papua (with a Christian majority) and Bali (with a Hindu majority) had opposed the bill. Similarly, even though the state had shown efficiency in busting the Poso network of Jemaah Islamiyah in 2007-08, it issued a joint ministerial decree in June 2008 that imposed a ban on public professing and propagation of Ahmadiyah, an Islamic sect that believes its founder Mirza Ghulam Ahmad to be a prophet. Following the decree, 16 provinces decided to impose a ban on Ahmadiyah.

Second, a somewhat long-term trend continuing in Indonesia is the growing debate within Indonesian Islam about what is sacred and what is profane, prompting people to shed those aspects of life-style that may not appear to be orthodox Muslim. There has been a growing tendency towards returning to the roots, to the Arab worldview on Islam with an emphasis on outward observation. As a result, Arabic has become fashionable. The circulation of Arabic texts, called *kitabkuning* (yellow books) has increased manifold during the last ten years. Similar growth can be noticed in the usage of head covers and scarfs among women in Java, the epicentre of Indonesian syncretism. It also appears that common Muslims, though not in favour of violence and radical Islam, are not averse to a purer version of their religion. This tendency also seems to have influenced the outlook of the national political parties and organisations. The experiences of ethno-religious violence also seemed to have hardened radicalised identities and entities.

Finally, the law-enforcement agencies have exhibited both their inability and unwillingness to act against the radical elements engaged in the persecution of religious minorities. In other words, law-enforcement agencies, especially the police, continue to demonstrate their partisan role that disrupted peace and harmony all over the country during the first few years of Indonesia's transition to democracy after the departure of Suharto.

Internal Balancing or Acquisition of "Hard Power" Fails to Take Off

Military capability forms the central component of any debate or discussion on a country's power. Two elements draw the maximum attention – the capability of the military to stave off internal subversion and external aggression, and the range of the projection of the military power beyond the country's geographical boundary. An effective military projection is considered to be an essential pre-requisite for a rising power with the ambition of playing regional and global roles. Therefore, any discussion over Indonesia as a rising power entails the consolidation and projection of its military power.

Indonesia has long been known for its inefficient, under-equipped and under-resourced military, which is responsible primarily for protecting against internal threats. The military's underperformance appears starker when compared to the wherewithal at the disposal of the Indonesian navy and the magnitude of responsibilities assigned in the form of protecting various sea-lanes, territorial waters, internal naval arteries and ports of an archipelagic maritime nation-state.

Indonesia's military modernisation programme has had a chequered history. The first concerted effort towards achieving self-sufficiency in terms of military modernisation and developing its capability was taken by the Suharto regime during the 1980s. Though the Suharto regime initiated the programme of developing its military strength during the 1980s, it failed to take off due to a lack of finances, governmental neglect and the lack of research and development capacities.[48] Moreover, while the reported brutality of the military invited international sanctions, the onset of the economic crisis in 1997-98 and the departure of Suharto's technocrat successor, B.J. Habibie, killed any scope for modernisation. The absence of any territorial dispute with any major power of Asia seems to have made the state somewhat indifferent to the need of force projection beyond the boundary.

Notwithstanding the confident tone and tenor of the current leadership towards advancing its military capability, the long-term planning of the government remains limited. Though the government has laid out a plan towards military modernisation by 2019, its implementation has been much slower and ad hoc in nature.

The modernisation drive requires a sustained supply of finances and effective implementation of policy pronouncements. Even though the Indonesian defence budget has increased, from US$2.4 billion (Rp23.1 trillion) in 2005 to US$8 billion (Rp77 trillion) in 2013, this figure still constitutes less than one per cent of the national GDP.[49] Indonesian Defence Minister, Purnomo Yusgiantoro, has agreed to raise the country's annual defence budget to 1.5 per cent of GDP by 2015.[50] Indonesia's defence budget in 2011 (US$5.42 billion) stood lower than that of even Singapore (US$9.66 billion) and Thailand (US$5.52 billion) and was much lower when compared to that of other Asian powers, such as China (US$89.76 billion), India (US$32 billion), Japan (US$58.42 billion), and South Korea (US$28.48 billion).[51]

Similar structural, financial and functional limitations plague the Indonesian navy that, otherwise, should have been an efficient agency, given the archipelagic character of the nation-state and over the fact that it straddles several important strategic waterways. Though maritime security has emerged as one of the most important security agendas, the deployment and future positioning of the Indonesian navy has not received much attention. Moreover, the 2005 plan of naval modernisation remains extremely modest in its long-term objectives and unclear in how to achieve those objectives.

The limited modernisation of the Indonesian military and its lack of projection as an important military power in the region can affect the country's overall strategic positioning in the regional and global matrix of power.

Reduced State Capacity for Governance

The efficiency of a developing state depends considerably on the available resources in terms of finances and personnel as well as institutional resources for service delivery, facilitating businesses and ensuring governance in the country. Even though Indonesia has emerged as one of the most favourable destinations for foreign investment, the country, especially its politico-administrative structure, has not provided a conducive atmosphere for faster and efficient business and governance. The evolving dynamic of coalition-driven vulnerability of the ruling government, rampant corruption in the political leadership and administrative institutions, and the lack of political will for large-scale politico-economic reforms are currently threatening to gobble up any prospect of it emerging as a rising Muslim democracy and a developing economy of the East. Two trends – the ills of coalition-based politics and the return of three headed monster of the KKN (Corruption, Collusion and Nepotism) – have emerged as major spoilers in rising Indonesia's success story.

The Ills of Coalition-Based Politics and Slowing-Down of Reforms

The six-party coalition that gives a two-thirds majority to President Yudhoyono in the legislature remains vulnerable to political pressure from its partners. The Yudhoyono government has increasingly caved in to the demands of its conservative partners to slow down the reform process. To quote the Economist Intelligence Unit report of June 2011, "The president, Susilo Bambang Yudhoyono, has a strong mandate to pursue his reformist policy agenda...but his reforms are encountering resistance from vested interests."[52] The coalition pressure, coming primarily from the Golkar party, the main political machine of the Suharto era with vested interests in various national financial ventures, has been a main source of this pressure to decelerate reforms.

The growing tussle between the reformists and the hardliners that threatens the reform process is exemplified by the issue of the financial bailout of the Bank Century. The issue involved two prominent reformists – Boediono, the Vice-President of Indonesia, and Mulyani Indrawati, the former Finance Minister. Though the parliamentary enquiry did not find the two guilty of corrupt practices, the pressure from constituent partners forced Ms. Indrawati to resign, further weakening the reform process. The Economist Intelligence Unit report of October 2010 blamed the whole episode on the Golkar machination.[53] The growing confrontation between these groups has also created an atmosphere of policy paralysis where the ruling government finds itself at the mercy of its coalition partners. The Yudhoyono government narrowly escaped efforts by two coalition partners – the Golkar and the PKS – for a full-scale parliamentary investigation against the tax department headed by Vice President Boediono in February 2011.[54] These efforts have been viewed primarily as an attempt on the part of the vested interests to discredit the reformists.[55]

The Return of Three-headed Monster: KKN (Corruption, Collusion and Nepotism)

Indonesia has historically suffered from the endemic problem of corruption that has affected the efficient delivery of governance and created public mistrust in the due process of law. The last decade of the Suharto regime saw an increase in the scale of corruption, including the top leaders of the country. Suhart's own party, the Golkar emerged as, perhaps, the most corrupt political party of its time. The intensity of the corruption can be gauged from the fact that Indonesia ranked 80th out of 85 as per the corruption-index by Transparency International, with 85th being the most corrupt country.[56] In fact, the issue of KKN emerged as an important catalyst in mobilising different segments of the Indonesian masses against the corrupt Suharto regime, ushering the country into a democratic future in the aftermath of the debilitating economic crisis that gripped the country in 1997.

The post-Suharto *Reformasi* politics saw an active electoral campaign from the political parties against corruption. Some of the parties achieved success and secured victory simply by projecting a clean image. The momentum for clean politics at the centre led to the formation of the Corruption Eradication Commission (KPK) in 2003 as per Law No. 30, which provided a comprehensive mandate to the commission in addressing the corruption problem. Yudhoyono rose to the presidency on the placard of clean politics and governance by combating corruption in national governance.

However, it is argued that the corruption did not die down. Rather, corruption is thought to have simply shifted from the centre to provinces, which received greater administrative and fiscal power as a result of decentralisation process initiated in 1999.[57] This trend is evident in the outbreak of large-scale ethno-communal violence, which is attributed to rampant corruption in provincial politics and governance.

Indonesian politics has once again found itself mired in various cases of corruption. As per the 2012 index of the Transparency International, Indonesia's rank went from 100th out of 183 countries in 2011 to 118th out of 176 countries in 2012, representing a trend towards greater corruption.[58] Important actors of the state and government – police, legislature, judiciary, political parties, and public officials and civil servants – have been found deeply embroiled in corrupt practices.[59] Moreover, this downward trend was reported despite several high-level attempts to combat corruption in the country.[60] The UN Office on Drugs and Crime attributes the problem of corruption to the prevailing culture of patronage and under-resourcing of the oversight mechanism.

Various controversies and corruption scandals have begun resurfacing during the second tenure of President Yudhoyono, compromising his and his government's integrity and resolve against corruption in the process.[61] Two sets of corruption issues have dominated the discourse – corruption scandals involving the ruling coalition, and the inability of the current government to counter growing corruption at the highest level. The government came under criticism over the corruption scandal involving the preparatory works for the coming Southeast Asian Games, leading to the sacking of the treasurer of Yudhoyono's party and the arrests of two of its officials.[62] The Yudhoyono government also came under criticism in August 2011 when two officials in the Ministry of Manpower and Transmigration were arrested for allegedly accepting US$175,000 as a bribe to divert the government project.[63] The Jakarta Corruption Court sentenced Ridwan Sanjaya, an official of the Energy and Mineral Resources Ministry, to six years of imprisonment for 'rigging a tender bid in 2009 for a home solar energy system project.'[64] Moreover, the Chairman of the ruling party, Anas Urbaningrum, was forced to resign in February 2013 after he was named by the Corruption Eradication Commission (KPK) as a suspect in a graft-case.[65] Another Democratic Party leader and Australian-born former model, Angelina Sondakh, was sentenced to an imprisonment of four and a half years in January 2013 for 'collecting bribes in return for awarding government education grants.'[66] Exposing another corruption scandal in the government, dubbed as the Beef-gate, the KPK reportedly summoned the elderly chief patron of Indonesia's leading Islamic-based political party, as well as a provincial governor, for interrogation in early May 2013.[67]

The second half of 2013 was rocked by two major corruption cases that implicated people who were supposed to be fighting against corruption in high places. The first shock came in August 2013 when the KPK arrested Rudi Rubiandini, Chief of the country's top oil-and-gas regulator, SKK Migas, on corruption charges. Many Indonesians had viewed him as 'a clean and upstanding figure – a respected academic and technocrat who had pledged to fight corruption in Indonesia's lucrative energy sector.'[68] Rubiandini has been accused of taking US$700,000 as a bribe from an oil-trading company. Another major shock came in October 2013, when the KPK arrested the Chief Justice of the Constitutional Court of Indonesia, Akil Mochtar over the issue of taking bribes for favourable judgements, shattering popular opinion that the judiciary was the only clean institution in the country. The KPK has initiated prosecution against more than 100 government officials, lawmakers, and corporate leaders since its formation in 2003.[69] In fact, one of the Deputy Commissioners of the KPK declared that the corruption today 'is bigger than in Suharto era.'[70]

These cases and controversies have revealed the all-pervasive character of corruption involving high level political and administrative functionaries and weakened both the claim as well as resolve of the current leadership in its fight against corruption. President Yudhoyono won his second tenure of presidency on the plank of his fight against corruption. Moreover, KKN had proved to be a precipitating factor during the 1997 economic crisis and subsequent process of democratisation. The return of KKN does not augur well for the 15-year old Indonesian democracy. At the same time, corruption has created a hostile climate for investment, an essential necessity for Indonesia's sustained growth story. The rampant scale of corruption can lead to wasteful investment of resources, deter foreign investment, render output less productive, delay and distort delivery of government services (especially at the level of common people), and kill entrepreneurship. An economy that is slowing down can not afford to be seen creating a hostile climate for foreign investment, efficiency and output.

Conclusion

What is worrisome is the continued existence of these challenges and the lack of political will and consensus within the country as to how they should be dealt with. It will be extremely detrimental for rising Indonesia's regional and global image to be a state incapable of providing security to its people and where law-enforcement agencies are seen as engaged in human rights violations. A weak state internally with no force projection externally may not remain a rising power for long.

ENDNOTES

1. Rizal Sukma, "Domestic Politics and International Posture: Constraints and Possibilities," in Anthony Reid, *Indonesia Rising: The Repositioning of Asia's Third Giant* (Singapore, ISEAS, 2012), p. 78.
2. Gareth Evans, "Foreword," in Anthony Reid, op.cit., p. xvi.
3. Anthony Reid, "Indonesia's New Prominence in the World," in Anthony Reid, op.cit., p. 10.
4. Arianto Patunru, Securing Prosperity: Building a more Equitable and Productive Indonesia," *East Asia Forum Quarterly*, vol. 5, no.4 (October-December 2013), p. 3; "Indonesia needs more investments for economic growth," *Antara News*, 19 August 2013, http://www.antaranews.com/en/news/90330/indonesia-needs-more-investments-for-economic-growth (accessed on 16 December 2013).
5. Arianto Patunru, op.cit., p. 3; International Monetary Fund, "Asia and Pacific Economic Outlook: October 2013 Update," *IMF Regional Economic Outlook Update*, 11 October 2013, http://www.imf.org/external/pubs/ft/reo/2013/apd/eng/areo1013.pdf (accessed on 16 December 2013); "UN reports subdued Asia-Pacific growth in 2013 as region faces developed world uncertainty," *United Nations Department of Economic and Social Affairs*, http://www.un.org/en/development/desa/news/policy/un-reports-subdued-asia-pacific-growth-in-2013-as-region-faces-developed-world-uncertainty.html (accessed on 16 December 2013).
6. International Monetary Fund, op.cit.; "UN reports subdued Asia-Pacific growth in 2013 as region faces developed world uncertainty," op.cit.; "Indonesia's Economy to Grow Slower," Antara News, 16 December 2013, http://www.antaranews.com/en/news/91805/indonesias-economy-to-grow-slower (accessed on 16 December 2013).
7. Andrew Mac Intyre and Maria Monica Wihardja (eds.), "Indonesia's Choices," *East Asia Forum Quarterly*, vol. 5, no.4 (October-December 2013), p. 2.
8. Kevin Lim, "Indonesia Faces 'Middle-Income Trap' Without Reform: IMF," *The Jakarta Globe*, 29 April 2013, http://www.thejakartaglobe.com/business/indonesia-faces-middle-income-trap-without-reform-imf/ (accessed on 14 January 2014); Raras Cahyafitri, "RI risks falling into middle-income trap," *The Jakarta Post*, 13 October 2012, http://

www.thejakartapost.com/news/2012/10/13/ri-risks-falling-middle-income-trap.html (accessed on 14 January 2014); Satria Sambijantoro, "RI at middle-income crossroad," *The Jakarta Post,* 13 December 2013, http://www.thejakartapost.com/news/2013/12/13/ri-middle-income-crossroad.html (accessed on 14 January 2014).

9. Nithin Coca, "How far can Indonesia's consumption-driven growth go?," *Penang Monthly,* 27 March 2013, http://penangmonthly.com/how-far-can-indonesias-consumption-driven-growth-go/ (accessed on 21 May 2013); Raoul Oberman, et.al. "The Archipelago Economy: Unleashing Indonesia's Potential," *Mckinsey Global InstituteReport,* September 2012, pp. 1-2, http://www.mckinsey.com/insights/asia-pacific/the_archipelago_economy (accessed on 21 May 2013); "Indonesia's Cement Consumption Grows 8.6% in January – April 2013," *Indonesia Investments,* 13 May 2013, http://www.indonesia-investments.com/nl/business/business-columns/inequality-of-the-regions-economic-significance-towards-indonesias-economy/item730 (accessed on 21 May 2013).
10. Raoul Oberman et.al. op.cit., pp. 1-2.
11. "Indonesia's Middle Class: Missing BRIC in the Wall," *The Economist,* 21 July 2011, http://www.economist.com/node/18989153 (accessed on 21 May 2013).
12. Ibid.
13. H. Aswicahyonoand D. Friawan, "Infrastructure Development in Indonesia," in N. Kumar (ed.), *International Infrastructure Development in East Asia – Towards Balanced Regional Development and Integration,* ERIA Research Project Report 2007-2 (Chiba: IDE-JETRO, 2008), pp.132-133.
14. Karishma Vaswani, "Poor infrastructure curbs Indonesian growth," *BBC News,* 07 October 2010, http://www.bbc.co.uk/news/business-11483541 (accessed on 22 May 2013).
15. "Poor infrastructure could hamper Indonesia's further growth," *Global Times,* 05 November 2012, http://www.globaltimes.cn/content/742392.shtml (accessed on 22 May 2013).
16. H. Aswicahyonoand D. Friawan, op.cit., pp.132-133.
17. "Poor infrastructure could hamper Indonesia's further growth," op.cit.
18. "Indonesia's Middle Class: Missing BRIC in the Wall," op.cit.
19. Ibid.
20. "Poor infrastructure could hamper Indonesia's further growth," op.cit.
21. Ibid.
22. Raoul Oberman et.al. op.cit.
23. "Indonesia's Cement Consumption Grows 8.6% in January – April 2013," op.cit.
24. Ibid.
25. Nithin Coca, op.cit.,
26. Andre Sinaga, "Income, a perilously widening gap," The Jakarta Post, June 05 2012, http://www.thejakartapost.com/news/2012/06/05/income-a-perilously-widening-gap.html (accessed on 18 December 2013).
27. Raoul Oberman et.al. op.cit., p. 31.
28. "Income Inequality – A Risk to Indonesia's Spectacular Growth?," *CEIC Data Blog,* 24 April 2012, http://blog.securities.com/2012/04/income-inequality-a-risk-to-indonesias-spectacular-growth/ (accessed on 21 May 2012).
29. Arianto Patunru, "Indonesia: reform and the people," *East Asia Forum,* 17th January 2013, http://www.eastasiaforum.org/2013/01/17/indonesia-in-2012-reform-and-the-people/ (accessed on 21 May 2013).
30. Andrew G. Berg and Jonathan D. Ostry, "Inequality and Unsustainable Growth: Two Sides of the Same Coin?," *IMF Staff Discussion Note,* no. SDN/11/08, 08 April 2011.

31. Ibid.
32. The Front Pembela Islam is led by Habib Rizieq Shihab and focuses on removing social impurities prevalent in the Indonesian society. These social impurities are discotheques, bars, nightclubs, and the FPI acts as a moral police. For details Noorhaidi Hasan, "Faith and Politics: The Rise of the Laskar Jihad in the Era of Transition in Indonesia," *Indonesia,* no. 73 (April 2002), pp. 145-169.
33. Greg Fealy, Virginia Hooker and Sally White, "Indonesia," in Greg Fealy and Virginia Hooker (eds.) *Voices of Islam in Southeast Asia: A Contemporary Sourcebook* (Singapore, ISEAS, 2006), p. 50.
34. Noohaidi Hasan, op.cit., p. 146.
35. For details on *Jemaah Islamiyah* see *White Paper: The Jemaah Islamiyah Arrests and the Threat of Terrorism,* Ministry of Home Affairs, Government of Singapore, 7 January 2003, http://www.mha.gov.sg/publication_details.aspx?pageid=35&cid=354; (accessed on 09 May 2013) *Indonesia Backgrounder: How the Jemaah Islamiyah Terrorist Network Operates,* International Crisis Group (ICG) Asia Report, no. 43, 11 December 2002; Sidney Jones, "The changing nature of Jemaah Islamiyah," Australian Journal of International Affairs, vol. 59, no. 2, June 2005, pp. 169-178; Zachary Abuza, "Tentacles of Terror: Al Qaeda's Southeast Asian Network," *Contemporary Southeast Asia,* vol. 24, no. 3 (December 2002), pp. 427-65.
36. "In Religion's Name: Abuses against Religious Minorities in Indonesia," *Human Rights Watch* (USA, Human Rights Watch, 2013), p. 2, http://www.hrw.org/sites/default/files/reports/indonesia0213_ForUpload_0.pdf; (accessed on 01 May 2013).
37. Aubrey Belford, "Indonesian Assault Victim Gets Harsher Sentence Than His Attackers," *The New York Times,* 15 August 2011, http://www.nytimes.com/2011/08/16/world/asia/16indonesia.html?_r=0 (accessed on 01 May 2013).
38. "Religious Intolerance Poisoning Indonesia," *The Jakarta Globe,* 02 May 2013, http://www.thejakartaglobe.com/news/religious-intolerance-poisoning-indonesia/ (accessed on 07 May 2013).
39. Sara Schonhardt, "Amid fear, Indonesian Atheists Build a Community of Support," *International Herald Tribune,* 26 April 2013, http://iht.newspaperdirect.com/epaper/viewer.aspx (accessed on 07 May 2013).
40. "In Religion's Name," op.cit., p. 28.
41. The Jakarta Post, 25 April 2010.
42. Paul J. Carnegie, *The Road from Authoritarianism to Democratization in Indonesia* (New York: Palgrave Macmillan, 2010).
43. "In Religion's Name," op.cit., pp. 28-30.
44. Matt Brown, "Indonesian military backs religious persecution," *Australian Broadcasting Corporation,* 16 March 2011, http://www.abc.net.au/lateline/content/2011/s3166034.htm(accessed on 01 May 2013).
45. "In Religion's Name: Abuses against Religious Minorities in Indonesia," op.cit., p. 98.
46. Olivia Rondonuwu and Telly Nathalia, "Indonesian parliament passes anti-porn bill," *Reuters,* 30 October 2008, http://in.reuters.com/article/2008/10/30/us-indonesia-pornography-idINTRE49T3M020081030 (accessed on 15 May 2013); "Indonesian Muslim leader gets jail for inciting violence," *Reuters,* 30 October 2008, http://in.reuters.com/article/2008/10/30/idINIndia-36221020081030 (accessed on 15 May 2013).
47. Olivia Rondonuwu and Telly Nathalia, op.cit.,
48. Vibhanshu Shekhar, "Indonesia's Military Modernisation," *ICWA Issue Brief,* 11 February 2013, http://www.icwa.in/pdfs/VPIndonesiamilitarymodernisation.pdf (accessed on 17 May 2013); "Indonesia's Naval Development and Maritime Cooperation," *RSIS Policy Report,*

05 July 2012, http://www.rsis.edu.sg/publications/policy_report/Indonesia_Naval_Development_Maritime_Cooperation_5_July_2012.pdf (accessed on 17 November 2012).

49. Rizal Sukma, "Strength in Numbers: Indonesia's Multiple Defense Relationships," *Strategic Review,* 27 March 2013, http://www.sr-indonesia.com/this-months-issue/cover-story/272-strength-in-numbers-indonesias-multiple-defense-relationships (accessed on 19 May 2013).
50. Ibid.
51. "Chapter Six: Asia," *The Military Balance*, vol. 112, no. 1, 2012, p. 209.
52. "Indonesia: June 2011," *Economist Intelligence Unit Country Report*, June 2011, p. 3.
53. "Indonesia: October 2010," *Economist Intelligence Unit Country Report*, October 2010, pp. 4-5.
54. "Indonesia: June 2011," op.cit., p. 4.
55. Ibid.
56. Fiona Robertson-Snape, "Corruption, Collusion and Nepotism in Indonesia," *Third World Quarterly*, vol. 20, No 3, 1999, p. 589.
57. "Corruption in Indonesia," Indonesia-Investments, http://www.indonesia-investments.com/doing-business/risks/corruption/item235 (accessed on 18 December 2013).
58. Gregory B. Poling and Blake Day, "Corruption in Indonesia and the 2014 Elections," *CSIS Critical Questions*, 07 NOV 2013, http://csis.org/publication/corruption-indonesia-and-2014-elections (accessed on 18 December 2013); "High Profile Corruption Cases in Indonesia," *Global Indonesian Voices*, 14 October 2013, http://www.globalindonesianvoices.com/10165/high-profile-corruption-cases-in-indonesia/ (accessed on 18 December 2013).
59. Gregory B. Poling and Blake Day, ibid,
60. Ibid.
61. Joe Cochrane, "Plague of Corruption Rises Anew in Indonesia," *The New York Times,* 31 May 2013, http://www.nytimes.com/2013/05/31/world/asia/31iht-indonesia31.html?ref=global-home&_r=0
62. Jason Tedjasukmana, "In Indonesia, Corruption Scandals Plague Anti-Graft President," *Time,* 26 September 2011, http://www.time.com/time/world/article/0,8599,2094188,00.html (accessed on 23 May 2013).
63. Ibid.
64. "High Profile Corruption Cases in Indonesia," op.cit.,
65. George Roberts, "Indonesian Party Chief Quits over Corruption Claims," *ABC News,* 23 February 2013, http://www.abc.net.au/news/2013-02-23/indonesian-politician-suspected-of-corruption/4535572 (accessed on 23 May 2013.
66. Ibid.
67. Joe Cochrane, "'Beef-gate' Transfixes Scandal-Prone Indonesia," *New York Times,* May 16, 2013, http://www.nytimes.com/2013/05/17/world/asia/beefgate-transfixes-scandal-prone-indonesia.html?pagewanted=all&_r=0 (accessed on 23 May 2013).
68. Yenni Kwok, "Shocking Arrest Underscores Endemic Corruption in Indonesia's Energy Sector," *Time World,* 15 August 2013, http://world.time.com/2013/08/15/shock-arrest-underscores-endemic-corruption-in-indonesias-energy-sector/ (accessed on 18 December 2013).
69. Ibid.
70. Ibid.

7

Interpreting Indonesia's Strategic Culture

A community or country sediments certain values, beliefs and wisdoms that it encounters in its historical experiences over different time-frames. These sedimented values and beliefs, over time, become a part of the accumulated wisdom and strategic prudence of the country and community and, therefore, are reflected in the national security debates and discourses of the country. These values and beliefs often interfere in the decision-making processes of the national elite and influence the choices and behaviour of the country in the form of its strategic culture. These value-systems can have both facilitating as well as restraining effects in the decision-making process.

In a similar fashion, rising Indonesia's strategic behaviour exhibits certain traits and characteristics that are reflective of its historical-cultural and somewhat universally acceptable beliefs and world-views. Indonesia's strategic community, political elite, and interest groups have often debated these sets of world-views both consciously and subconsciously while prescribing visions for Indonesia's long-term foreign policy formulation. They involve larger questions regarding the national security and threat perceptions of the country, its image and identity, the underlying principles and normative orientations shaping the views and choices of its national elite, and grand visions about what a country should seek to achieve in the world and how in the long run. In other words, Jakarta's strategic choices and behaviour while engaging the outside world are representative of its own evolving strategic culture rooted in its historical (civilisational, colonial and post-colonial) experiences.

Understanding Strategic Culture

The idea of a strategic culture has emerged as an important conceptual framework among both practitioners and academics in terms of its utility in understanding the strategic choices and behaviour of a country.[1] The concept was used, for the first time, by Jack Snyder in 1977 in explaining the Soviet military strategy in building up the theory of strategic culture.[2] The idea has gained currency during the last two decades as an important tool of foreign policy analysis in deciphering why different states, operating in similar strategic environment, demonstrate divergent strategic choices and behaviour. The limited applicability of structural realism in explaining the divergent state behaviour and the increasing importance and contribution of domestic variables in shaping the foreign policy of a country provided additional stimuli to the research on strategic culture.

Alastair Johnston has identified three generations of scholarship on strategic culture and today the concept is being analysed and explored from various schools and perspectives of international relations, such as culturalism, constructivism and neo-classical realism.[3] The debate on strategic culture has, since then, become much more rigorous, revolving around definitional approaches, methodologies, objects of analysis, its historicity or temporality, and actors shaping the strategic culture.[4] Several pertinent questions confront us. What constitutes strategic culture? How historical or how evolutionary should the strategic culture be? Who are key domestic actors shaping the strategic culture? In what ways can once ascertain whether strategic culture is influencing or shaping strategic choices and behaviours of a country?

While discussing the meaning and definitional aspects of what constitutes the strategic culture, Jack Snyder provided its first authoritative definition. He identified strategic culture as "the body of attitudes and beliefs that guides and circumscribes thought on strategic questions, influences the way strategic issues are formulated, and sets the vocabulary and the perceptual parameters of strategic debate."[5] An open-ended and somewhat simplistic and comprehensive nature of this definition provided an important reference point for discussion and debates on what constitutes strategic culture. Snyder's definition, however, did not locate the issue in any historical and time-specific context.[6]

Alastair Johnston, on the contrary, offered a much more rigorous definition of strategic culture and placed it in the historical-cultural contexts. He sought to explain what strategic culture should problematize, what its objects of analysis should be, and how it evolves. According to him, "strategic culture as a system of symbols embodies assumptions about what the security problematique is, and therefore, about how to best deal with it. In principle, then, strategic culture ought to embody preferred methods for responding to the threat environment. Moreover, preferences established in the past become part of the symbol system that is learned and reproduced, thus becoming part of the strategic culture milieu at time *t*."[7] By focusing on the historical-cultural inheritance or acquisition of strategic culture, Johnston also tried to provide a time framework for any set of belief and values to become part of a country's strategic culture.

A somewhat related question that requires discussion concerns the sources wherefrom the strategic culture emanates, or who should be the actual repository of such values and beliefs – people at large or the decision makers, and how these values and beliefs are transferred from generation to generation. While Snyder identified the strategic elite as the repository of strategic culture, Colin Grey focused on dominant national beliefs available with people at large.[8]

Both Johnston and Colin Dueck have tried to find a middle ground, with Johnston identifying the strategic elite and decision-makers as the final repository of strategic culture and public beliefs as a part of strategic sub-culture. Dueck, on the other hand, locates the source among the 'politically interested people.'[9] He defines strategic culture as an interlocking set of values and beliefs held by the politically interested people of each nation-state that relate to strategic affairs, a set of beliefs that can be referred to as a nation's "strategic culture."[10] In other words, the ultimate decision on what constitutes the strategic culture rests with the national elite and strategic community of the country.

Moreover, one could also raise questions regarding the process of embodiment. Is it an unbroken chain of memorising those values and beliefs? Can values and beliefs, which appear in two disjointed time-frames, be understood as a part of the strategic culture? These values and beliefs are acquired and inherited by domestic actors, especially the political elite and strategic community, and transferred through the generations in what is understood as an extremely complex process of socialization, both at the conscious as well as subconscious level.[11]

Dueck identifies two processes through which strategic culture could lead to a particular type of state behaviour. First, "strategic choices when framed within culturally acceptable framework both in terms of either new formulations or departure form the existing ones, remain acceptable to the public opinion, and therefore there is greater likelihood of popular support."[12] Such a trend is more pervasive in any democratic political structure, such as Indonesia. Second, the national elite may 'actually share, or come to share, or even shape the cultural preferences and perceptions held by their constituents.'[13] It is through these beliefs and values that the political elite shares or shapes grand visions for any country. In other words, it is both the fear of popular backlash as well as deep-seated beliefs of the national elite that affect the strategic choices of the decision makers and, in turn, influence the state behaviour.

These values are often articulated in the form of rhetorics and speeches or serious doctrines, debates and discussions by the strategic community or the country's national elite. In other words, these become intrinsic to what can be considered the national psyche of any country, informing and defining the debates and discussions within the country. An important yardstick to discern national psyche is to identify the paranoia or obsession that engulfs the national elite, generating a national debate on the issue. The elite opinion feeds into the national debate on the threat perceptions, national security or strategic doctrine of the country. It is this debate that plays a critical role in shaping the foreign policy priorities or strategic behaviour of the country. In other words, the leaders could be shaping the foreign policy with a set of mandates as well as restrictions imposed on them by these all-pervasive beliefs or wisdoms, understood as strategic culture.

Viewed from this perspective, Indonesia's strategic culture could be a set of values and beliefs shared and shaped by its national elite and strategic community regarding its threat perceptions, grand visions, and the way it should engage with and behave within the prevailing international order.

Current Debates on Indonesia's Strategic Culture

The debate over the notion and components of Indonesia's strategic culture, though sparse, has gained traction during the last twenty years among the strategic community. This debate has revolved around a few key issues – the existence or absence of a strategic culture within the country, sources of the country's strategic culture, and elements of the strategic culture. Three sets of consciousness – historical-cultural traditions (especially among the

Javanese), the colonial experience and nationalist movement, and the post-colonial nation-building processes – are believed to have been playing critical roles in shaping Indonesia's strategic behaviour. Over the decades and centuries, they have become very much a part of the national psyche and public consciousness in terms of Indonesia's strategic culture. One can discern a continuum in Indonesia's strategic behaviour in terms of its consciousness of its archipelagic destiny, national identity, regional centrality, and global posturing. Reflecting on the impact of historical traditions on Indonesia's foreign policy, Rizal Sukma wrote in 1995, "contemporary Indonesian foreign policy should be understood as a product of continuous historical consciousness, not as 'emerging from a certain historical context'."[14]

One can discern two distinct phases – pre-democratic and democratic – in the debate on Indonesia's strategic culture. The debates during both the phases have taken place in the backdrop of Indonesia's growing regional and global profile, domestic politico-economic consolidation and greater politico-societal attention towards developing long-term foreign policy objectives. However, it must be stated at the outset that the two-phase classification of the debate is due partly to the qualitative change in the content and contexts of the debate and largely because of the sudden rupture in the flow of the debate that occurred in the aftermath of the politico-economic crises in the country.

The first phase of the debate began to take shape during the early 1990s, when Indonesia, after the end of the Cold War era, had emerged as a pivotal state in the regional strategic discourses, the leader of ASEAN, a critical player in the APEC process with the outcome of Bogor Declaration of 1994, and a rapidly growing economy.[15] Under the leadership of Suharto, Indonesia was emerging as one of the champions of the 'Asian values,' a semi-authoritarian form of governance, and democracy as an unnecessary political quagmire. Notwithstanding the unfolding crises in the Indonesian peripheries of East Timor, Aceh and West Papua, the Javanese military elite remained in the driving seat, espousing a military dominated and archipelago-centric security doctrine.

Quite logically, the pre-democratic debate on Indonesia's strategic culture revolved around (a) a Java-centric worldview, (b) the geography-driven 'threats from within' worldview, and (c) a military-dominated worldview. Moreover, these worldviews were often understood and expressed in an inter-related and mutually reinforcing manner.[16] In fact, they explained Indonesia's conceptualization of its national interest, threat perceptions and security formulations, thereby, shaping the contours of Indonesian foreign policy. They always figured, either individually or conceptually entwined, as key reference points in discussions on Indonesia's strategic doctrine.

The Java-centric worldview identifies Java as the centre of the Indonesian universe, and traces political and military philosophies in the experiences and doctrines of Javanese political and military leaders. It has been argued that the Javanese concepts of power, authority and leadership have received a great deal of attention as a critical intellectual tradition in explaining the 'attitudes, behaviours and perceptions of the Indonesian state and its key actors such as the military.'[17] This perspective has been expounded and perpetuated by the long lineage of political and military leaders coming from Java – Sudirman, Sukarno, Suharto, Moertopo, Moerdani, Wahid, Megawati, and Yudhoyono.[18] Amidst the dominant Javanese leadership, one can safely surmise that other important leaders, such as Sjahrir, Hatta and Nasution (all from Sumatra) were either presenting an overarching Indonesian strategic doctrine or advocating philosophies along the lines of the Javanese leaders.

The geography-driven approach has presented Indonesia's archipelagic character as the critical point of security debate and a source of continued instability and divisibility. The simultaneity of the processes of national integration, the problem of internal subversion, and fears of secession underscore the extremely troubled nature of Indonesia's nation-building process. In fact, post-colonial Indonesia's critical vulnerability has remained rooted in its archipelagic character, which has been seen as a divisive element, reinforcing its social and political divisions.[19] In other words, Indonesia's security doctrine has aimed at managing its archipelagic vulnerabilities and preventing these divisions from affecting the territorial integrity of the country.

The military-dominated worldview has its genesis in the Javanese politico-military philosophy, the guerilla warfare strategy of the Indonesian armed forces before and after the end of the Dutch colonial rule, and three decades of the military-led authoritarianism of Suharto.[20] The domination of the military in the pre-democratic Indonesian politics presented an intrusive role for the military to play in shaping the country's threat perceptions and security doctrine. This perspective has two critical components – the military as the promulgator of Indonesia's security doctrine, and a restrictive, inward-looking, guerilla warfare and land-based defensive strategic doctrine.[21]

Representing one of the earliest studies, Dewi Fortuna Anwar, a prominent Indonesian scholar, offered the most extensive narrative on Indonesia's strategic culture in 1996. She identified three doctrinal discourses of Indonesia's foreign policy as elements of its strategic culture – *Ketahanan Nasional* (National Resilience), *Wawasan Nusantara* (Archipelagic Outlook), and *Hankamrata* (Total People's Defence).[22] These three elements sequentially highlight (a) the nation's strength and resources, (b) the main source of the country's vulnerability or threat perception emanating from the archipelagic nature of the country, and (c) the strategy to maintain the country's territorial integrity and sovereignty. She traced these elements to the articulation of national security – national unity, territorial integrity and national development – as perceived and prescribed predominantly by the politico-military elite of the country. The main rationale came from the country's archipelagic vulnerability, accentuated by its ethno-cultural diversity, and the somewhat contested nature of the nation-building process threatened by its internal instabilities and challenges. These principles have played an important role in shaping post-Colonial Indonesia's strategic thinking regarding its national security and the threat environment of Southeast Asia.

Alan Dupont, while discussing Indonesia's strategic doctrine, identified two issues: (a) the indispensability of somewhat inseparable notions of archipelagic vulnerability and the military's defence doctrine of *Hankamrata* in any discussion on Indonesia's strategic thinking; and (b) the limited applicability of these strategic concepts to appreciate Indonesia's changing security needs in the 21st century. He traced these strategic concepts and defence doctrines to 'the memories and experiences of the immediate post-colonial period,' and viewed them as 'inadequate, conformist, and insufficient in providing a conceptual underpinning of Indonesian security in the 21st century.'[23] Highlighting the all-pervasive influence of *Hankamrata* on Indonesian strategic thinking, Alan Dupont declared that '*Hankamrata* has now become an article of faith doctrinally' and 'Indonesia will find it extremely difficult to move away from the strategic dictates of its post-colonial past unless there is an external shock, of sufficient magnitude, to cause the political and military leadership to reassess the utility of the doctrine.'[24]

These elements of strategic culture borrowed elements from Indonesia's historical-cultural traditions, long-standing military-dominated political culture, and troubled experiences encountered during the nation-building process. Though these traditions remain paramount in the country's security considerations and strategic doctrine, they represented an insular, vulnerability-driven, internal security-centric, and archipelagic posturing – a somewhat limited worldview or strategic thinking of the Indonesian national elite, deeply concerned with internal security and political stability.[25] Moreover, the focus of the foreign policy remained centered around Southeast Asia with a special focus on the ASEAN region.

The debate on strategic culture dried up during the late 1990s in the wake of Indonesia's worst economic and political crises. The debate soon shifted towards domestic politics –the departure of Suharto, the ascent of a weak and unstable democracy, insurgencies and the independence movement in the peripheries, widespread ethnic violence in the outer islands, and the possible internal implosion of the country. Amidst the chaos, the foreign policy debates remained somewhat marginal, with few writings on the strategic culture.

The rise of democratic Indonesia not only revived the strategic culture debate, but also introduced some critical elements – the issue of democratic identity in foreign policy projections, the expanded geographical canvas of the concentric circles, the broader notion of threat perceptions and security beyond its archipelagic and internal vulnerabilities, the reinvigoration of the principle of strategic autonomy and growing demands for greater discussions on Jakarta's global projections.[26] In other words, there is a trend away from the military-dominated insular strategic outlook towards an outward-oriented debate on identifying a holistic approach to Indonesia's strategic culture. There is also a trend away from personalised wisdoms of political leaders towards growing institutionalisation of foreign policy decision-making process, widening the national constituencies of the debate on Indonesia's strategic culture and strategic behaviour.

An important reflection on the country's democratic identity debate comes from the statement of Indonesia's former Foreign Minister, Hasan Wirajuda, when he described Indonesia as the third largest democratic country, possessing 'a natural affinity to democracy.'[27] Similarly, Jakarta's concentric circles, as discussed later in the chapter, have undergone remodeling and expansion both in terms of its inner as well as immediate circles, with the global circle receiving attention as well. Even though the 2008 Defence White Paper of Indonesia represents traditional army-dominated defence doctrine, the strategic community has begun questioning the viability of 1940s' defence doctrine in the 21st century on the ground of its irrelevance and the strategic necessity of better military preparedness and force projection.[28] A major contribution to the debate on some of the salient aspects of the Indonesian strategic culture has come from the recent writings of Daniel Novotny and Anothony Reid.[29]

Elements of Indonesia's Strategic Culture

A holistic picture of Indonesia's strategic behaviour brings out some of the following elements of Indonesia's strategic culture: (a) the perceived destiny of the country as a strategic archipelago, (b) national leadership to regional leadership, (c) an emphasis on maintaining its long-standing strategic autonomy, (d) its Muslim democratic identity, (e) its underbalancing and limited force projection, (f) the focus on a rule-based, and liberal global and regional order, and (g) solidarity with the Global South. The genesis of these elements of strategic culture lies in the political and military philosophy of Javanese kingdoms, the shared experiences of Indonesia's national liberation movement, its post-colonial experiences in foreign policy, and its democratic and demographic outlook. These beliefs and values have been shaped by the national elite of the country and its strategic community, and reinforced by the popular assumptions and beliefs, which can be understood as what Iain Johnston calls 'strategic sub-cultures.'[30]

Wawasan Nusantara: Indonesia's Destiny as a 'Strategic Archipelago'[31]

An important consciousness that has shaped the worldview of Indonesia's strategic community and the national elite is the idea of *Wawasan Nusantara* (archipelagic outlook), viewing Indonesia as 'destined by its geography to be a passageway between oceans and continents,' symbolizing the unity of water and land.[32] Prime Minister Djoeanda Kartawidjaja declared on 13 December 1957 that the country 'should be seen as one nation consisting of land, maritime and space areas.' Since then the Djoenda Declaration has come to reinforce Indonesia's archipelagic credentials.[33] The declaration laid a new maritime boundary for Indonesia with outer points of the outlying islands forming the archipelagic baseline. Indonesia commemorated 13 December 2011 as *Hari Nusantara* (Archipelagic day).

Its archipelagic character has come to define the country's sources of threats, primarily in the form of 'continuing fear of dismemberment' and the basic reference point of national security in the form of preserving the

Tanah-Air Kitah (out homeland) that has come to characterize the territoriality of Indonesia.[34] The concept symbolizes unity and harmony between the land and water, making an inter-connected archipelago the only viable option for the survival of the country. The concept has also been viewed as 'a way for Indonesia to look at itself (geographically) as a unity of ideology, politics, economy, socio-cultural, security and defense issues.'[35]

To quote Michael Leifer, "The experience of upholding independence in both domestic and international dimensions generated an abiding concern for the integrity of a state beset by social diversity and physical fragmentation. A common and consistent theme of Indonesia's foreign policy has been the need to overcome an intrinsic vulnerability."[36] It is this archipelagic vulnerability of the country that convinced its leaders to develop a centralised state structure, to embrace the principle of *Negara Kesatuan Republik Indonesia* (Unitary State of the Republic of Indonesia), to continue the territorial command structure of the military, and to advocate for the principle of unity in diversity (*Bhinneka Tunggul Ika*).[37]

The sensitivity of its archipelagic vulnerability has weighed high in the minds of its freedom fighters and subsequent generation of leaders. The Indonesian national leaders under Sukarno had rejected the Dutch proposal of creating a federal nation-state as a colonial design to break up the nascent Indonesian republic. National unity, under a centralized state structure, has always been viewed as indispensable for the political survival and emergence of Indonesia as a strong and powerful nation. Sukarno 'indeed, put it at the center of their political ideas and worked to ensure that a single political system would prevail over the whole of Indonesia and over all Indonesians.'[38]

Leonard Sebastian and Imran Lanti argue that the process of developing a shared national identity for an archipelagic Indonesia was 'the project of two authoritarian leaders, Sukarno and Suharto, who sought a centralized model based on cooptation and if necessary coercion to construct an "imagined community" based on *Pancasilaist* norms within a unitary state structure.'[39] While Sukarno perceived threats to its archipelagic nation-state emanating primarily from the imperialist and colonial powers and the Cold-War based global structure of power, Suharto viewed threats to the Indonesia archipelago coming primarily from internal sources. As a result, while Sukarno talked about OLDEFOs (Old Established Forces) versus NEFOs (new Emerging Forces) and called for an Afro-Asian solidarity, Suharto called for national resilience. While laying down the basic contours of Indonesia's foreign policy in his epochal writing, Mohammad Hatta, the then foreign minister of Indonesia, emphasised the archipelagic destiny of Indonesia and its existence in the Indonesian cultural consciousness. He wrote:

> Nature has ordained that Indonesia, lying between two continents – the Asian Mainland and Australia – and washed by the waters of two vast oceans – the Indian and the Pacific – must maintain intercourse with lands stretching in a great circle around it. From time immemorial, it has had relationships with all of them, varied as they are. Its position at the very heart of a network of communications has for centuries made the archipelago a halting place for all races and a staging base in international travel. When one considers that the territory of Indonesia extends for more than 3000 miles and is composed of thousands of islands, large and small, the magnitude of the problem of maintaining the security of the country is apparent. So extensive an area cannot be defended purely by military strength.[40]

Hatta's words were a continuation of the country's long-standing historical narrative and its distinct identity that its fixed geography has bestowed on it both in terms of strategic advantages as well as geo-strategic challenges. It also appears that the country's archipelagic consciousness is instilled at a very early stage as a part of school curriculum at the primary and secondary levels.[41]

In addition to its archipelagic consciousness, another important idea or strategic sub-culture that seems to have shaped geo-spatial consciousness of Indonesia and its strategic thinking in terms of the threat environment and security is the *Mandala* doctrine.[42] It recommends the management of inter-state relations in the form of concentric circles. Though the idea has emanated from the Indian Kautilyan concept of *Mandala* or concentric circles, it has come to permeate political and foreign policy thinking of many Southeast Asian countries, including Indonesia. The reference to *Mandala* theory is traced to two powerful Hindu-Buddhist kingdoms of Java and Sumatra – Srivijaya kingdom (Sumatra) and Majapahit kingdom (Java). A noted Indonesian writer Soemarsaid Moertono explained the concept of *Mandala* (circle namely of influence, interests or ambitions) as follows:

> ...a complex of geopolitical relations, relating to boundaries and to contact with foreign countries. The doctrine emphasizes the cult of expansion, a necessary spur to the struggle for existence, self-assertion and world domination, and the dynamics factor calculated to disturb the equilibrium of inter-state relations. A state's belligerence is in the first place directed towards its closest neighbour(s), thus making

> necessary the friendship of the state next to the foe, which, because of its proximity, is also a natural enemy of the foe. But if the mutual foe should be conquered, the two allies would become close neighbours, which would create a new enmity. So this circle of alignment and alienation would steadily expand until a universal peace is reached by the establishment of a world-state with a sole and supreme ruler (*chakravartin*).[43]

The *Mandala* theory combines elements of Javanese politico-cosmological consciousness – the idea of the Cosmos – in the form of concentric circles as perceived from the Javanese Core, the essence of archipelagic vulnerability, sources of security and strength, and the responsibility of the core to provide leadership, wisdom and security to its larger populace.

While the archipelagic nation-state forms the first circle and therefore, the circle and source of vulnerability, the region of Southeast Asia has formed the second circle, or the circle of strength and security. In other words, 'the primary security concern has always been the state itself or the state's very existence, its unity and territorial integrity and its security.'[44] Leonard Sebastian identifies two important inter-related aspects of the doctrine: (a) the immediate outer rings (in a series of radiating rings of security) must be secured if the centre (the Indonesian state) was to be secure; and (b) Indonesian foreign policy must first and foremost serve the nation itself (national unity, national security, and the national interest).

Indonesia's military strategists have used this concept extensively, whereby its archipelagic character forming the inner circle has been viewed as the main source of threats and Southeast Asia, being the intermediary circle, as the most important source of strength.[45] This notion has also been applied in the context of Indonesia's leadership of ASEAN. The contemporary leaders of Indonesia seem to have placed a good deal of emphasis on the *Mandala* theory in their articulation of foreign policy, understood as circles, a theatre, or a part of a larger cosmos.[46] The 1995 Defence White Paper of Indonesia states,

> In a geostrategic context, Indonesia's basic defence and security strategy is one providing for layered security. The deepest layer is domestic security, followed by sub-regional (ASEAN) security, regional (South East Asia) security and security of neighbouring regions, in that order. This strategy is also called defense-in-depth.[47]

Moreover, the boundary of these circles does not always remain the same and may expand or shrink depending on the strength and vulnerabilities of the core. According to Wolters, "*mandalas* would expand or contract in concertina like fashion. Each one contained several tributary rulers, some of whom repudiate their vassal status when the opportunity arose and try to build up their own networks of vassals."[48]

In fact, the foreign policy debates during the Suharto regime covered only two concentric circles of Indonesia's worldview and overlooked the third *mandala* of global relationships – an important component of the post-colonial Indonesia's foreign policy projections. Moreover, the first two concentric circles also represented limited geographical canvas. While the domestic politics referred to the first concentric circle, Southeast Asia represented the second concentric circle.[49]

Today, the official website of the Ministry of Foreign Affairs of Indonesia places ASEAN or the entire Southeast Asia as the innermost concentric circle or 'prime pillar in carrying out its foreign policies.'[50] The official website goes on to identify ASEAN+3 as the second concentric circle. Though the official description does not mention India, Australia or the South Pacific in the country's concentric circles, one could assume that given their geographic proximity, shared maritime space, common security concerns, and intense diplomatic engagement, they would form part of the second concentric circle along with ASEAN+3. Viewed from this perspective, the much broader geo-politics of the Asia-Pacific seems to be representing the second/immediate circle of rising Indonesia's foreign policy and its real source of strength. Further buttressing the similar fungible character of each of these circles, Rizal Sukma identified the dynamic and fast-growing East Asia as one of the *Mandalas* or theatres for Indonesia's foreign policy.[51] Both the USA and EU lie beyond these two concentric circles. Finally, like-minded developing countries form the third concentric circle. However, these countries remain unenumerated, leaving further scope in the expansion of these concentric circles.

National Resilience: From National to Regional Preparedness

It is a long-standing and widespread belief that the leadership provides strength to the country and plays a critical role in building the country's national resilience, which is essential for country's internal consolidation and external projection. Leaders or kings, according to the Javanese cultural traditions, have been viewed as perhaps the most important source of power and wisdom with the capability to lead (*tut wuri handayani*).[52] Indonesia has always projected its power and influence successfully when under stable leadership. As a result, Indonesia's foreign policy has often been guided by the visions of its leaders, reflecting the predilections of its leaders in both long-term and short-term foreign policy strategies.

It is believed that the stronger and more powerful the leadership, the better the foreign policy articulation of the government. As a result, popular perceptions draw comprehensively from the visions and worldviews of the leaders. The country has experienced fundamental transformation in the preferences and choices of the country with the change in the leadership. For example, the vocal, normative, post-colonial and anti-imperialist, world-focused and somewhat assertive foreign policy of Sukarno (Indonesia's first President) was replaced with much more benign, low-profile, pragmatic, region-centric, ASEAN-based and pro-West policy of Suharto.

Moreover, leaders are expected to offer grand visions and wisdoms, embodying the notion of Javanese kingship. As a result, we have seen each important leader of Indonesia bring out a vision of Indonesia's foreign policy and its place in the region and the world, often expressed in the form of catch-phrases. While Mohammad Hatta contributed the *Bebas dan Aktif* doctrine of foreign policy, Sukarno focused on Post-Colonial Afro-Asian Solidarity and the Non-Aligned Movement. Suharto's image as *Bapak Pembangunan* (the father of Indonesia development), as well as his benign leadership and activism in the regional cooperation seems to have merged with Yudhoyono's 'Million Friends Zero Enemies' policy and Marty Natalegawa's 'Dynamic Equilibrium.'

One could extend the leadership argument to Indonesia's leadership role or its centrality in the regional strategic and cooperative discourse under the aegis of ASEAN, thereby translating national resilience into regional resilience. Dewi Fortuna Anwar argues that three major Javanese concepts – *tut wuri handayani* (leading from behind), *nglurug tampa bala* (marching forward without an army) and *menagng tanpa ngasorake* (winning without defeating) – have shaped contemporary Indonesia's policy towards ASEAN and regionalists.[53] Indonesia's intellectual contribution to ASEAN emanates from that notion of leadership and strategic centrality.

Anthony Smith points out that Suharto may have treated himself as an incarnation of the Javanese king, as evident from some of the provisions of the Indonesian Legal Code, which prohibits common Indonesian citizens from deliberately disrespecting the President, Vice-President and several other government officials and leaders.[54]

Suharto's advocacy of national resilience extended the principle of roles and responsibilities of Indonesia's leaders to include Indonesia's leadership role in shaping the regional strategic discourses. To quote Suharto:

> ...the national resilience concept is the only answer to the challenges posed by a world still dominated by tension. National resilience encompasses ideological resilience, based on a nation's own identity which receives the full support of entire nation, economic resilience capable of meeting the nation's own basic needs, social resilience, which ensures a feeling of solidarity and harmony among the peoples, and an appropriate military resilience to face aggression from outside. Without national resilience, we shall always be afraid.[55]

Only a strong and resilient Indonesia could secure its strategic interests in the region that was experiencing instability, great power interventions and inter-state conflicts and hostilities. The idea of national resilience aimed at projecting Indonesia's strength and capabilities or its comprehensive national power onto the regional strategic discourses and validating Indonesia's leadership role in the ASEAN cooperative processes. By supporting the formation of ASEAN, Indonesia was only trying to secure its interests in the circle of strength. Anwar identifies two important aspects of national resilience. First, the idea represents an inward-looking security doctrine and connotes a strong sense of nationalism, leading to self-reliance and regional strategic autonomy away from great power interventions.[56] These were often seen as important ASEAN strategies towards maintaining peace and stability in the region. In fact, the idea of resilience envisaged collective efforts on the part of the individual member-state and the entire regional grouping. The conversion of national resilience into regional resilience was viewed as an effective strategy to deal with a myriad of security challenges – traditional and non-traditional, home-grown and external, intra-state and inter-state, and intra-regional and extra-regional. The Declaration of ASEAN Concord, adopted in 1976 at Bali, Indonesia, identified national resilience as 'a step towards the strengthening of regional resilience, which, in turn, will contribute towards international peace and solidarity.'[57]

Michael Leifer has highlighted that the setting up of ASEAN truly marked "Indonesia's assumption of a primary role in promoting a system of regional order 'involving' a refusal in principle to accept the need for the role of an external power to fill any so-called power vacuum created within Southeast Asia by the retreat of colonialism. Indeed, the concept of a regional power vacuum was alien to a strategic perspective, which spanned the administration of Sukarno and Suharto."[58] In other words, ASEAN was viewed by the Indonesian elite also 'as a contributor to Indonesia's good name' and 'an enhancer of Indonesia's international stature.'[59]

Moreover, the strong and stable leadership in Indonesia has also meant a stable and powerful ASEAN, emanating from a deep-seated conscientious awareness among the Indonesian leaders that they have to maintain peace and stability in the circle of strength in order to ensure peace and stability at the core, and demonstrate their leadership roles in the region in order to secure Jakarta's leadership position. The stability and strength of the core is reflected in the dynamic of its interactions with the external settings and the way it is respected by others. Anthony Smith argues that both Sukarno and Suharto wanted to ensure Indonesia's pre-eminence in regional strategic discourses, even though their means and methodologies may have differed.[60] While Sukarno followed a power-driven discourse of strategic assertiveness, Suharto followed a cooperation-driven strategy of regional benign hegemon, seeking to dissuade mistrust and insecurity among the smaller neighbours and win over their support for cooperation, which ensures regional pre-eminence for Indonesia. What Sukarno sought to achieve through *Konfrontasi*, Suharto tried to achieve through ASEAN.[61]

The political elite of Indonesia, somewhat pre-eminently placed in the regional strategic discourse due to the country's strategic centrality and its regional profile, view themselves as obligated to contribute substantially to the regional strategic debates and efforts towards regional cooperation. Leonard Sebastian points out that Indonesian leaders have always given prominence to the idea that 'maintaining national regional security is the fundamental right and responsibility of the countries of the region themselves, acting separately and in concert with one another.'[62] This has often convinced the Indonesian elite to offer its good offices for deliberation over regional issues and alternative wisdoms for discussion. It is no surprise, therefore, to know that all the ASEAN summits in Indonesia have strived to offer grand visions and strategies while dealing with regional challenges. Anwar argues that though Indonesia seems to have maintained a low profile role in ASEAN, its 'voice nonetheless had often been decisive.[63]

ASEAN got the first important breath of relevance and continued existence in 1976 in Bali when it adopted some fundamental structural and functional steps to guide the functioning of the grouping. Since then, each of the ASEAN summits in Bali, Indonesia, whether it be in 2003, 2008 or 2011, have had profound implications in terms of objectives, directions, and strategies of ASEAN regional cooperation. Besides, three ASEAN concepts, derived from Indonesian political traditions, merit discussion here. The ASEAN Way derives its normative strength from the cultural traditions of Indonesia. The ideas of *musyawarah* (deliberation) and *mufakat* (consensus) find their genesis in the political culture of Indonesia.

Indonesia as a Moderate Muslim Democracy

Indonesia, as a multi-ethnic and pluralistic democracy, exists along multiple faultlines – social, regional, geographic, cultural, ethnic, religious, linguistic, native versus migrant, highlanders versus lowlanders, and so on. These lines have come to shape both Indonesia's internal and external expressions. Today, a rising Indonesia exudes a different sense of confidence in its global projection as a moderate, Muslim democracy, living somewhat in harmony with its multi-layered and multi-pronged diversities. To quote Hasan Wirajuda, the former Foreign Minister of Indonesia, "Indonesia today stands proud as the third largest democracy in the world. As a nation with an overwhelmingly Muslim population, Indonesia is a living refutation of the erroneous notion that Islam and democracy are incompatible."[64]

Indonesia's democracy promotion is primarily a result of two mutually reinforcing processes of international image-building and the need to construct a national identity built around a democratic value system.[65] Underscoring the growing importance of these processes, the political leadership decided to blend its international image with its democratic national identity. Even though two of the longest serving leaders of Indonesia – Sukarno and Suharto – developed an authoritarian structure of governance, they always camouflaged them as a variant of democracy, with the main objective of securing greater societal and political legitimacy. While Sukarno called his non-democratic presidential regime a 'Guided Democracy', Suharto called his authoritarian regime as '*Pancasila* Democracy.'

A major boost to the democratic consciousness of Indonesia came from the first major foreign policy speech given by President Yudhoyono when he declared that 'Indonesia's international identity must be rooted in a strong sense of who we are.'[66] According to Dewi Fortuna Anwar, "Indonesia's identity as the third largest democracy in the world needs to be constructed as the primary image of the country. In order for foreign policy to reflect national identity and priorities, democracy and respect for human rights that have become central to Indonesia's domestic politics should become the values that serve as the basis for Indonesia's foreign policy."[67] Rizal Sukma argues that the question of international identity became central to Indonesia's foreign policy, and the government devoted itself to solving its image problem.[68]

Three characteristics of rising Indonesia have received global attention. First, Indonesia has been viewed as a model Muslim democracy and an alternative blueprint for other Muslim societies to follow. The moderate Muslims of Indonesia have emerged as the vanguard of Indonesia's democratic resurgence. Scholars like Joshua Kurlantzik and magazines with global outreach like *the Economist* were prescribing the Indonesian model of Muslim democracy for the Arab countries amidst the revolution initiated at Tahrir Square in Egypt in 2011.[69] Indonesia's former Foreign Minister, Hasan Wirajuda, while taking part in the Bali Democracy Forum in 2011, indicated his country's desire to 'share its experience with the Arab countries and learn from each other's mistakes.'[70]

Second, the Indonesian leadership has projected itself as an important bridge-builder between the West and Muslim world and a facilitator of dialogue between the two world-views. The then Indonesian Ambassador to the United States, Dino Patti Djalal characterised Indonesia-US partnership as a 'constructive 21st-century partnership between the West and the Islamic world.'[71] Moreover, the West also seems to have acknowledged Indonesia's bridge-building capacity. While delivering his address at *Istiqlal* mosque in Jakarta in November 2000, the American President, Barrack Obama called upon Indonesia to play a greater role in facilitating dialogue between the West and Muslim world and build trust. The international Conference on Cultural Diplomacy in the European Union, Brussels in December 2011 identified Indonesia as a bridge between Islam and the West and a model of compatibility between Islam and democracy.

Finally, what has drawn the attention of the international community is Indonesia's image as a moderate Muslim society where the state has proven extremely effective against terrorism. Post-Suharto Indonesia has projected its successful counterterrorist campaigns against the home-grown terror network with regional and global linkages. So far, the democratic Indonesia is known to have launched the most effective measures against the terrorist networks. Notwithstanding being the largest Muslim country in the world, 'Indonesia is neither an Islamic state nor is Islam the official religion of the state.'[72] At the same time, in pursuance of this objective, Jakarta has also emphasised its credentials as a Muslim society and expressed strong opinions on the issues confronting the global Muslim community. The Megawati government of Indonesia openly criticized the US interventions in Afghanistan and Iraq. Indonesian leadership has shown activism in the deliberations of the OIC (Organisation of Islamic Countries). Moreover, President Yudhoyono had called upon the need for greater global sensitisation about the Islamic values and an international anti-blasphemy Code to prevent insult to the global religions during his speech at the UN General Assembly.

Indonesia is Underbalancing

Another debate that has travelled along the 'Indonesia rising' discourse: has the Indonesian leadership deliberately maintained a low force-projection in an strategic atmosphere marked by conflicts of interests, major power rivalries, territorial claims, and instability? Is Indonesia's arms build-up much less compared to what is required to ensure its national security? Is Indonesia articulating its threat perceptions primarily in terms of Non-Traditional Security threats or non-military threats and overlooking threats emanating from any foreign power? In other words, is Indonesia underbalancing?

Randall L. Schwller identifies balancing as "a situation in which a state is not directly menaced by a predatory state but decides to balance against it anyway to protect its long-term security interests."[73] In this context, the underbalancing behaviour occurs when 'threatened countries fail to recognize a clear and present danger or, more typically, simply not react to it or, more typically still, respond in paltry and imprudent ways.'[74] Viewed in this context, states may sometimes interpret differently national security and threats to their national security and, therefore, prioritise them differently.

When pitched in this context, underbalancing seems to be an important part of Indonesia's strategic culture. The state seems to have, on occasions encapsulated its security threats and its long-term military modernisation programme. One could look at three narratives to buttress the argument that Indonesia has been underbalancing, deliberately overlooking its security concerns or taking minimum efforts to engage in either internal or external balancing.

The first situation relates to an unstable external security environment of Indonesia under Suharto. Why did Indonesia maintain an extremely low level of arms build-up even when the national elite under the leadership of Suharto had pronounced a strong 'China-threat theory'? One could surmise the level of threat perception due to the complete severance of any diplomatic relationship with the People's Republic of China until 1990. Why did Jakarta not enter into any formal alliance with any major power, including the US? It was under the Suharto regime that the indigenous military industry reached its lowest point in terms of output and innovation.

The second situation relates to growing menace of maritime piracy and armed robbery in the Indonesian territorial waters in the 1990s and early years of 21st century. Both the Strait of Malacca and Indonesian waters had become notorious for unsafe ship transit. The situation worsened to a new level in 2005 when the UK-based insurance company, the Lloyd Agency, declared the Strait of Malacca and Indonesian territorial waters to be war-zone. Even at the height of these situations, Indonesian military spending on better policing of its territorial waters remained low.

Finally, even when Indonesia is facing similar security challenges in 2014 in the form of multi-layered rivalries, territorial claims (China's nine dotted lines include Indonesia's Natuna islands), and regional instability, its military build-up remains one of the lowest in the region. Notwithstanding being the regional pivot and the largest and most powerful player of Southeast Asia, Jakarta's military and arms build-up remains much lower than that of many smaller powers of Southeast Asia. The Indonesian navy and air-force remain underdeveloped. Smaller states like Malaysia and Singapore have much better navies and air-forces.[75] Even the idea of self-sufficiency and MEF (Minimal Essential Force) of Indonesia entail essentially rudimentary upgradation. Moreover, Jakarta has desisted from entering into any formal alliance system with any major power of the world, including the United States, with which the former shared strong politico-strategic relations during the Cold War era.

The Indonesian navy reported several military intrusions by 'a number of Malaysian warships and military airplanes' in December 2006 and February 2007 into the Indonesian territory around the oil-rich Ambalat region.[76] The then Indonesian Defence Minister, Juwono Sudarsono 'acknowledged the inadequacy of the Indonesian deterrence force in addressing the issues of border disputes and foreign attacks' and declared, 'we have to live with the fact that we have a low level of effectiveness in acting against trespassers on our land, sea and air territories.'[77]

The real reason for this posturing marked by underbalancing lies in its long-standing understanding of the nature of threats facing the archipelagic country and the level of willingness on the part of its leaders to strengthen the country's military capability. The paranoia that guides the country's political elite in defining its long-term national security is focused, in case of Indonesia, away from threats emanating from other powers and towards threats from within.

Nevertheless, one can also argue that because Indonesia is surrounded by weak neighbours, its geopolitical strategy includes a deliberate effort to ensure that its military might should not be seen as a threat. This calculation may have contributed to the country's decision not to develop its military strength. It is argued that Indonesia has consciously maintained a low military profile in the region even though it has a clear power advantage.[78]

In fact, the idea of military modernisation needs to be closely connected with Indonesia's long-term strategic thinking, its security agenda and its changing geo-strategic profile in the region. An Indonesian analyst, Andy Widjajanto, points out that the real hurdle in the realisation of the MEF is the inability of the country to 'initiate doctrinal innovation.'[79] He argues:

> Indonesia has failed to transform its way of warfare due to a collective belief within the military organization that Indonesia is a weak state that must rely on the doctrine of defensive warfare...This mentality became a strategic culture that caused stagnation within the military doctrine, prohibiting any policy initiatives to develop a more advanced military force. As a weak state, Indonesia could not develop and modernize its Armed Forces to a level that could significantly challenge major powers.[80]

The disconnect between the changing geopolitical realities and Jakarta's security doctrine and limited resources on defence expenditure continues to define the country's limited build-up, and therefore, its underbalancing strategy.

Strategic Autonomy in International Affairs

An important consciousness that has weighed heavily on the leadership of post-colonial Indonesia is the ability to take a position on any international issue without coming under any pressure. The idea of strategic autonomy has figured prominently in the choices of the decision-makers ever since its encapsulation by Mohammad Hatta, the promulgator of Indonesia's foreign policy in 1948 characterised as *Bebas dan Aktif* (independent and active) foreign policy. He wrote in 1953:

> The policy of the Republic of Indonesia is not one of neutrality, because it is not constructed in reference to belligerent states but for the purpose of strengthening and upholding peace. Indonesia plays no favourites

> between the two opposed blocs and follows its own path through the various international problems. It terms this policy "independent," and further characterises it by describing it as "independent (bebas)" and "active (aktif)." By active is meant the effort to work energetically for the preservation of peace and the relaxation of tension generated by the two blocs, through endeavours supported if possible by the majority of the members of the United Nations.[81]

Since then, the doctrine of *Babas dan Aktif* has come to serve as an important component of Indonesia's strategic culture and shaped Indonesia's strategic preferences. The decision-makers have taken recourse to this aspect whenever faced with situations of international coercion, dilemmas posed by great power rivalries or any other matters of international concern. Indonesia's sustained refusal towards any security agreement involving the major powers during the 1990s attests to Indonesia's pursuit of autonomy in its strategic behaviour.

Such a policy, according to Rizal Sukma, 'allowed Indonesia to not only follow a non-aligned approach without joining any bloc, but also to mitigate any internal dissent that could have arisen in the course of policy actions.'[82] The policy of *Bebas dan Aktif* has continued to form the central component of Indonesia's foreign policy, notwithstanding several important changes in the policy pronouncements, such as the centrality of ASEAN in Indonesian foreign policy. Dewi Fortuna Anwar argues that its ASEAN membership was partly 'a means of introducing its free and active foreign policy doctrine into a wider region.'[83]

Reflecting on the improvisations within its long-avowed foreign policy philosophy and its continued relevance in the changing global context, Foreign Minister Natalegawa characterised the independent and active (*bebas dan aktif*) approach as 'a capacity to make up our own mind in terms of issues – in other words, room for us to be able to maneuver, being able to reach positions and to have positions independent of any other powers and interests.'[84] For him, reaching such a position entails developing a 'dynamic equilibrium' involving multiple players, regions and issues. The doctrine of 'dynamic equilibrium' postulates a long-term strategic framework of an emerging power with the desire to (a) play greater role in the regional and global strategic discourses, (b) negotiate parity in its strategic engagement with important global players, and (c) act as an interlocutor and mediator in the issues of both intra-national and international disputes. There is a growing desire among the leadership to play at the bigger table and, therefore, project its importance. These debates and discussions have brought forth several important components of Indonesia's strategic vision in the 21st century. Similarly, the Indonesian emphasis on multilateralism either at the regional level under the aegis of ASEAN or at the global level under the aegis of the UN, can be viewed as an important strategy towards maintaining strategic autonomy in both regional and global affairs.

A characteristic feature of post-colonial Indonesia's global projection has been its active participation in international institutions and summits, whether it be the UN, the WTO, climate change negotiations or other international initiatives. Moreover, its leaders have called for these institutions to become more inclusive and representative, to function efficiently, and to take on global welfare as their main objectives. While doing so, Indonesian decision makers have projected the country as a global citizen abiding by international norms, rules and laws. The incorporation of the principle of internationalism in the Indonesian doctrine of *Pancasila* has helped further permeate the idea of multilateralism in the national psyche of Indonesia, evolving as an element of the country's strategic culture.

The genesis of Indonesia's multilateralist approach lies in its emphasis on collective wisdom and its advocacy for the collective management of global affairs. Sukarno's advocacy of the Non-Aligned Movement and the UN multilateralism provided one of the fundamentals of Indonesia's strategic behaviour in the global politics. Indonesia's participation in the UN came to symbolize the idea of global multilateralism. Indonesia's support for the UN multilateralism is best expressed in the words of Mohammad Hatta when he declared that one of the objectives of the country's foreign policy was 'to strengthen principles of international law and to aid in achieving social justice on an international scale, in line with the UN Charter, with special reference to articles 1, 2, and 55, in particular by endeavouring within the UN framework to help people still living within the colonial system to achieve freedom.'[85] The pursuit of the Non-Aligned Movement brought out another element of Indonesian strategic thinking – solidarity with the global sub-alterns or the Global South.

One can discern a different type of multilateralism at the regional level during the authoritarian regime of Suharto, when institution-building and rule-making under ASEAN acquired greater prominence in the then strategic thinking of the national elite and strategic community. Indonesia under the leadership of Suharto played an active role in facilitating the evolution and subsequent growth of ASEAN as a regional cooperative process.

Four instances further testify to Indonesia's advocacy for global multilateralism – its participation and performance in the UN peacekeeping processes, its call for democratization and comprehensive reforms in the international institutions, its emphasis on Indonesia's role in the G-20, and Jakarta's call for global efforts to mitigate global challenges and protect the Global Commons. In order to project rising Indonesia's multilateralist image, the Directorate of Multilateral Affairs has set the program of year 2010-2014 under the frame of 'Improvement of Indonesia's Role and Diplomacy in Multilateral Affairs' with the desirable outcome of 'improving Indonesia's role and diplomacy in addressing multilateral issues.'[86] The basic objectives of Indonesia's multilateralism as outlined on the website of the Department of Foreign Affairs, Republic of Indonesia are as follows:

(a) improve Indonesia's participation and initiative in multilateral forums that includes becoming host to multilateral conferences;
(b) synergize Indonesia's participation in G-20 through participation in other forums;
(c) formulate policy concept/ grand design of South-South cooperation; and
(d) intensify diplomacy on the establishment of international norms.[87]

These elements are gradually gaining prominence in the country's foreign policy, strengthening, in the process, ideational component of Indonesia's foreign policy.

Conclusion

Rising Indonesia's strategic behaviour represents inspiration from the country's historical-cultural traditions, its experiences during the national liberation movement, its post-colonial regional and global roles and its experiences as a democratic nation-state during the first decade of the 21st century. The national elite and the strategic community today are trying to stitch these traditions and choices together in the form of Indonesia's evolving strategic culture. The debates over these values and beliefs are going to further intensify in the coming years with its national elite and the strategic community ponders over long-term directions in the strategic choices and grand strategy. Indonesia's regional and global roles, though not the sum-total of its strategic culture, represent a continuous interplay between these elements of strategic culture and the strategic environment in which the decision makers are finding the country situated today.

ENDNOTES

1. For details on strategic culture see, Jack Snyder, *The Soviet Strategic Culture: Implications for Nuclear Options*, Rand R-2154-AF (Santa Monica, Rand Publications, 1977); Alastair Iain Johnston, *Cultural Realism: Strategic Culture and Grand Strategy in Chinese History* (New Jersey, Princeton University Press, 1995), pp. 1-60; Alastair Iain Johnston, "Thinking about Strategic Culture," *International Security*, vol. 19, no. 4 (1995), pp. 32-64; Colin Gray, 'Strategic Culture as Context: The First Generation of Theory Strikes Back', *Review of International Studies*, vol. 25, no. 1 (1999), pp. 49-69; Alastair Iain Johnston, 'Strategic Cultures Revisited: Reply to Colin Gray', *Review of International Studies*, vol. 25, no. 3, 1999, pp. 519-523; Jeffrey S. Lantis, "Strategic Culture and National Security Policy," International Studies Review, vol. 4, no. 3, December 2002, pp. 87-113; Stuart Poore, 'What is the Context? A Reply to the Gray-Johnston Debate on Strategic Culture', *Review of International Studies*, vol. 29, no. 2 (2003), pp. 279-284; Colin Dueck, *Reluctant Crusaders: Power, Culture, and Change in American Grand Strategy* (New Jersey, Princeton, 2006), pp. 15-20.
2. Jeffrey S. Lantis, ibid, p. 93.
3. Alastair Iain Johnston, *Cultural Realism: Strategic Culture and Grand Strategy in Chinese History*, op.cit., pp. 1-31; Colin Dueck, op.cit.; Jeffrey S. Lantis, "Strategic Culture: from Clausewitz to Constructivism," *Defense Threat Reduction Agency*, SAIC, 31 October 2006, http://www.fas.org/irp/agency/dod/dtra/stratcult-claus.pdf (accessed on 27 May 2013).
4. Alastair Iain Johnston, op.cit., pp. 1-60.
5. Jack Snyder, op.cit., p. 9.
6. Alastair Iain Johnston, op.cit., p. 6.
7. Ibid, p. 39.
8. Ibid, pp. 6-7.
9. Ibid, p. 8; Colin Dueck, op.cit., pp. 18-20.
10. Colin Dueck, ibid, p. 15.
11. Alastair Iain Johnston, op.cit., p. 8; Colin Dueck, op.cit., pp. 18-20.
12. Colin Dueck, ibid, p. 19.
13. Ibid.
14. Rizal Sukma, "The Evolution of Indonesia's Foreign Policy: An Indonesian View," *Asian Survey*, vol. 35, no. 3 (March 1995), p. 305.
15. Donald E Weatherbee, "Indonesian Foreign Policy: A Wounded Phoenix," *Southeast Asian Affairs*, vol. 2005, p. 152; Donald K Emmerson, "Is Indonesia Rising: It Depends," in Anthony Reid (ed.), *Indonesia Rising: The Repositioning of Asia's Third Giant* (Singapore, ISEAS, 2012), p. 52; Ross Garnaut, "Indonesia in the New World Balance," in Anthony Reid (ed.), *Indonesia Rising: The Repositioning of Asia's Third Giant* (Singapore, ISEAS, 2012), pp. 18-21.
16. Patrick Chee Keong Lim, "Impact of Javanese culture on Indonesia's strategic outlook and on the Indonesian armed forces (TNI)," RSIS Theses, 2000, http://repository.ntu.edu.sg/handle/10356/14276?show=full (accessed on 22 December 2013).
17. Ibid.
18. Emmet McElhatton, "Guerrilla Warfare and the Indonesian Strategic Psyche," *Small Wars Journal*, May 2008, http://smallwarsjournal.com/jrnl/art/guerrilla-warfare-and-the-indonesian-strategic-psyche (accessed on 23 December 2013).
19. Evan A Laksmana, "The Enduring Strategic Trinity: Explaining Indonesia's Geopolitical Architecture," *Journal of the Indian Ocean Region*, vol. 7, no. 1, June 2011, pp. 98-100.

20. Emmet McElhatton, op.cit.
21. Evan A Laksmana, The Enduing Strategic Trinity, op.cit., p. 97; Ali Abdullah Wibisono, "Rethinking RI defense policy," *The Jakarta Post*, 12 January 2009, http://www.thejakartapost.com/news/2009/01/12/rethinking-ri-defense-policy.html (accessed on 30 December 2013).
22. Dewi Fortuna Anwar, *Indonesia's Strategic Culture: Ketahanan Nasional, Wawasan Nusantara And Hankamrata* (Griffith, Griffith University Press, 1996).
23. Alan Dupont, "Indonesian Defence Strategy and Security: Time for a Rethink?," *Contemporary Southeast Asia*, vol. 18, no. 3 (December 1996), pp. 275-297.
24. Ibid.
25. Ali Abdullah Wibisono, op.cit.; Andy Widjajanto, "Indonesia's Military Doctrinal Stagnation," *Strategic Review*, 20 March 2012, http://www.sr-indonesia.com/2011-08-09-22-09-10/commentaries/157-indonesias-military-doctrinal-stagnation (accessed on 19 May 2013).
26. N. Hasan Wirajuda, "The Democratic Response," *The Brown Journal of World Affairs*, vol. IX, no. 1 (Spring 2002), pp. 15-21; Leonard C. Sebastian, "Domestic Security Priorities, "Balance of Interests" and Indonesia's Management of Regional Order," in Joseph Chinyong Liow and Ralf Emmers, *Order and Security in Southeast Asia: Essays in Memory of Michael Leifer* (Oxon: Routledge, 2006); Dewi Fortuna Anwar, "Foreign Policy, Islam and Democracy in Indonesia," *Journal of Indonesian Social Sciences and Humanities*, vol. 3, 2010, pp. 37-54; Evan A Laksmana, "The Enduing Strategic Trinity: Explaining Indonesia's Geopolitical Architecture," *Journal of the Indian Ocean Region*, vol. 7, no. 1, June 2011, p. 97; Rizal Sukma, "Indonesia Finds a New Voice," *Journal of Democracy*, vol. 22, no. 4, October 2011, pp. 110-123.
27. N. Hasan Wirajuda, op.cit., p. 16.
28. Andy Widjajanto, op.cit.; Ali Abdullah Wibisono, op.cit.,
29. Daniel Novotny, *Torn between America and China, Elite Perceptions and Indonesian Foreign Policy* (Singapore, ISEAS, 2010); Anthony Reid, op.cit.,
30. Alastair Iain Johnston, op.cit., p. 6.
31. Anthony Reid, "Indonesia's New Prominence in the World," in Anthony Reid, op.cit., p. 2.
32. Dewi Fortuna Anwar, *Indonesia's Strategic Culture: Ketahanan Nasional, Wawasan Nusantara And Hankamrata*, op.cit.; Michael Leifer, Indonesia's Encounters with China and the Dilemmas of Engagement," in Alastair Iain Johnston and Robert S. Ross (eds.) *Engaging China: Management of an Emerging Power* (New York, Routledge, 1999), p. 92; "Anthony Reid, op.cit., p. 2; Yayan G H Mulyana, "Developing an archipelagic foreign policy," *The Jakarta Post*, 09 January 2012, p. 6; Leonard C. Sebastian and Imran J. Lanti, "Perceiving Indonesian Approaches to International Relations Theory," in Amitav Acharya and Barry Buzan (eds.), *Non-Western International Relations Theory : Perspectives on and beyond Asia* (London, Routledge, 2010), http://www.ditchley.co.uk/assets/media/7%20Indonesia-Sebastian%20and%20Lanti.pdf (accessed on 28 May 2013), p. 26.
33. I Made Andi Arsana, "Celebrating a hundred years of Maritime Nation," *The Jakarta Post*, 26 April 2008.
34. Leonard C. Sebastian, op.cit., p. 178.
35. Frederick Situmorang, "'Wawasan nusantara' vs UNCLOS," *The Jakarta Post*, 29 January 2013, p. 6.
36. Michael Leifer, *Indonesia's Foreign Policy* (London, Allen & Unwin, 1983), p. 173; also cited in Leonard C. Sebastian, op.cit., p. 177.

37. The idea of Bhinneka Tunggul Ika (Unity in Diversity) is attributed to Mpu Tantular, the poet-sage of Majapahit kingdom. Ian Chalmers, *Indonesia: An Introduction to Contemporary Traditions* (Victoria, Oxford University Press, 2006), p. 8; M C Ricklefs, "Unity and Disunity in Javanese Political and Religious Thought of the Eighteenth Century," *Modern Asian Studies*, vol. 26, no. 4 (1992), p. 663.
38. Robert Cribb and Colin Brown, *Modern Indonesia: A History Since 1945* (London, Longman, 1995), p.32.
39. Leonard C. Sebastian and Imran J. Lanti, op.cit., p. 2.
40. Mohammad Hatta, "Indonesia's Foreign Policy," *Foreign Affairs: an American Quarterly Review*, vol. 31, no. 1/4 (1952/1953), p.450.
41. Farish A. Noor, "How Indonesia Sees ASEAN and the World: A Cursory Survey of the Social Studies and History textbooks of Indonesia, from Primary to Secondary Level," *RSIS Working Paper*, no. 233, 22 February 2012, http://www.rsis.edu.sg/publications/workingpapers/wp233.pdf (accessed on 28 May 2013).
42. For details of discussion on manadala, see Nicholas Tarling, *Status and Security in Southeast Asian State Systems* (Oxon, Routledge, 2013), pp. 20-24; Leonard C. Sebastian, op.cit., pp. 180-182.
43. Soemarsaid Moertono, *State and Statecraft in Old Java: A Study of the Later Mataram Period, 16th to 19th Century* (Cornell, Cornell Southeast Asia Program Publications, 1968), f.n. 207, p. 81.
44. Leonard C. Sebastian, op.cit., p. 177.
45. Jürgen Rüland, "Constructing Regionalism Domestically: Local Actors and Foreign Policymaking in Indonesia," *University of Freiburg Occasional Paper*, no. 6 (December 2011), http://www.southeastasianstudies.uni-freiburg.de/Content/files/occasional-paper-series/op-ruland-no.6_2011 (accessed on 28 May 2013).
46. Dewi Fortuna Anwar referred to the importance of Mandala as circles in Indonesia's foreign policy while delivering a lecture at Indonesian Embassy, New Delhi in 2005.
47. *The Policy of the State Defence and Security of the Republic of Indonesia* (Jakarta, Ministry of Defence and Security, 1995), pp. 16-17 cited in Leonard C. Sebastian, op.cit., p. 181.
48. O.W. Wolters, *History, Culture and Region in Southeast Asian Perspectives* (Singapore, ISEAS, 1982), pp. 27-28 cited in Nicholas Tarling, op.cit., p. 22
49. Anthony L. Smith, *Strategic Centrality: Indonesia's Changing Role in ASEAN* (Singapore, ISEAS, 2000), p. 14.
50. "Ministry of Foreign Affairs – Multilateral Cooperation," *Government of Indonesia*, http://www.kemlu.go.id/Pages/IFP.aspx?P=Regional&l=en (accessed on 09 December 2013).
51. Rizal Sukma, "Domestic Politics and International Posture: Constraints and Possibilities," in Anthony Reid, op.cit., pp. 90-91.
52. Ian Chalmers, op.cit., p. 9; Dewi Fortuna Anwar, *Indonesia in ASEAN: Foreign Policy and Regionalism* (Sinagproe, ISEAS, 1994), p. 222.
53. Dewi Fortuna Anwar, *Indonesia in ASEAN: Foreign Policy and Regionalism* (Sinagproe, ISEAS, 1994), p. 222.
54. Anthony L. Smith, *Strategic Centrality: Indonesia's Changing Role in ASEAN* (Singapore, ISEAS, 2000), fn. 14, p. 78.
55. Dewi Fortuna Anwar, "National versus Regional Resilience: An Indonesian Perspective," in Derek Da Cunha, *Southeast Asian Perspectives on Security* (Singapore, ISEAS, 2000), p. 83.
56. Ibid, pp. 82-83.
57. Ibid, p. 82.

58. Michael Leifer, *Indonesia's Foreign Policy* op.cit., pp. 119-120; also cited in Leonard C. Sebastian, op.cit, p. 183.
59. Dewi Fortuna Anwar, *Indonesia in ASEAN: Foreign Policy and Regionalism,* op.cit., p. 197.
60. Anthony L. Smith, op.cit., p. 8.
61. Ibid, p. 8.
62. Leonard C. Sebastian, op.cit., p. 182.
63. Dewi Fortuna Anwar, *Indonesia in ASEAN: Foreign Policy and Regionalism,* op.cit., p. 223.
64. N. Hasan Wirajuda, op.cit., p. 16.
65. Dewi Fortuna Anwar, "Foreign Policy, Islam and Democracy in Indonesia," op.cit., p. 39.
66. Susilo Bambang Yudhoyono, "Speech Before The Indonesian Council on World Affairs (ICWA) http://www.presidenri.go.id/index.php/pidato/2005/05/19/332.html
67. Quoted in Rizal Sukma, "Indonesia Finds a New Voice," op.cit., p. 112.
68. Ibid, pp. 110-123.
69. Thomas Carothers, "The New Republic: A Lesson for Egypt In Indonesia," *National Public Radio,* 03 February 2011, http://www.npr.org/2011/02/03/133461179/the-new-republic-a-lesson-for-egypt-in-indonesia; Joshua Kurlantzik, "Is Egypt the Next Indonesia?," *Council on Foreign Relations,* 07 February 2011, http://blogs.cfr.org/asia/2011/02/07/is-egypt-the-next-indonesia/; "The Indonesian example: Remember 1998," *The Economist,* 07 February 2011, http://www.economist.com/blogs/asiaview/2011/02/indonesian_example
70. Shada Islam, "Indonesian example," *The Dawn,* 10 December 2012, http://dawn.com/2011/12/10/indonesian-example/ (accessed on 20 December 2012).
71. "Indonesia-U.S. Relations: A Comprehensive Partnership," *Metropolitan Corporate Counsel,* vol. 19, no. 3, 28 February 2011, p. 45, 48, http://www.metrocorpcounsel.com/pdf/2011/March/45.pdf
72. Azymardi Azra, "Islam, Indonesia and Democracy," *Strategic Review,* vol. 1, no. 1, August 2011, p. 74.
73. Randall L. Schweller, "Unanswered Threats: A Neoclassical Realist Theory of Underbalancing," *International Security* vol. 29, no. 2 (Fall 2004), p. 164.
74. Ibid, p. 159.
75. James Goldrick and Jack McCaffrie, *Navies of South-East Asia: A Comparative Study* (New York, Routledge 2013), pp. 12-13.
76. "RI Lacks Deterrence Force: Juwono," *The Jakarta Post,* 22 March 2007.
77. Ibid.
78. Dewi Fortuna Anwar, *Indonesia in ASEAN: Foreign Policy and Regionalism,* op.cit., pp. 196-199.
79. Andy Widjajanto, op.cit.,
80. Ibid.
81. Mohammad Hatta, op.cit., p.440.
82. Rizal Sukma, "the Evolution of Indonesia's Foreign Policy" op.cit., p. 305.
83. Dewi Fortuna Anwar, *Indonesia in ASEAN: Foreign Policy and Regionalism,* op.cit., p. 174.
84. "A Conversation with Marty Natalegawa, Minister of Foreign Affairs, Republic of Indonesia," *Council on Foreign Relations,* 20 September 2010, http://www.cfr.org/indonesia/conversation-marty-natalegawa-minister-foreign-affairs-republic-indonesia/p22984 (accessed on 20 May 2013).
85. Mohammad Hatta, op.cit., p. 442.
86. "Ministry of Foreign Affairs – Multilateral Cooperation," *Government of Indonesia,*http://www.kemlu.go.id/Pages/IFP.aspx?P=Multilateral&l=en (accessed on 16 December 2012).
87. Ibid.

CONCLUSION

Rising Indonesia is riding on its newfound confidence emanating from its domestic consolidation, its geo-strategic positioning in the region and its emerging identity at the global level. The Indonesian foreign policy establishment is working overtime to ensure a pivotal role in the regional strategic discourses and a place of prominence in the debates and discussions about restructuring the global order. Three Ms define Indonesia's present outlook – moderate Muslim democracy, multipolarity and multilateralism. While the first element – moderate Muslim democracy – manifests the broad contour of national priorities, the last two traits – multipolarity and multilateralism – seem to be shaping Indonesia's regional and global agenda. Indonesia's democratic tryst seems to be proving right the contested assumption that 'there is absolutely no contradiction between democracy, modernity, Islam and women's rights.'[1] The leadership is rightfully boasting about disproving a commonly-held myth across the globe, a myth that seems to have vitiated Islam's relations with the world and changed the course of international relations in the aftermath of the terrorist attack on 11 September 2001 in the United States.

At this juncture, one could ask two questions. First, what are the key trends that are going to have an impact on Indonesia's future strategic outlook? Second, how well can Indonesia respond to those trends in the coming years and decades? Though correctly reading the regional and global trends is the first step, the real litmus test of Indonesia's national elite and strategic community lies in making right choices for the country as it engages the world from the position of privilege. Though Indonesia's regional and global debates raise several pertinent questions, their answers have been shrouded in the uncertainties of the future, further compounding the complexities of the prevailing regional order. Indonesia's strategic behaviour should take cognisance of its evolving vulnerability emanating from its still incomplete project of national development, regional uncertainty, challenges facing global governance, and supra-global challenges such as climate change and natural disasters. While these trends continue to shape Indonesia's emerging profile, the story is far from complete. The critical factor lies with the role and direction of the leadership and its focus on the structural consolidation of the country and the dynamic of interaction with the systemic processes.

Indonesia's regional priorities and responses need to also address an emerging, unique dynamic of the 21st century facing the country's immediate concentric circle that covers the entire Indo-Pacific – namely, the shifting gravity of power to this part of the world. During the Cold War era and even during the 1990s, the system-shaping factors or processes were originating elsewhere, and Indonesia, Southeast Asia and even Asia were merely responding to these global developments rather than influencing them. The US-USSR Cold War rivalry is a standard example. Today, not only are the system-shaping factors originating in close vicinity, but also Jakarta has become an important mover and shaker in the global structure of power. The Sino-US rivalry in the Indo-Pacific region characterises the new power relationships at the global level, and Indonesia is understood to play a pivotal role in influencing their relationship. Since regional developments are going to influence overwhelmingly the global structure of power, Indonesia will be playing a critical role at the regional level and therefore can influence the global *bodypolitik* both directly and indirectly.

Indonesia's changing outlook is going to have more impact on the region than on the nation itself or its global position because its national security concerns will remain undiluted and its system-shaping capabilities will be limited in the short-to-medium term. Indonesia can ill-afford to stay out of this new process given its huge stake in addressing the negative fall-outs of the new power relationships. The real catalyst may emerge in the form of how the new Indonesian leadership after 2014 interprets the idea of national resilience and translates it into a substantial policy approach for Indonesia's regional roles.

Viewed from the prism of *Mandala,* or circles, rising Indonesia is positioning its normative power and its model global citizenship in the outermost circle at the global level. Furthermore, it is assuming a pro-active leadership role in the second circle or the "circle of strength" at the regional level, and engaging in underbalancing in the inner circle. While the inner circle of vulnerability remains the same, it is the second circle (region boundary), whose definition, development, and outlook have experienced substantial alteration and expansion demanding new attention and more complex diplomacy from its leaders while projecting the country's regional leadership. Its regional focus goes beyond the perimeters of Southeast Asia and covers what is referred to as the Indo-Pacific world, perhaps the most dynamic region today, filled with emerging challenges and prospects for stability and development. At the same time, the Indonesian leadership is exploring every possibility for steering the country and region clear of continuing uncertainties and vulnerabilities. In fact, Natalegawa's two-ocean 'Pacific Indo-Pacific' doctrine is an attempt to articulate the regional challenges and their possible solutions and initiate a region-wide debate on these issues engaging all the important stakeholders, including great powers, rising powers, middle powers, small powers, island states, regional organisations, international organisations, and national and international NGOs.

Natalegawa's Two-Ocean 'Pacific Indo-Pacific' Doctrine

The discourse on the Indo-Pacific region gained new momentum in May 2013 when the Indonesian Foreign Minister, Dr. R.M. Marty M. Natalegawa, called upon the countries to build an Indo-Pacific Treaty of Friendship and Cooperation as a viable means of creating what he characterised as the 'Pacific Indo-Pacific' region. He was delivering an address at the Washington-based Center for Strategic and International Studies entitled "An Indonesian Perspective on the Indo-Pacific." The Indo-Pacific Treaty by Dr. Natalegawa offers a broader regional canvas that places Indonesia at the centre and therefore obligates it to play an important role in shaping the regional strategic discourse.

The new doctrine underscores Jakarta's growing strategic ambition that appears to transcend the two long-standing geo-political classifications of Southeast Asia and the Asia-Pacific. While Southeast Asia dealt with a somewhat smaller geopolitical canvas, the Asia-Pacific kept Indonesia focused on the Pacific Ocean. For the first time, Indonesian leadership has begun looking at a region encompassing an interconnected world of two Oceanic systems – the Indo-Pacific. While the Pacific Ocean has always factored importantly in Indonesia's regional diplomacy, the Indian Ocean has, of late, come to figure prominently in Jakarta's regional strategic thinking for several reasons, such as great power politics, maritime security, greater economic integration, and the idea of a shared vulnerability from the NTS threat.[2] Similarly, the integrative processes that are taking place in the region have further bound together the destiny of countries in the region. Jakarta is becoming more and more aware of its stakes and interests in the entire Indo-Pacific. In fact, Indonesian leadership has shown its flexibility in dealing with the complexities of each of these constructs and also retaining their exclusive strategic significance.

Situated at the core of this new geo-political formulation, Indonesia's articulation offers a new justification for the relevance of the Indo-Pacific region and raises several pertinent questions regarding what the region means to Indonesia. The first and foremost question is regarding the Indonesian definition of the term. Natalegawa identifies the region as 'a triangular space spanning two oceans, the Pacific and Indian Oceans, bounded by Japan in the north, Australia in the South-east and India in the south-west, notably with Indonesia at its center.'[3] This spatial construct highlights the trend towards a growing integration of people, government and businesses involving the two maritime worlds of the Indian and Pacific Ocean. The region is characterised today by its emergence as a global economic hub and an arena of great power rivalries, the shrinkage of distance and space connecting the two oceans, the evolving multi-polarity marked by the rise of new powers, and, above all, the emergence of unstable relationship structures amidst growing integration.

Indonesia's archipelagic character places it as a bridge between the two maritime systems and positions it to play critical role in shaping the strategic discourses in the region.[4] An archipelagic Indonesia finds itself equally involved in the developments taking place in the Indian Ocean, the Southwest Pacific and the East China Sea. The Indian Ocean Tsunami of 2004 affected not only Indonesia, but also India, Sri Lanka and Thailand. The idea of stand-alone vulnerability seems to have become a relic of the past and can be pursued at one's own peril. Indonesia is perhaps the only country that could form the nucleus of the region straddling the Indian Ocean in the West and Pacific in the East. Anindya Novyan Bakrie, the Vice-Chairman of Indonesian Chamber of Commerce and Industry, argues that Indonesia, though ambivalent for now, will have to wake up to these game-changing developments taking place in the Indo-Pacific.[5] Dewi Fortuna Anwar, a well-known Indonesian expert on international affairs, argues that Indonesia is a 'global swing state' since it straddles strategic choke points between the Indian and Pacific Oceans, and that it will therefore exercise considerable influence in regional and international affairs.[6] Indonesia's status as a founding member of the IOR-ARC (Indian Ocean Rim Association for Regional Cooperation) and APEC further justifies its roles in this geo-political landscape of the Indo-Pacific. Indonesia will replace Australia in 2015 as the IOR-ARC Chair for 2015-17.

As an Indo-Pacific power, Natalegawa argues, Indonesia has to grapple with three critical challenges – the all-pervasive trust-deficit that lies at the heart of regional relationships, unresolved territorial disputes, and managing the impact of change.[7] The region can move towards peace and stability provided that its stakeholders make a concerted effort towards 'building and nurturing trust and confidence, exercising restraint in case of involvement in the territorial disputes, and developing and adhering to a specific code of behaviour.'[8] Only then a 'Pacific Indo-Pacific' world can be built.

Indonesia's Responsible Global Citizenry

The democratic Indonesia has shown a great deal of alacrity in presenting its image and role as a responsible stakeholder in global deliberations over critical challenges.[9] Indonesia's new activism aims at advocating reforms in the existing international order, calling upon the urgent necessity of a greater exchange of wisdom from diverse civilizational worldviews and value systems, and building a democratic and representative global order. The normative components of democratic Indonesia's global posturing are evident in its support for democracy, efforts towards strengthening the international institutions, participation in peace-building processes, including UN peacekeeping operations, and advocacy for the advanced world to take greater responsibility for poverty eradication, climate change and the protection of the environment.

As the democratic Indonesia consolidates its national resources, it finds itself more effectively projecting its international image. At the same time, the shifting gravity of power to the Indo-Pacific and growing power of the global South have brought Indonesia into the limelight, provided adequate wherewithal and strategic capital, and placed it in an atmosphere conducive for the rising Indonesia's global projection. Moreover, Indonesia's global positioning has gained more teeth as its normative positioning is getting mixed with practical concerns and interests, such as permanent membership in the UN Security Council and capture of the emerging market.

However, Indonesia would require mobilising huge national resources to keep abreast of the changing global landscape and to provide intellectual support on issues confronting the world. An investment in the human resources and national foreign policy debates is required. The Indonesian leadership could do this by augmenting new institutions and initiating comprehensive debates within the country with participation from different segments of society including the national elite, the strategic community and common people. There is a need to broad-base the debate over strategic thinking and foreign policy in the country. Some of the critical issues such as the grand strategy or the strategic culture have been largely missing from the foreign policy debates that are taking place within the country. At the same time, Indonesia has to put its own house in order since its global normative projections have revolved around various factors of national identity. It is imperative that a multi-religious, moderately Muslim, democratic, fast-growing, and institutionalising Indonesia addresses challenges, which can, otherwise, undercut a somewhat perfectly crafted success story of a civilizational power from the East.

ENDNOTES

1. The speech of Indonesian Ambassador to the United States, Dino Patti Djalal, at USINDO Welcoming Dinner, Washington DC, 16 September 2010, http://www.embassyofindonesia.org/press/docpdf/speech/AmbDinoPattiDjalal_Remarks_USINDO_Welcoming_Dinner.pdf (accessed on 01 June 2013).
2. Evan A. Lakshamana, "The Enduring Strategic Trinity: Explaining Indonesia's Geopolitical Architecture," *Journal of Indian Ocean Region,* vol. 7, no. 1, June 2011, p. 110.
3. Marty Natalegawa, "An Indonesian perspective on the Indo-Pacific," *The Jakarta Post,* 20 May 2013, http://www.thejakartapost.com/news/2013/05/20/an-indonesian-perspective-indo-pacific.html (accessed on 15 June 2013).
4. Anindya Novyan Bakrie, "US Pivot to the Region has Changed the Game," *The Jakarta Globe,* 03 January 2012, http://www.thejakartaglobe.com/columnists/us-pivot-to-the-region-has-changed-the-game/488796 (accessed on 18 September 2012).
5. Ibid.
6. Dewi Fortuna Anwar, "A Problem of Mixed Messages," *The Asialink Essays 2012,* vol. 4, no. 6, August 2012, p. 2.
7. Marty Natalegawa, op.cit.
8. Op.cit.,
9. Anthony L. Smith, "Indonesia's Foreign Policy under Abdurrahman Wahid: Radical or Status Quo State?," *Contemporary Southeast Asia,* vol. 22, no. 3 (December 2000), pp. 499-504.

Select Bibliography

Primary Sources

"A Conversation with Marty Natalegawa, Minister of Foreign Affairs, Republic of Indonesia," Council on Foreign Relations, 20 September 2010, http://www.cfr.org/indonesia/conversation-marty-natalegawa-minister-foreign-affairs-republic-indonesia/p22984 (accessed on 03 January 2013)

Annual Press Statement of the Foreign Minister of the Republic of Indonesia Dr. R.M. Marty M. Natalegawa 2011, http://www.indonesiavancouver.org/speeches-a-statements/582-annual-press-statement-of-the-foreign-minister-of-the-republic-of-indonesia-dr-rm-marty-m-natalegawa-2011 (accessed on 04 March 2012)

Association of Southeast Asian Nations, *The ASEAN Charter* (Jakarta, ASEAN Secretariat, 2008)

"ASEAN Framework for Regional Comprehensive Economic Partnership," ASEAN Secretariat, no. 26744, http://www.aseansec.org/26744.htm (accessed on 25 October 2012)

"ASEAN Plus Three Cooperation," ASEAN Secretariat, no. 16580, 16 April 2012, http://www.aseansec.org/16580.htm (accessed on 14 October 2012)

"Background Notes: Indonesia," State Department Press Release, Government of the United States of America, 03 November 2010, http://www.state.gov/r/pa/ei/bgn/2748.htm#foreign (accessed on 23 December 2012)

"Bali Climate Change Conference – December 2007," United Nations Framework Convention on Climate Change, http://unfccc.int/meetings/bali_dec_2007/meeting/6319.php (accessed on 16 December 2012)

"Building Security Partnership in Asia," Speech of H.E. Purnomo Yusgiantoro, Minister of Defence of the Republic of Indonesia at CSIS seminar, Centre for Strategic and International Studies, Washington D.C. 16 May 2013, http://csis.org/files/attachments/130516_PurnomoYusgiantoro_Speech.pdf (accessed on 10 June 2013)

"Declaration of ASEAN Concord II (Bali Concord II)," ASEAN Secretariat, no. 15159, http://www.aseansec.org/15159.htm (accessed on 25 October 2012)

"Declaration on the New Asian-African Strategic Partnership," http://www.kbri-canberra.org.au/lains/Hasil%20KTT%20AA%202005.pdf (accessed on 26 December 2012)

"Defending Australia in the Asia-Pacific Century: Force 2030," Defence White Paper 2009.Department of Australia, Commonwealth of Australia, http://www.defence.gov.au/whitepaper/docs/defence_white_paper_2009.pdf. (accessed on 14 October 2012)

"First Meeting of India-Indonesia Joint Working Group on Counter-Terrorism," Ministry of External Affairs, Government of India, no. 9051, 25 February 2005, http://meaindia.nic.in/pressrelease/2005/02/25pr01.htm (accessed on 10 May 2010)

"Full Text of Final Communique of the Bandung Conference, April 18-24 1955," quoted in Ide Anak Agung Gde Agung, Twenty Years of Indonesian Foreign Policy 1945-65, Appendices 13, p. 583 (The Hague, Mouton, 1973)

"Full text of Kevin Rudd's Speech to the Asia Society Australasia", *The Australian*, 05 June 2008, http://www.theaustralian.com.au/politics/full-text-of-kevin-rudds-speech/story-e6frgczf-1111116541962 (accessed on 13 December 2012)

G-20 Communique. 1999. Meeting of the G-20 Finance Ministers and Central Bank Governors, Berlin, 15-16 December, http://www.g20.org/Documents/1999_germany.pdf (accessed on 17 May 2010)

Hatta, Mohammad *Kumpulan Pidato* [collected speeches] (Jakarta: Yayasan Idayu, 1981)

"IMF Managing Director Visits Indonesia, Meets President Susilo Bambang Yudhoyono," IMF Press Release, no. 12/254, 10 July 2012, http://www.imf.org/external/np/sec/pr/2012/pr12254.htm (accessed on 17 December 2012)

"Indonesia and the United Nations: Working Together for Peace and Development," *Permanent Mission of the Republic of Indonesia to the United Nations* (New York, 2005)

"Indonesia Calls for G-77 Countries and China to Push Agenda of Global Economy," *Embassy of The Republic of Indonesia in Seoul – South Korea*, 24 September 2011, http://www.kemlu.go.id/seoul/Pages/News.aspx?IDP=5169&l=en (accessed on 26 December 2012)

"Indonesia Crisis Prevention and Recovery Update," *United Nations Development Programme*, http://www.undp.or.id/programme/cpr/ (accessed on 15 September 2012)

"Indonesia's Foreign Policy," *Embassy of the Republic of Indonesia in Ottawa*, Canada, http://www.indonesia-ottawa.org/discover-indonesia/foreign-policy/ (accessed on 25 December 2012)

"Indonesia: EU Bilateral Trade and Trade with the World," IMF (DoTS), DG TRADE, 8-Jun-11, http://trade.ec.europa.eu/doclib/docs/2006/september/tradoc_113391.pdf (accessed on 30 December 2012)

"Joint Declaration between the Republic of India and the Republic of Indonesia," *Ministry of External Affairs*, Government of India, 23 November 2005, http://meaindia.nic.in/ (accessed on 13 March 2010)

Lipscobm, Laura et. al., "Indonesia: Select Issues," *International Monetary Fund Country Report*, no. 10/285, September 2010, http://www.imf.org/external/pubs/ft/scr/2010/cr10285.pdf (accessed on 30 December 2012)

"List of Representative offices of Indian Banks as on November 30, 2007," Reserve Bank of India, Government of India, http://rbidocs.rbi.org.in/rdocs/Content/pdfs/71206.pdf (accessed on 10 May 2010)

Mendayung Di Antara Dua Karang (Rowing Between Two Reefs) (Jakarta: Ministry of Information, 1951)

"Ministry of Foreign Affairs – Multilateral Cooperation," *Government of Indonesia*, http://www.kemlu.go.id/Pages/IFPDisplay.aspx?Name=MultilateralCooperation&IDP=11&P=Multilateral&l=en (accessed on 17 December 2012)

"Opening Statement by the President of Republic of Indonesia at the Bali Democracy Forum V," *Presidential Secretariat*, 8 November 2012, http://www.presidenri.go.id/index.php/eng/pidato/2012/11/08/1999.html (accessed on 10 December 2012)

Panetta, Leon "The US Rebalance towards the Asia-Pacific," *Shangri La Dialogue Plenary Speech*, 02 June 2012, http://www.iiss.org/en/events/shangri%20la%20dialogue/archive/sld12-43d9/first-plenary-session-2749/leon-panetta-d67b (accessed on 15 September 2012)

"Remarks by H.E. Dr. R.M. Marty M. Natalegawa, Minister for Foreign Affairs Republic of Indonesia," Opening Session of the Fourth Ministerial Conference of the Bali Process on People Smuggling, Trafficking in Persons and Related Transnational Crime

"Speech of the Minister of Foreign Affairs," Ministry of Foreign Affairs, Republic of Indonesia, http://www.deplu.go.id/Pages/Speeches.aspx?IDP=Menteri&l=en (Accessed on 21 January 2012)

"Speech of Indonesian Ambassador to the United States, Dino Patti Djalal, at USINDO Welcoming Dinner," Washington DC, 16 September 2010, http://www.embassyofindonesia.org/press/docpdf/speech/AmbDinoPattiDjalal_Remarks_USINDO_Welcoming_Dinner.pdf (accessed on 01 June 2013)

"Statement of ASEAN Foreign Ministers on ASEAN's Six-Point Principles on the South China Sea," Ministry of Foreign Affairs and International Cooperation, Kingdom of Cambodia, 20 July 2012, http://www.mfaic.gov.kh/mofa/default.aspx?id=3206 (accessed on 28 October 2012)

"Statement by Mr. Biren Nanda, Ambassador of India to Indonesia and Head of Delegation at New Asia-Africa Strategic Partnership Ministerial Conference on Capacity Building for Palestine at Jakarta," Ministry of External Affairs, Government of India, no. 14080, 14 July 2008, http://meaindia.nic.in/speech/2008/07/14ss01.htm (accessed on 06 May 2010)

Statement by H.E. Mrs. Adiyatiwidi A. Adiwoso, Deputy Permanent Representative of the Republic of Indonesia to the United Nations at the Meeting of the Open-ended Working Group on the Question of Equitable Representation on and Increase in the Membership of the Security Council and Other Matters related to the Security Council, New York, 2 September 2008, http://www.indonesiamission-ny.org/NewStatements/ps090208.htm (accessed on 15 December 2012).

"South-South Cooperation of Republic of Indonesia," Coordination Team on South-South Cooperation, Government of Indonesia, http://www.ssc-indonesia.org/

The Policy of the State Defence and Security of the Republic of Indonesia (Jakarta, Ministry of Defence and Security, 1995)

Yudhoyono, Susilo Bambang "The Confluence of Civilisations," Common Ground News Service, 13 October 2009,http://www.commongroundnews.org/article.php?id=26530&lan=en&sp=0 (Accessed on 21 January 2012)

"What is the Bali Democracy Forum," *Bali Democracy Forum*, Department of Foreign Affairs, Republic of Indonesia

"White Paper: The Jemaah Islamiyah Arrests and the Threat of Terrorism," Ministry of Home Affairs, Government of Singapore, 7 January 2003, http://www.mha.gov.sg/publication_details.aspx?pageid=35&cid=354; (accessed on 09 May 2013)

Yong, Ong Keng "ASEAN and Pan-Asian integration," *ASEAN Secretariat*, no. 18861, 2011,http://www.asean.org/18861.htm (accessed on 25 October 2012)

Yudhoyono, Susilo Bambang "An Architecture for Durable Peace in the Asia-Pacific," *Shangri La Dialogue Keynote Address*, 01 June 2012, http://www.iiss.org/en/events/shangri%20la%20dialogue/archive/sld12-43d9/opening-remarks-and-keynote-address-9e17/keynote-address-7244 (accessed on 10 January 2013)

Yudhoyono, Susilo Bambang "Indonesia's Role as Regional and Global Actor," *The Wilton Park Annual Address*, London, 2 November 2012, http://

www.presidenri.go.id/index.php/eng/pidato/2012/11/02/2001.html (accessed on 12 December 2012)

Yudhoyono, Susilo Bambang "Speech Before The Indonesian Council on World Affairs (ICWA),"http://www.presidenri.go.id/index.php/pidato/2005/05/19/332.html (accessed on 22 May 2013)

Yudhoyono, Susilo Bambang "The Big Shift and the Imperative of 21st Century Globalism," *Keynote Speech at World Economic Forum 2011*, Davos, 27 January 2011, http://www.embassyofindonesia.org/press/docpdf/THE%20BIG%20SHIFT%20AND%20THE%20IMPERATIVE%20OF%2021ST%20CENTURY%20GLOBALISM.pdf (12 December 2012)

Books

Acharya, Amitav, *Constructing a Security Community in Southeast Asia: ASEAN and the Problem of a Regional Order* (London: Routledge, 2001)

Agung, Ide Anak Agung Gde, *Twenty Years of Indonesian Foreign Policy (1945-65)* (The Hague: Mouton, 1968)

Agus P. Sari (ed.), *Indonesia and Climate Change: Current Status and Policies* (Jakarta: Peace, 2007)

Alatas, Ali, *A Voice for a Just Peace: A Collection of Speeches by Ali Alatas* (Singapore, ISEAS, 2001)

Anwar, Dewi Fortuna, *Indonesia and the Security of Southeast Asia* (Jakarta: Centre for Strategic and International Studies, 1992)

Anwar, Dewi Fortuna, *Indonesia and ASEAN: Foreign Policy and Regionalism* (Singapore: ISEAS, 1994)

Anwar, Dewi Fortuna, *Indonesia's Strategic Culture: Ketahanan Nasional, Wawasan Nusantara And Hankamrata* (Griffith, Griffith University Press, 1996)

Buzan, Barry and Waever, Ole, *Regions and Powers: The Structure of International Security* (Cambridge: Cambridge University Press, 2003)

Carnegie, Paul J., *The Road from Authoritarianism to Democratization in Indonesia* (New York: Palgrave Macmillan, 2010)

Chalmers, Ian, *Indonesia: An Introduction to Contemporary Traditions* (Victoria, Oxford University Press, 2006)

Chase, Robert, Emily Hill and Paul Kennedy (eds.), *The Pivotal States: a New framework for U.S. Policy in the Developing World* (New York: W.W. Norton, 1999)

Cooper, A.F. (ed.), *Niche Diplomacy: Middle Powers after the Cold War* (New York: Macmillan, 1997)

Cribb, Robert and Colin Brown, *Modern Indonesia: A History Since 1945* (London, Longman, 1995)

Cunha, Derek Da, *Southeast Asian Perspectives on Security* (Singapore, ISEAS, 2000)

Dueck, Colin, *Reluctant Crusaders: Power, Culture and Change in American Grand Strategy* (Princeton, N.J.: Princeton University Press, 2006)

Esposito, John L., *Unholy War: Terror in the Name of Islam* (New York, Oxford University Press, 2002)

Fassbender, Bardo, *UN Security Council Reform and the Right of Veto: A Constitutional Perspective* (Netherlands: Martinus Nijhoff Publishers, 1998)

Friedberg, Aaron L., *A Contest for Supremacy: China, America, and the Struggle for Mastery in Asia* (New York: Norton, 2011)

Gilpin, Robert, *War and Change in World Politics* (New York: Cambridge University Press, 1981)

Goldrick, James and Jack McCaffrie, *Navies of South-East Asia: A Comparative Study* (New York: Routledge, 2013)

Hart, B.H. Liddell (second revised edition), *Strategy* (New York: Meridian, 1991)

Hein, Gordon, *Suharto's Foreign Policy: Second Generation Nationalism in Indonesia*, PhD dissertation, University of California, Berkeley, CA, 1986 (Ann Arbor: UMI Dissertation Information Service, 1988)

Holbraad, C., *Middle Powers in International Politics* (London: Macmillan, 1984)

Jr., Charles V. Kegley and Eugene R. Wittkopf, *World Politics: Trend and Transformation* (New York: Worth Publishers, 1999)

Jr., Joseph S. Nye, *The Future of Power* (New York: Public Affairs, 2011)

Kaplan, Robert D., *Monsoon: The Indian Ocean and the Future of American Power* (New York: Random House, 2010)

Katzenstein, Peter J. (ed.), *The Culture of National Security: Norms and Identity in World Politics* (New York: Columbia University Press, 1996)

Kegley Jr., Charles V. and Eugene R. Wittkopf, *World Politics: Trend and Transformation* (New York: Worth Publishers, 1999)

Kennedy, Paul M., *Grand Strategies in Time of War and Peace* (New Haven: Yale University Press, 1991)

Kennedy, Paul M., *Rise and Fall of Great Powers* (London: Unwin Hyman, 1988)

Kerr, Pauline and Geoffrey Wiseman (eds.), Diplomacy in a Globalizing World: Theories and Practice (New York: Oxford University Press, 2012)

Kimche, D., *The Afro-Asian Movement: Ideology and Foreign Policy of the Third World* (New York: Halsted Press, 1973),

Legro, Jeffrey W., *Rethinking the World: Great Power Strategies and International Order* (Ithaca, NY: Cornell University Press, 2005)

Leifer, Michael, *ASEAN and the Security of Southeast Asia* (London: Routledge, 1989)

Leifer, Michael, *Indonesia's Foreign Policy* (London: Allen & Unwin, 1983)

Lim, Patrick Chee Keong, *Impact of Javanese Culture on Indonesia's Strategic Outlook and on the Indonesian Armed Forces (TNI)* (Singapore: Institute of Defence and Strategic Studies, 2000)

Mearsheimer, John J., *The Tragedy of Great Power Politics* (New York: W.W. Norton, 2001)

Mehbubani, Kishore, *The New Asian Hemisphere: The Irresistible Shift of Global Power to the East* (New York: Public Affairs, 2008)

Moertono, Soemarsaid, *State and Statecraft in Old Java: A Study of the Later Mataram Period, 16th to 19th Century* (Cornell: Cornell Southeast Asia Program Publications, 1968)

Nanda, Prakash, *Rediscovering India: Evolution of India's Look East Policy* (New Delhi: Lancer Publishers & Distributors, 2003)

Naim, Moises, *The End of Power: From Boardrooms to Battlefields and Churches to States, Why Being In Charge Isn't What It Used to Be* (Philadelphia: Basic Books, 2013)

Nau, Henry R. and Deepa M. Ollapally (eds.), *Worldviews of Aspiring Powers: Domestic Foreign Policy Debates in China, India, Iran, Japan, and Russia* (Kindle Edition) (Kindle Locations 4-6: Oxford University Press, 2012)

Nayyar B.R. and Paul, T.V., *India in the World Order: Searching for a Major Power Status* (Cambridge: Cambridge University Press, 2003)

Neumann, Iver B., *Regional Great Powers in International Politics* (London: Macmillan, 1992)

Novotny, Daniel, *Torn between America and China, Elite Perceptions and Indonesian Foreign Policy* (Singapore, ISEAS, 2010)

Nye, Jr., Joseph S., *The Future of Power* (New York, Public Affairs, 2011)

Peou, Sorpong, *Peace and Security in the Asia-Pacific: Theory and Practice* (California: Praeger, 2010)

Ping, Jonathan H., *Middle Power Statecraft: Indonesia, Malaysia and the Asia-Pacific* (Aldershot: Ashgate Publishing, 2005)

Posen, Barry R., *The Sources of Military Doctrine: France, Britain and Germany between the World Wars* (Ithaca: Cornell University Press, 1985)

Reid, Anthony (ed.), *Indonesia Rising: The Repositioning of Asia's Third Giant* (Singapore: ISEAS, 2012)

Reinhardt, Jon M., *Foreign Policy and National Integration: The Case of Indonesia*, monograph series no. 17 (New Haven: Yale University, 1971)

Roberts, Christopher B., *ASEAN Regionalism: Cooperation, Values and Institutionalization* (New York: Routledge, 2012)

Smith, Anthony L., *Strategic Centrality: Indonesia's Changing Role in ASEAN* (Singapore: ISEAS, 2000)

Snyder, Jack, *The Soviet Strategic Culture: Implications for Nuclear Options*, Rand R-2154-AF (Santa Monica: Rand Publications, 1977)

Storey, Ian, *Southeast Asia and the Rise of China: The Search for Security* (New York: Routledge, 2011)

Suryadinata, Leo, *Indonesia's Foreign Policy: Aspiring to International Leadership* (Singapore: Times Academic Press, 1996)

Tarling, Nicholas, *Status and Security in Southeast Asian State Systems* (Oxon: Routledge, 2013)

Waltz, Kenneth N., "Theory of International Politics (Massachusetts: Addison Wesley, 1979)

Weinstein, Franklin B., *Indonesian Foreign Policy and the Dilemma of Dependence: From Sukarno to Suharto* (Jakarta: Equinox Publishing, 2007)

Wolters, O.W., *History, Culture and Region in Southeast Asian Perspectives* (Singapore: ISEAS, 1982)

Journals/Magazines/Newspapers/Book Chapters

Abdussalam, Andi, "Indonesia Eager to Become Regional Power through APEC, *The Jakarta Globe*, 05 October 2013, http://www.antaranews.com/en/news/91012/indonesia-eager-to-become-regional-power-through-apec (accessed on 10 December 2013)

Abuza, Zachary, "Tentacles of Terror: Al Qaeda's Southeast Asian Network," *Contemporary Southeast Asia*, vol. 24, no. 3 (December 2002), pp. 427-65

"A clear Signal of "Core Interests" to the World," *China Daily*, 02 August 2010, http://www.chinadaily.com.cn/usa/2010-08/02/content_11083124.htm (accessed on 12 October 2012)

"Accommodating the Growing Middle Class," *The Jakarta Globe*, 21 December 2012, http://www.thejakartaglobe.com/editorials/editorial-accommodating-the-growing-middle-class/562912 (accessed on 27 December 2012)

Acharya, Amitav, "What Obama's second term means for Asia," *East Asia Forum*, 11 November 2012, http://www.eastasiaforum.org/2012/11/11/what-obamas-second-term-means-for-asia/ (accessed on 11 November 2012)

Acharya, Amitav, "Will Asia's Past Be Its Future?" *International Security*, vol. 28, no. 3 (Winter 2003-2004), pp. 149-164

Afrida, Nani, "Indonesia to send peacekeeping battalion to Darfur," *The Jakarta Post*, 08 June 2012, http://www.thejakartapost.com/news/2012/06/08/indonesia-send-peacekeeping-battalion-darfur.html (accessed on 15 December 2012)

Alexandra, Lina, "Indonesia Emerging," *The Diplomat*, 11 August 2011, http://thediplomat.com/asean-beat/2011/08/11/indonesia-emerging/ (accessed on 15 August 2012).

Alford, Peter, "Fifteen years after Humiliation, Indonesia turns the tables on IMF," *The Australian*, 11 July 2012, http://www.theaustralian.com.au/news/world/fifteen-years-after-humiliation-indonesia-turns-the-tables-on-imf/story-e6frg6so-1226422907171 (accessed on 17 December 2012)

Allard, Tom, "Indonesia fears US forces could create 'vicious circle of tension'," *Sydney Morning Herald*, 17 November 2011, http://www.smh.com.au/world/indonesia-fears-us-forces-could-create-vicious-circle-of-tension-20111117-1nk0e.html (accessed on 03 January 2013)

Andrew, Michael and Peng Yali, "The Rise of the Middle Class in Asian Emerging Markets," *KPMG Report*, April 2012, http://www.kpmg.com/cn/en/IssuesAndInsights/ArticlesPublications/Documents/Middle-Class-Asia-Emerging-Markets-201206-2.pdf (accessed on 27 December 2012)

Anjaiah, Veeramalla, "Relations between RI and India reach 'historic high' in 2009," *The Jakarta Post*, 04 January 2010, http://www.thejakartapost.com/news/2010/01/04/relations-between-ri-and-india-reach-%E2%80%98historic-high%E2%80%99-2009.html (accessed on 05 September 2011)

Anjaiah, Veeramalla and Yassine Majdi, "Russia's Relations with RI growing in a 'Dynamic Way'," *The Jakarta Post*, 12 June 2009, http://www.thejakarta post.com/news/2009/06/12/russia039s-relations-with-ri-growing-a-dynamic-way039.html (accessed on 12 December 2012)

Anwar, Dewi Fortuna, "A Problem of Mixed Messages," *The Asialink Essays* 2012, vol. 4, no. 6, August 2012, http://www.asialink.unimelb.edu.au/__data/assets/pdf_file/0004/614425/Mixed_Messages-Anwar.pdf (accessed on 19 December 2012)

Anwar, Dewi Fortuna, "Foreign Policy, Islam and Democracy in Indonesia," *Journal of Indonesian Social Sciences and Humanities*, vol. 3, 2010, pp. 37-54

Anwar, Dewi Fortuna, "Key Aspects of Indonesia's Foreign Policy" in Trends in Southeast Asia Series, no. 9 (Singapore, ISEAS, 2003)

Anwar, Dewi Fortuna, "National versus Regional Resilience: An Indonesian Perspective," in Cunha, Derek Da *Southeast Asian Perspectives on Security* (Singapore: ISEAS, 2000), pp. 81-96

"APEC Strengthens Indonesia's Position as Regional Power," *The Jakarta Post*, 05 October 2013, http://www.thejakartapost.com/news/2013/10/05/apec-strengthens-indonesias-position-regional-power.html (accessed on 10 December 2013)

Ardiyansyah, Fitrian, "Durban climate talks bring mixed results for Indonesia," *East Asia Forum*, 20 December 2011, http://www.eastasiaforum.org/2011/12/20/durban-climate-talks-bring-mixed-results-for-indonesia/ (accessed on 16 December 2012)

Armstrong, David, "The Next Yugoslavia? The Fragmentation of Indonesia," *Diplomacy & Statecraft*, vol. 15, no. 4 (2004), pp. 783-808

Arnold, Wayne, "Surprise Pressure From Myanmar's Neighbors," *The New York Times*, 20 November 2007, http://www.nytimes.com/2007/11/20/world/asia/20asean.html?_r=1&oref=slogin (accessed on 25 October 2012)

Arsana, I Made Andi, "Celebrating a hundred years of Maritime Nation," *The Jakarta Post*, 26 April 2008, http://www.thejakartapost.com/news/2008/04/26/celebrating-a-hundred-years-maritime-nation.html (accessed on 16 May 2013)

Art, Robert J., "A Defensible Defense: America's Grand Strategy after the Cold War," *International Security*, vol. 15, no. 4 (Spring 1991), pp. 5-53

Aswicahyono, H. and D. Friawan, "Infrastructure Development in Indonesia," in N. Kumar (ed.), International Infrastructure Development in East Asia – Towards Balanced Regional Development and Integration, *ERIA Research Project Report 2007-2* (Chiba: IDE-JETRO, 2008)

Ayoob, Mohammad, "Southeast Asia in Indian Foreign Policy: Some Preliminary Observations," *Contemporary Southeast Asia*, vol. 9, no. 1 (June 1987), pp. 1-11

Azra, Azyumardi, "Islam, Indonesia and Democracy," *Strategic Review*, vol. 1, no. 1, August 2011, p. 74

Azra, Azyumardi, "Islam in Indonesian foreign policy: assessing impacts of Islam revivalism during the Soeharto era," *Studia Islamika: Indonesian Journal for Islamic Studies*," vol.7, no.3, 2000, pp. 1-29

Bakrie, Anindya Novyan, "US Pivot to the Region has Changed the Game," *The Jakarta Globe*, 03 January 2012, http://www.thejakartaglobe.com/columnists/us-pivot-to-the-region-has-changed-the-game/488796 (accessed on 18 September 2012)

Bandoro, Bantarto, "Democracy and Indonesian Diplomacy Beyond 2009," *Jurnal Diplomasi*, vol. 1, no. 1 (June 2009), p. 36

Bedi, Rahul, "A new Doctrine for the Navy," *Frontline*, vol. 21, no. 14 (03-16 July 2004), http://www.hinduonnet.com/fline/fl2114/stories/20040716002104600.htm (accessed on 10 May 2010)

Belford, Aubrey, "Indonesian Assault Victim Gets Harsher Sentence Than His Attackers," *The New York Times*, 15 August 2011, http://www.nytimes.com/2011/08/16/world/asia/16indonesia.html?_r=0 (accessed on 01 May 2013)

Bellman, Eric and Martin Vaughan, "Indonesia Seeks Larger Role in Asean," *Wall Street Journal*, 9 May 2011, http://online.wsj.com/article/SB10001424052748703864204576310613441920214.html

Berg, Andrew G. and Jonathan D. Ostry, "Inequality and Unsustainable Growth: Two Sides of the Same Coin?," *IMF Staff Discussion Note*, no. SDN/11/08, 08 April 2011.

Bolton, John R., "Indonesia: Asia's Yugoslavia," *Far Eastern Economic Review*, vol. 162, no. 13, 1 April 1999, p. 31

Brown, Jessica, "Jakarta's Juggling Act: Balancing China and America in the Asia-Pacific, *CIS Foreign Policy Analysis*, no. 5, 3 February 2011, http://www.cis.org.au/publications/foreign-policy-analysis/article/2342-jakartas-juggling-act-balancing-china-and-america-in-the-asia-pacific (accessed on 18 May 2013)

Brown, Matt, "Indonesian military backs religious persecution," *Australian Broadcasting Corporation*, 16 March 2011, http://www.abc.net.au/lateline/content/2011/s3166034.htm (accessed on 01 May 2013)

Bundo, Joana, "The Middle Class Problem that Threatens Indonesia," *Asia House*, 19 December 2012, http://asiahouse.org/news-and-analysis/detail?id=141 (accessed on 28 December 2012)

Bush, Robin, "Indonesia: An Example for Egypt, or a Democracy in Retreat?," *The Asia Foundation*, 16 February 2011, http://asiafoundation.org/in-asia/2011/02/16/indonesia-an-example-for-egypt-or-a-democracy-in-retreat/ (accessed on 20 December 2012)

Bussière, Matthieu and Arnaud Mehl, "China's and India's Roles in Global Trade and Finance: Twin Titans for the New Millenium?" *ECB Occasional Papers*, no. 80, January 2008, European Central Bank, http://www.ecb.int/pub/pdf/scpops/ecbocp80.pdf (20 September 2012)

Cahyafitri, Raras, "RI risks falling into middle-income trap," *The Jakarta Post*, 13October 2012, http://www.thejakartapost.com/news/2012/10/13/ri-risks-falling-middle-income-trap.html (accessed on 14 January 2014)

Camroux, David, "Asia . . . whose Asia? A 'Return to the Future' of a Sino-Indic Asian Community," *The Pacific Review*, vol. 20, no. 4, December 2007, pp. 551–575;

Camroux, David, "Towards an Asian Community: the East Asian Summit, Kuala Lumpur," *CERi Sciences Po*, January 2006, http://www.ceri-sciences-po.org (accessed on 14 October 2012)

Carothers, Thomas, "The New Republic: A Lesson for Egypt In Indonesia," *National Public Radio*, 03 February 2011, http://www.npr.org/2011/02/03/133461179/the-new-republic-a-lesson-for-egypt-in-indonesia (accessed on 20 December 2012)

Carothers, Thomas, "The New Republic: A Lesson for Egypt In Indonesia," *National Public Radio*, 03 February 2011, http://www.npr.org/2011/02/03/133461179/the-new-republic-a-lesson-for-egypt-in-indonesia (accessed on 21 May 2013)

Chandra, Kartika, "Russia Proposes Indonesia Join BRIC," *Tempo Interactive*, 19 April 2010, http://www.tempo.co.id/hg/nasional/2010/04/19/brk,20100419-241568,uk.html (accessed on 09 May 2010)

"Chapter Six: Asia," *The Military Balance*, vol. 111, no. 1, 2011, pp. 195-292

"Chapter Ten: Current trends in Asia-Pacific defence industries," *The Military Balance*, vol. 109, no. 1, 2009, p. 455-460;

"CIL Plans to Invest in Overseas Coalmines (in 15-20 coalmines in the US, Indonesia and Australia," *India Business Insight*, 01 February 2010 (accessed on 07 May 2010 via Lexis Nexis Academic)

Cheng-Chwee, Kuik, "Multilateralism in China's ASEAN Policy: Its Evolution, Characteristics, and Aspiration," *Contemporary Southeast Asia*, vol. 27, no. 1, 2005, pp. 102-122;

Cheng-Chwee, Kuik, "The Essence of Hedging: Malaysia and Singapore's Response to a Rising China," *Contemporary Southeast Asia*, vol. 30, no. 2 (August 2008), pp. 159-185;

"China Since 1990: Facts and Figures Tell of Rising Prosperity," *People's Daily*, 16 September 2002, http://english.peopledaily.com.cn/200209/16/eng20020916_103251.shtml (accessed on 15 September 2012)

"China, Indonesia Expand Military Cooperation," *Defence Update*, 29 July 2012, http://defense-update.com/20120729_china-indonesia-military-cooperation.html (accessed on 20 October 2012)

"China, Vietnam, Philippines press maritime claims," *Reuters*, 07 June 2011, http://in.reuters.com/article/2011/06/07/idINIndia-57541120110607 (accessed on 07 October 2012)

"Chinese, Indonesian Presidents Meet on Cooperation," *Xinhuanet*, 08 September 2012, http://news.xinhuanet.com/english/china/2012-09/08/c_131835517.htm (accessed on 20 October 2012)

Christensen, Thomas J., "Fostering Stability or Creating a Monster?: The Rise of China and U.S. Policy toward East Asia," *International Security*, vol. 31, no. 1 (Summer 2006), pp. 81-126

Ciorciari, John David (2009), "The Balance of Great-Power Influence in Contemporary Southeast Asia," *International Relations of the Asia-Pacific*, vol. 9, no. 1, pp. 157-196

Coca, Nithin "How far can Indonesia's consumption-driven growth go?," *Penang Monthly*, 27 March 2013, http://penangmonthly.com/how-far-can-indonesias-consumption-driven-growth-go/ (accessed on 21 May 2013)

Cochrane, Jow, "'Beef-gate' Transfixes Scandal-Prone Indonesia," *New York Times*, May 16, 2013, http://www.nytimes.com/2013/05/17/world/asia/beefgate-transfixes-scandal-prone-indonesia.html?pagewanted=all&_r=0 (accessed on 23 May 2013)

Cooper, Andrew F., "The G8 as Complex Diplomacy," http://g8heiligendamm.wordpress.com/2007/06/07/the-g8-as-complex-diplomacy/ (accessed on 13 October 2012)

"Corruption in Indonesia," *Indonesia-Investments*, http://www.indonesia-investments.com/doing-business/risks/corruption/item235 (accessed on 18 December 2013)

Dalby, Simon, "Critical Geopolitics: Discourse, Difference, and Dissent," in Klaus Dodds (ed.) *Geopolitics*, second volume (New Delhi: Sage Publications, 2009), pp.

Darmosumarto, Santo, "Indonesia: A New 'Middle Power'," *The Jakarta Post,* 30 October 2009,http://www.thejakartapost.com/news/2009/10/30/indonesia-a-new-middle-power039.html (accessed on 18 May 2013)

Deskar, Barry, "Russia looks to boost its Asia-Pacific credentials," *Today Online*, 06 September 2012, http://www.todayonline.com/World/EDC120906-0000023/Russia-looks-to-boost-its-Asia-Pacific-credentials (accessed on 08 October 2012)

Djalal, Dino Pati, "Promise of the 21st Century," 16 March 2011, http://www.youtube.com/watch?v=IdGciEyAOGA (accessed on 20 January 2013)

Drysdale, Peter, "China and India as Strategic Partners," *East Asia Forum*, 16 July 2012, http://www.eastasiaforum.org/2012/07/16/china-and-india-as-strategic-partners/ (accessed on 13 October 2012)

Dupont, Alan, "Indonesian Defence Strategy and Security: Time for a Rethink?," *Contemporary Southeast Asia*, vol. 18, no. 3 (December 1996), pp. 275-297

"East Asia and Australasia," *The Military Balance*, vol. 107, no. 1, 2007, pp. 331-384

"East Asia Pacific Economic Update, October 2013 – Rebuilding Policy Buffers, Reinvigorating Growth," *The World Bank Economic Update,* October 2013, http://www.worldbank.org/en/region/eap/publication/east-asia-pacific-economic-update-october-2013 (accessed on 23 December 2013)

Evans, Gareth, "Foreword," in Anthony Reid (ed.), *Indonesia Rising: The Repositioning of Asia's Third Giant* (Singapore, ISEAS, 2012), pp. xv-xvii

Emmerson, Donald K., "Is Indonesia Rising: It Depends," in Anthony Reid (ed.), *Indonesia Rising: The Repositioning of Asia's Third Giant* (Singapore, ISEAS, 2012), pp. 49-76

Farrell, Maureen, "Indonesia: The newest BRIC?," *CNN Money*, 15 October 2012, http://money.cnn.com/2012/10/15/investing/indonesia-bric/index.html (accessed on 27 December 2012)

Fealy, Greg Virginia Hooker and Sally White, "Indonesia," in Greg Fealy and Virginia Hooker (eds.) *Voices of Islam in Southeast Asia: A Contemporary Sourcebook* (Singapore, ISEAS, 2006), p. 50

Ferry Akbar Pasaribu, "Scientific and economic diplomacy a pressing agenda," *The Jakarta Post*, 24 February 2012, http://www.thejakartapost.com/news/

2012/02/24/scientific-and-economic-diplomacy-a-pressing-agenda.html (accessed on 4 March 2012)

Fravel, M. Taylor, "International Relations Theory and China's Rise: Assessing China's Potential for Territorial Expansion," *International Studies Review*, vol. 12, no. 4 (December 2010), pp. 505–532

Frederick Situmorang, "'Wawasan nusantara' vs UNCLOS," *The Jakarta Post*, 29 January 2013, p. 6

Fogarty, David, "Indonesia Approves Landmark Forest Protection Project, *TheJakarta Globe*, 05 December 2012, http://www.thejakartaglobe.com/home/indonesia-approves-landmark-forest-protection-project/559941 (accessed on 16 December 2012)

Fontaine, Richard and Daniel M. Kliman, "International Order and Global Swing States," *The Washington Quarterly*, vol. 36, no. 1 (Winter 2013), pp. 93-109

Gallagher, Michael G., 'Future Indian-South Korean ties: can Seoul use India to balance China?," *Korean Journal of Defense Analysis*, vol. 22, no. 1, 2010, pp. 43-56

Ganesan, S., "Call for Global Pact on Disaster Risk Reduction," *The Hindu*, 27 October 2012, http://www.thehindu.com/sci-tech/energy-and-environment/call-for-global-pact-on-disaster-risk-reduction/article4038619.ece (accessed on 29 October 2012)

Garnaut, Ross, "Indonesia in the New World Balance," in Anthony Reid (ed.), *Indonesia Rising: The Repositioning of Asia's Third Giant* (Singapore, ISEAS, 2012), pp. 14-27

Glosney, Michael A., "Heading towards a Win-Win Future?: Recent Developments in China's Policy toward Southeast Asia," *Asian Security*, vol. 2, no. 1, 2006, pp. 24-57

Goh, Evelyn, "Institutions and the Great Power Bargain in East Asia: ASEAN's Limited "brokerage" Role," *International Relations of the Asia-Pacific*, vol. 11, no. 3, 2011, pp. 373-401.

Goh, Evelyn, "Meeting the China Challenge: The U.S. in Southeast Asian Regional Security Strategies," *East-West Center Policy Studies*, no. 16, 2005

Goh, Evelyn, "Singapore's Reaction to Rising China: Deep Engagement and Strategic Adjustment," *RSIS Working Papers*, no.67, 2004, http://www.rsis.edu.sg/publications/WorkingPapers/WP67.pdf (accessed on 12 October 2012)

Goh, Evelyn, "Great Powers and Hierarchical Order in Southeast Asia: Analyzing Regional Security Strategies" *International Security*, vol. 32, no. 3 (Winter 2007-08), pp. 113-157

Gray, Colin, 'Strategic Culture as Context: The First Generation of Theory

Strikes Back', *Review of International Studies*, vol. 25, no. 1, 1999, pp. 49-69.

Guharoy, Debnath, "Analysis: How big is Indonesia's middle-class today?," *The Jakarta Post*, 28 February 2012, http://www.thejakartapost.com/news/2012/02/28/analysis-how-big-indonesia-s-middle-class-today.html (accessed on 27 December 2012)

Gujaral, I.K., "Lands of the Asian Miracle," *The Hindu*, 10 August 1996

Hao, Su, "Harmonious World: the Conceived International Order in Framework of China's Foreign Affairs," in Masafumi Iida (ed.) *China's Shift: Global Strategy of the Rising Power* (Tokyo, National Institute for Defense Studies, 2009), pp. 29-56

Hart, Andrew F. and Bruce D. Jones, "How do Rising Powers Rise?" *Survival*, 52, no. 6 (2010): 63-88

Hasan, Noorhaidi, "Faith and Politics: The Rise of the Laskar Jihad in the Era of Transition in Indonesia," *Indonesia*, no. 73 (April 2002), pp. 145-169.

Hatta, Mohammad, "Indonesia's Foreign Policy," *Foreign Affairs: an American Quarterly Review*, vol. 31, no. 1 (1952-53), pp. 441-452

Hatta, Mohammad (1958), "Indonesia between the Power Blocs," *Foreign Affairs*, vol. 36, no. 3 (April), pp. 480-490

He, Kai, "Indonesia's Foreign Policy after Soeharto: International Pressure, Democratization, and Policy Change," *International Relations of the Asia-Pacific*, vol. 8, no. 1, 2008, pp. 47-72

"High Profile Corruption Cases in Indonesia," *Global Indonesian Voices*, 14 October 2013, http://www.globalindonesianvoices.com/10165/high-profile-corruption-cases-in-indonesia/ (accessed on 18 December 2013)

Hodgson, An "Indonesia's Rising Middle Class to Transform the Country's Consumer Market," *Euromonitor International*, 3 July 2012, http://blog.euromonitor.com/2012/07/indonesias-rising-middle-class-to-transform-the-countrys-consumer-market.html (accessed on 28 December 2012)

"Hot Growth Markets in the Spotlight Indonesia: Hidden Treasure – Indonesia," *Ernst & Young*, http://www.ey.com/Publication/vwLUAssets/Hot_growth_markets_in_the_spotlight_-_Hidden_treasure-Indonesia/$FILE/Hidden_Treasure_Indonesia.pdf (accessed on 27 December 2012)

"How to gracefully step aside," *The Economist*, 10 January 2011, http://www.economist.com/blogs/freeexchange/2011/01/china (accessed on 15 September 2012)

Huei, Pang Yang, "The Four Faces of Bandung: Detainees, Soldiers, Revolutionaries and Statesmen," *Journal of Contemporary Asia*, vol. 39, no. 1 (February 2009), p. 63-86

Hurrell, Andrew, "Hegemony, Liberalism and Global Order: What Space for Would-be Great Powers?," *International Affairs*, 82, no. 1, 2006, 1-19;

Hussain, Zakir, "Indonesia Seeks to Boost Arms Industry," *The Jakarta Globe*, 24 March 2012, http://www.thejakartaglobe.com/news/indonesia-seeks-to-boost-arms-industry/506923 (accessed on 30 December 2012)

Ikenberry, G. John, "The Rise of China: Power, Institutions and the Western Order," in Robert S. Ross, Feng Zhu (eds.), *China's Ascent: Power, Security, and the Future of International Politics* (Ithaca: Cornell University Press 2008)

Ikenberry, G. John, "The Rise of China and the Future of the West: Can the Liberal System Survive?," *Foreign Affairs*, vol. 87, no. 1 (January-February 2008), http://www.foreignaffairs.com/articles/63042/g-john-ikenberry/the-rise-of-china-and-the-future-of-the-west (accessed on 14 November 2013)

In Religion's Name: Abuses against Religious Minorities in Indonesia," *Human Rights Watch* (USA: Human Rights Watch, 2013), http://www.hrw.org/sites/default/files/reports/indonesia0213_ForUpload_0.pdf (accessed on 01 May 2013)

"Indonesia Backgrounder: How the Jemaah Islamiyah Terrorist Network Operates," *International Crisis Group (ICG) Asia Report*, no. 43, 11 December 2002, http://www.crisisgroup.org/~/media/Files/asia/south-east-asia/indonesia/043%20-%20Indonesia%20Backgrounder%20-%20How%20The%20Jemaah%20Islamiyah%20Terrorist%20Network%20Operates.pdf (accessed on 20 March 2013)

"Income Inequality – A Risk to Indonesia's Spectacular Growth?," *CEIC Data Blog*, 24 April 2012, http://blog.securities.com/2012/04/income-inequality-a-risk-to-indonesias-spectacular-growth/ (accessed on 21 May 2012)

"India, Indonesia Mull Joint Defense Hardware Production," *India Defence Online*, 15 June 2007, http://www.india-defence.com/reports-3311 (accessed on 05 May 2010)

"India's Nalco To Invest Big In Indonesia's Aluminium Project," *Bernama*, 12 April 2010, www.bernama.com/bernama/v5/newsbusiness.php?id=489803 (accessed on 08 May 2010)

"Indonesia Calls for UN Reform," *Antara News*, 27 September 2011, http://www.antaranews.com/en/news/76041/indonesia-calls-for-un-reform (accessed on 16 December 2012)

"Indonesia enjoys relations with almost all UN member states: FM," *People's Daily Online*, 04 January 2012, http://english.peopledaily.com.cn/90777/7695887.html (accessed on 16 December 2012)

"Indonesia to Send 4,000 Troops, Helicopters to UN Peacekeeping Missions," *The Jakarta Globe*, 20 March 2012, http://www.thejakartaglobe.com/home/indonesia-to-send-4000-troops-helicopters-to-un-peacekeeping-missions/506100 (accessed on 15 December 2012)

"Indonesia Wants Regional Bloc to be 'Strong Voice'," *Bangkok Post*, 17 December 2010 http://www.burmanet.org/news/2010/12/17/bangkok-post-indonesia-wants-regional-bloc-to-be-strong-voice/ (accessed on 18 May 2013)

"Indonesia wants to advance peacekeeping role in 2011," *The Jakarta Post*, 08 January 2011, http://www.thejakartapost.com/news/2011/01/08/indonesia-wants-advance-peacekeeping-role-2011.html (accessed on 15 December 2012)

"Indonesia-Russia Relations Bolstered Through Real Cooperation Agreement," *The President Post*, 26 March 2012, www.thepresidentpost.com/?p=16194 (accessed on 25 October 2012)

"Indonesia-U.S. Relations: A Comprehensive Partnership," *Metropolitan Corporate Counsel*, vol. 19, no. 3, 28 February 2011, http://www.metro corpcounsel.com/pdf/2011/March/45.pdf (accessed on 18 December 2012)

"Indonesia, Countries urge UN to Implement cease fire in Libya," *People's Daily Online*, 28 March 2011, http://english.peopledaily.com.cn/90001/90777/ 90855/7333132.html (accessed on 16 December 2012)

"Indonesia, India consider joint production of military equipment," *Agence France Presse*, 26 November 2006,

"Indonesia, Indian Navies Conduct Joint Patrols in Malacca Strait," *BBC Monitoring Asia Pacific – Political*, 12 March 2010,

"Indonesia: Defending Democracy – A Global Survey of Foreign Policy Trends 1992-2002," *Democracy Coalition Project*, http://www.demcoalition.org/pdf/ Indonesia.pdf (accessed on 01 December 2012)

"Indonesia: June 2011," *Economist Intelligence Unit Country Report*, June 2011

"Indonesia: October 2010," *Economist Intelligence Unit Country Report*, October 2010

"Indonesia's Cement Consumption Grows 8.6% in January – April 2013," *Indonesia Investments*, 13 May 2013, http://www.indonesia-investments. com/nl/business/business-columns/inequality-of-the-regions-economic-significance-towards-indonesias-economy/item730 (accessed on 21 May 2013)

"Indonesia's Economic Competitiveness Improving: WER Report," *Asia Pulse*, 08 June 2011 (accessed via Lexis Nexis Academic)

"Indonesia's Economy to grow slower," *Antara News*, 16 December 2013, http:/ /www.antaranews.com/en/news/91805/indonesias-economy-to-grow-slower (accessed on 16 December 2013);

"Indonesia's Middle Class: Missing BRIC in the wall," *The Economist*, 21 July 2011, http://www.economist.com/node/18989153 (accessed on 27 December 2012)

"Indonesia's Naval Development and Maritime Cooperation," *RSIS Policy Report*, 05 July 2012, http://www.rsis.edu.sg/publications/policy_report/Indonesia_Naval_Development_Maritime_Cooperation_5_July_2012.pdf (accessed on 17 November 2012)

"Indonesia needs more investments for economic growth," *Antara News*, 19 August 2013, http://www.antaranews.com/en/news/90330/indonesia-needs-more-investments-for-economic-growth (accessed on 16 December 2013)

"Indonesian Muslim leader gets jail for inciting violence," *Reuters*, 30 October 2008, http://in.reuters.com/article/2008/10/30/idINIndia-36221020081030 (accessed on 15 May 2013)

"Indonesian police say bomb being prepared for terrorist attack explodes, 2 suspects escape," *The Washington Post*, 09 September 2012, http://www.washingtonpost.com/world/asia_pacific/indonesian-police-say-bomb-being-prepared-for-terrorist-attack-explodes-injuring-5-people/2012/09/09/e0499e6a-fa3a-11e1-a0a1-b07778c66e04_story.html (accessed on 16 September 2012)

Indrakesuma, Rizali "Indonesia-India relations: Some updates," *The Jakarta Post*, 11 October 2013, http://www.thejakartapost.com/news/2013/10/11/indonesia-india-relations-some-updates.html (accessed on 22 December 2013)

International Monetary Fund, "Asia and Pacific Economic Outlook: October 2013 Update," *IMF Regional Economic Outlook Update*, 11 October 2013, http://www.imf.org/external/pubs/ft/reo/2013/apd/eng/areo1013.pdf (accessed on 16 December 2013)

Islam, Shada "Indonesian example," *The Dawn*, 10 December 2012, http://dawn.com/2011/12/10/indonesian-example/ (accessed on 20 December 2012)

Itzkowitz-Shifrinson, Joshua "Assessing China's Rise: Power and Influence in the 21st Century" Massachusetts Institute of Technology Workshop Report, 27-28 February, 2009, http://web.mit.edu/ssp/publications/conf_reports/china_rising_workshop_report.pdf (accessed on 10 October 2013)

Jaffrelot, Christophe "India's Look East Policy: an Asianist Strategy in Perspective," *India Review*, vol. 2, no.2, (April 2003), pp. 35-68;

"Jakarta is Affirmed to be a Diplomatic Capital City," *ASEAN Secretariat*, 31 May 2012, no. 27026, http://www.aseansec.org/27026.htm (accessed on 27 October 2012)

"Japan-Indonesia Summit Meeting (Summary)," Ministry of Foreign Affairs of Japan, 19 June 2012, http://www.mofa.go.jp/region/asia-paci/indonesia/meeting1206_pm.html (accessed on 13 December 2013)

Jemadu, Aleksius, "Parts Washington, Beijing and Delhi: The Jakarta Consensus," *The Jakarta Globe*, 13 September 2010, http://www.thejakartaglobe.com/opinion/parts-washington-beijing-and-delhi-the-jakarta-consensus/395920 (accessed on 20 January 2013)

Jha, Ganganath "A Brief Survey of India-Indonesia Relations," *Contemporary Southeast Asia*, vol. 17, no. 4 (March 1996), pp. 389-405

Johnson, Michael "Indonesia looks to Africa, the Middle East to sell military equipment," *Asia-Pacific Defense Forum*, 05 October 2012, http://apdforum.com/en_GB/article/rmiap/articles/online/features/2012/10/05/indonesia-arms-export (accessed on 30 December 2012)

Johnston, Alastair Iain, 'Strategic Cultures Revisited: Reply to Colin Gray', *Review of International Studies*, vol. 25, no. 3, 1999, pp. 519-523

Johnston, Alastair Iain, "Thinking about Strategic Culture," *International Security*, vol. 19, no. 4, 1995, pp. 32-64;

Johnston, Alastair Iain, *Cultural Realism: Strategic Culture and Grand Strategy in Chinese History* (New Jersey: Princeton University Press, 1995)

Jones, Sidney, "The changing nature of Jemaah Islamiyah," *Australian Journal of International Affairs*, vol. 59, no. 2, June 2005, pp. 169-178;

Jordaan, Eduard (2003), "The concept of a middle power in international relations: distinguishing between emerging and traditional middle powers," *Politikon*, vol. 30, no. 1, pp. 165-181

Jorgensen-Dahl, Arnfinn "Indonesia as a Regional Great Power," in Neumann, Iver B. *Regional Great Powers in International Politics* (London: Macmillan, 1992)

Jotzo, Frank, "Indonesia a key player in climate deal?," *East Asia Forum*, 08 February 2009, http://www.eastasiaforum.org/2009/02/08/indonesia-a-key-player-in-climate-deal/ (accessed on 16 December 2012)

"KS Oils buys palm plantation in Indonesia," *The Hindu Business Line*, 27 March 2010

Kang, David C., "Hierarchy, Balancing, and Empirical Puzzles in Asian International Relations' *International Security*, vol. 28, no. 3 (Winter 2003-04), pp. 165-180

Kang, David C., "Getting Asia Wrong: The Need for New Analytical Frameworks," *International Security*, vol. 27, no. 4 (Spring 2003), pp. 57-85

Kaplan, Robert D., "The Geography of Chinese Power: How Far Can Beijing Reach on Land and at Sea?," *Foreign Affairs*, vol. 89, no. 3, May-June 2010, pp. 22-41

Keating, Joshua, "The Stories you Missed in 2010," *Foreign Policy Special Report*, 28 November 2010, http://www.foreignpolicy.com/articles/2010/11/29/

the_stories_you_missed_in_2010?page=0,0#sthash.hzXnJn9J.dpbs (accessed on 22 December 2013)

Kelemen, R. Daniel, "The Study of Critical Junctures: Theory, Narrative and Counterfactuals in Institutional Theory in Historical Institutionalism," *World Politics*, vol. 59, no. 3 (April 2007), pp. 341–69

Khalik, Abdul and Desy Nurhayati, "RI Wants NAM to Play Greater Role on World Stage," *The Jakarta Post*, 26 May 2011, http://www.thejakartapost.com/print/325293 (accessed on 13 September 2011)

Khurana, Gurpreet S., "Maritime Security in the Indian Ocean: Convergence Plus Cooperation Equals Resonance," *Strategic Analysis*, vol. 28, no 3 (July-September 2004), p. 418

Kimura, Ehito, "Indonesia in 2011: A Glass Half-Empty," *Asian Survey*, vol. 52, no. 1, p. 186

Kliman, Daniel M., "Global Swing States and U.S. Strategy," GMF Policy Brief, August 2013, http://www.gmfus.org/wpcontent/blogs.dir/1/files_mf/1377879312Kliman_GSSandUSStrategy_Aug13.pdf (accessed on 22 December 2013)

Koh, Tommy, 'Australia's Asia Pacific Community Proposal: Some Issues for Discussion', Conference on the Asia-Pacific: A Community for the twenty-first Century, Sydney, 3-5 December 2009, http://www.apc2009conference.org/userfiles/Koh.pdf (accessed on 15 September 2012)

Kroef, Justus M. van der, "Entrepreneur and Middle Class in Indonesia," *Economic Development and Cultural Change*, vol. 2, no. 4, 1954, pp. 297-325

Kuntjoro, Irene and Sofiah Jamil, "Triple Trouble in Indonesia: Strengthening Jakarta's Disaster Preparedness," *RSIS Commentary*, no. 138/2010, 1 November 2010, www.rsis.edu.sg/publications/Perspective/RSIS1382010.pdf (accessed on 15 September 2012)

Kurlantzik, Joshua, "Is Egypt the Next Indonesia?," *Council on Foreign Relations*, 07 February 2011, http://blogs.cfr.org/asia/2011/02/07/is-egypt-the-next-indonesia/ (accessed on 20 December 2012)

Kwok, Yenni, "Shocking Arrest Underscores Endemic Corruption in Indonesia's Energy Sector," *Time World*, 15 August 2013, http://world.time.com/2013/08/15/shock-arrest-underscores-endemic-corruption-in-indonesias-energy-sector/ (accessed on 18 December 2013)

Laksmana, Evan A., "Indonesia's Rising Regional and Global Profile: Does Size Really Matter?," *Contemporary Southeast Asia: A Journal of International and Strategic Affairs*, vol. 33, no. 2 (August 2011), pp. 157-182

Laksmana, Evan A., "The Enduring Strategic Trinity: Explaining Indonesia's Geopolitical Architecture," *Journal of Indian Ocean Region*, vol. 7, no. 1, June 2011, pp. 95-116

Lantis, Jeffrey S., "Strategic Culture and National Security Policy," *International Studies Review*, vol. 4, no. 3, December 2002, pp. 87-113

Legro, Jeffrey W., "What China will Want: The Future Intentions of a Rising Power," *Perspectives on Politics*, vol. 5, no. 3, September 2007, pp. 515-534

LI, Chenyang, "China–Myanmar Comprehensive Strategic Cooperative Partnership: A Regional Threat?," *Journal of Current Southeast Asian Affairs*, vol. 31, no. 1, 2012, pp. 53-72

Lim, Kevin, "Indonesia Faces 'Middle-Income Trap' Without Reform: IMF," *The Jakarta Globe*, 29 April 2013, http://www.thejakartaglobe.com/business/indonesia-faces-middle-income-trap-without-reform-imf/ (accessed on 14 January 2014)

Litke, Mark, "SARS Virus Devastating Asia's Economies," *ABC News*, 19 April 2003, http://abcnews.go.com/Health/story?id=116746&page=1#.Uased5Xkbdk (accessed on 16 September 2012)

Lutfia, Ismira, "Indonesia Leads from the Front on ASEAN," *The Jakarta Globe*, 08 August 2012, http://www.thejakartaglobe.com/home/indonesia-leads-from-the-front-on-asean/536384 (accessed on 28 October 2012)

Malik, Mohan, "The East Asia Summit," *Australian Journal of International Affairs*, vol. 60, no. 2 (June 2006), pp. 207-211

Malik, Mohan, 'The East Asia Community and the Role of External Powers: Ensuring Asian Multilateralism is not Shanghaied', *Korean Journal of Defense Analysis*, vol. 19, no. 4 (Winter 2007), pp. 29-50

Maull, Hanns W., "The Rise of New Powers: Implications for the Transatlantic World," in Daniel S. Hamilton and Kurt Volker, *Transatlantic 2020: A Tale of Four Futures* (Washington, DC: Center for Transatlantic Relations, 2011), pp. 71-92

McBeth, John, "Indonesia's Quiet Welcome of US Troops in Region," *Straits Times*, 18 September 2012

Mearsheimer, John J., "The Rise of China will not be Peaceful at all," *The Australian*, 18 November 2005, http://mearsheimer.uchicago.edu/pdfs/P0014.pdf (accessed on 10 October 2012)

Mietzner, Marcus, "The Politics of Military Reform in Post-Suharto Indonesia: Elite Conflict, Nationalism, and Institutional Resistance," *East West Centre Policy Studies*, no. 23, 2006, East West Centre, http://www.eastwestcenter.org/fileadmin/stored/pdfs/PS023.pdf

Mocuta, Simona, "S&P Upgrades Indonesia's Sovereign Risk Rating to Just Below Investment Grade," *Global Insight*, 11 April 2011 (accessed via Lexis Nexis Academic)

Maulia, Erwida, "Economy remains priority for RI diplomacy in 2012," *The Jakarta Post*, 05 January 2012, http://www.thejakartapost.com/news/2012/

01/05/economy-remains-priority-ri-diplomacy-2012.html-0 (accessed on 04 March 2012)

Mohan, C. Raja, "India in East Asia," *Australia-India Strategic Lecture Series 2007*, Lowy Institute for International Policy, Melbourne, 21 February 2007, http://www.lowyinstitute.org/Publication.asp?pid=548 (accessed on 10 October 2012)

Moss, Trefor, "Indonesia Talks Defense With China," *The Diplomat*, 01 August 2012, http://thediplomat.com/flashpoints-blog/2012/08/01/indonesia-talks-defense-with-china/ (accessed on 20 October 2012)

Mozur, Paul Mitsuru Obe and Alexander Kolyandr, "Territorial Spats Overshadow Asian-Pacific Summit," *Wall Street Journal*, 09 September 2012, http://online.wsj.com/article/SB10000872396390444554704577641301712512154.html (accessed on 07 October 2012)

Mulyana, Yayan G.H., "Developing an archipelagic foreign policy," *The Jakarta Post*, 09 January 2012, p. 6

Mulyana, Yayan G.H., "Peacekeeping operations and Indonesian Foreign Policy," *The Jakarta Post*, 03 January 2012, http://www.thejakartapost.com/news/2012/01/03/peacekeeping-operations-and-indonesian-foreign-policy.html (accessed on 15 December 2012)

Murphy, Ann Merie, "Democratization and Indonesian Foreign Policy: Implications for the United States," *Asia Policy*, number 13 (January 2012), pp. 83–111

"Non-Aligned Movement (NAM)," Nuclear Threat Initiative, http://www.nti.org/treaties-and-regimes/non-aligned-movement-nam/ (accessed on 26 December 2012)

Natalegawa, Marty, "An Indonesian perspective on the Indo-Pacific," *The Jakarta Pos*t, 20 May 2013, http://www.thejakartapost.com/news/2013/05/20/an-indonesian-perspective-indo-pacific.html (accessed on 15 June 2013)

Noor, Farish A., "How Indonesia Sees ASEAN and the World: A Cursory Survey of the Social Studies and History textbooks of Indonesia, from Primary to Secondary Level," *RSIS Working Paper*, no. 233, 22 February 2012, http://www.rsis.edu.sg/publications/workingpapers/wp233.pdf (accessed on 28 May 2013)

Nossal, K.R. and Stubbs, R. (1997), "Mahathir's Malaysia: An Emerging Middle Power?," in Cooper (ed.) *Niche Diplomacy: Middle Powers after the Cold War* (New York, Macmillan)

Novotny, Daniel, "Indonesia's Foreign Policy: in Quest for the Balance of Threats," presented to the 15th Biennial Conference of the Asian Studies Association of Australia, Canberra (29 June – 2 July 2004), http://coombs.anu.edu.au/SpecialProj/ASAA/biennial-conference/2004/Novotny-D-ASAA2004.pdf (accessed on 17 May 2013)

Osius, Ted, "Global Swing States: Deepening Partnerships with India and Indonesia," *Asia Policy*, no. 17 (January 2014), http://www.nbr.org/publications/asia_policy/AP17/Advance/AP17_SwingStates_110413.pdf (accessed on 22 December 2013)

Oberman, Raoul et. al., "The Archipelago Economy: Unleashing Indonesia's Potential," *Mckinsey Global Institute Report*, September 2012, http://www.mckinsey.com/insights/asia-pacific/the_archipelago_economy (accessed on 21 May 2013)

Odgaard, Liselotte, "The South China Sea: ASEAN's Security Concerns about China," *Security Dialogue*, vol. 34, no. 4 (March 2003), pp. 11-24

Onishi, Norimitsu, "US and China vie to win over Jakarta: With Visit to Indonesia, Obama tries to secure strategic edge in region," *The International Herald Tribune*, 10 November 2010, p. 1

"On regional tour, Ban salutes Indonesia's commitment to UN peacekeeping," *UN News Centre*, 20 March 2012, http://www.un.org/apps/news/story.asp?NewsID=41589&Cr=Indonesia&Cr1#.UMwig6V33dk (accessed on 15 December 2012)

Pangestu, Mari Elka, in Sudhir T. Devare and Vibhanshu Shekhar, *Delhi Dialogue III: Beyond the First Twenty Years of India-ASEAN Engagement* (New Delhi: Manohar, 2012)

Parlina, Ina, "Indonesia, India take further steps to strengthen relationship," *The Jakarta Post*, 12 October 2013, http://www.thejakartapost.com/news/2013/10/12/indonesia-india-take-further-steps-strengthen-relationship.html (accessed on 22 December 2013)

Paul, Shutapa, "CIL Plans to Invest in Overseas Coalmines," Livemint, 31 January 2010, http://www.livemint.com/Companies/KsJg6c5qQYDM9N9wrzjWxI/CIL-plans-to-invest-in-overseas-coal-mines.html (accessed on 05 May 2013)

Piccone, Ted, "Global Swing States and the Human Rights and Democracy Order," *GMF Global Swing States Working Paper*, November 2012, http://www.brookings.edu/~/media/research/files/papers/2012/11/27%20global%20swing%20states%20piccone/27%20global%20swing %20states%20piccone.pdf (accessed on 22 December 2013)

Primanita, Arientha Francezka Nangoy and Tito Summa Siahaan, "Indonesia's Pledge of $1 Billion to IMF Marks an Era Of Financial Independence: SBY," *The Jakarta Globe*, 11 July 2012, http://www.thejakartaglobe.com/news/indonesias-pledge-of-1-billion-to-imf-marks-an-era-of-financial-independence-sby/529871 (accessed on 17 December 2012)

Patunru, Arianto, "Indonesia: reform and the people," *East Asia Forum*, 17th January 2013, http://www.eastasiaforum.org/2013/01/17/indonesia-in-2012-reform-and-the-people/ (accessed on 21 May 2013)

Patunru, Arianto, "Securing Prosperity: Building a more Equitable and Productive Indonesia," *East Asia Forum Quarterly*, vol. 5, no. 4 (October-December 2013), pp. 2-4

Peou, Sorpong (2002), "Realism and Constructivism in Southeast Asian Security Studies Today: a Review Essay," *The Pacific Review*, vol. 15, no. 1, 2002, pp. 119-138

Perwita, Anak Agung Banyu, "Islam 'Symbolic Politics,' Democratization and Indonesian Foreign Policy," *Centro Argentino de Estudios Internacionales*, vol. 4, no. 1, 1999,http://www.caei.com.ar/sites/default/files/04_2.pdf (accessed on 12 September 2012)

Perwita, Anak Agung Banyu (2010), "RI as a new Middle Power?," *The Jakarta Post*, 12 November, http://www.thejakartapost.com/print/246554 (accessed on 14 October 2012)

Poling, Gregory B. and Blake Day, "Corruption in Indonesia and the 2014 Elections," *CSIS Critical Questions*, 07 November 2013, http://csis.org/publication/corruption-indonesia-and-2014-elections (accessed on 18 December 2013)

Pitsuwan, Surin, "Charter is Key for ASEAN Revitalization," *East-West Center Press Release*, 24 January 2008, http://www.eastwestcenter.org/news-center/east-west-wire/surin-charter-is-key-for-asean-revitalization (accessed on 14 October 2012)

Poore, Stuart, 'What is the Context? A Reply to the Gray-Johnston Debate on Strategic Culture', *Review of International Studies*, vol. 29, no. 2 (2003), pp. 279-284;

"Poor infrastructure could hamper Indonesia's further growth," *Global Times*, 05 November 2012, http://www.globaltimes.cn/content/742392.shtml (accessed on 22 May 2013)

"President: Indonesia supports nuclear disarmament," *Antara News*, 25 November 2009, http://www.antaranews.com/en/news/1259137727/president-indonesia-supports-nuclear-disarmament (accessed on 16 December 2012)

Puri, Hardeep S., "Rise of the Global South and Its Impact on South-South Cooperation," *World Bank Special Report*, October 2010, http://siteresources.worldbank.org/WBI/Resources/213798-1286217829056/puri.pdf

Rao, P.V. Narasimha, "India and the Asia-Pacific: Forging a New Relationship," Singapore Lecture, *Strategic Digest* (October 1994), p. 1412

"Recent Natural Disasters in Indonesia," www.disaster-report.com/.../recent-natural-disasters-in-indonesia.html (accessed on 10 September 2012)

Reid, Anthony, "Indonesia's New Prominence in the World," in Anthony Reid,

Indonesia Rising: The Repositioning of Asia's Third Giant (Singapore, ISEAS, 2012)

"Reliance Power buys 3 coal mines in Indonesia," *The Financial Express*, 03 May 2008

"Religious Intolerance Poisoning Indonesia," *The Jakarta Globe*, 02 May 2013, http://www.thejakartaglobe.com/news/religious-intolerance-poisoning-indonesia/ (accessed on 07 May 2013)

"Revitalizing Indonesia's Defence Industrial Base: Agenda for Future Action," *RSIS Policy Report*, 05 July 2012, http://www.rsis.edu.sg/publications/policy_report/Revitalizing_Indonesia_Defence_Industrial_Base_—_Agenda_for_Future_Action_5_July_2012.pdf (accessed on 30 December 2012)

"RI Elected to UN Human Rights Council for Third Time," *Antara News*, 21 May 2011, http://www.antaranews.com/en/news/71746/ri-elected-to-un-human-rights-council-for-third-time (accessed on 16 December 2012)

"RI Invites India to help Maintain Malacca Strait Security," *Antara News*, 05 March 2009, Jakarta (accessed via Lexis Nexis Academic)

"RI Lacks Deterrence Force: Juwono," *The Jakarta Post*, 22 March 2007

"RI to open 21 diplomatic relations in 2011," *Antara News*, 8 January 2011, http://www.antaranews.com/en/news/66764/ri-to-open-21-diplomatic-relations-in-2011

"RI, India Increase Mily Cooperation," *Antara News*, 09 February 2009 (accessed via Lexis Nexis Academic)

"Russia asserts its power in the Asia-Pacific at APEC summit," *The China Post*, 05 September 2012, http://www.chinapost.com.tw/commentary/afp/2012/09/05/353297/Russia-asserts.htm (accessed on 08 October 2012)

Ricklefs, M.C., "Unity and Disunity in Javanese Political and Religious Thought of the Eighteenth Century," *Modern Asian Studies*, vol. 26, no. 4, 1992, pp. 663-678

Roberts, George, "Indonesian Party Chief Quits over Corruption Claims," *ABC News*, 23 February 2013, http://www.abc.net.au/news/2013-02-23/indonesian-politician-suspected-of-corruption/4535572 (accessed on 23 May 2013)

Robertson-Snape, Fiona, "Corruption, Collusion and Nepotism in Indonesia," *Third World Quarterly*, vol. 20, no. 3, 1999, pp. 589-602,

Rohde, David, "Indonesia Unravelling," *Foreign Affairs*, vol. 80, 2001, pp. 110-124

Rondonuwu, Olivia and Stuart Grudgings, "Bali attack plot shows Indonesia terror threat evolving," *Reuters*, 22 March 2012, http://www.reuters.com/article/2012/03/22/us-indonesia-militants-idUSBRE82L0FS20120322 (accessed on 16 September 2012)

Rondonuwu, Olivia and Telly Nathalia, "Indonesian parliament passes anti-porn bill," *Reuters*, 30 October 2008, http://in.reuters.com/article/2008/10/30/us-indonesia-pornography-idINTRE49T3M020081030 (accessed on 15 May 2013)

Ross, Robert S., "China's Naval Nationalism: Sources, Prospects, and the U.S. Response," *International Security*, vol. 34, no. 2 (Fall 2009), pp. 46-81

Ross, Robert S., "Balance of Power Politics and the Rise of China: Accommodation and Balancing in East Asia," *Security Studies*, vol. 15, no. 3, 2006, pp. 355-395

Rüland, Jürgen, "Constructing Regionalism Domestically: Local Actors and Foreign Policymaking in Indonesia," *University of Freiburg Occasional Paper*, no. 6 (December 2011), http://www.southeastasianstudies.uni-freiburg.de/Content/files/occasional-paper-series/op-ruland-no.6_2011 (accessed on 28 May 2013)

Rumley, Dennis, "The Geopolitics of Asia-Pacific Regionalism in the twenty-first Century," *The Otemon Journal of Australian Studies*, vol. 31, 2005, pp. 5-27

Sambijantoro, Satria, "RI at middle-income crossroad," *The Jakarta Post*, 13 December 2013, http://www.thejakartapost.com/news/2013/12/13/ri-middle-income-crossroad.html (accessed on 14 January 2014)

Santoso, Lie Nathanael, "Defining Indonesia's Need for a Grand Strategy," *The Jakarta Post*, 19 August 2011, http://www.thejakartapost.com/news/2011/08/19/defining-indonesia's-need-a-grand-strategy.html (accessed on 18 May 2013)

Saragih, Bagus BT and Yohanna Ririhena, "Composition in UNSC no longer Relevant," *The Jakarta Post*, 01 October 2012, http://www.thejakartapost.com/news/2012/10/01/composition-unsc-no-longer-relevant.html (accessed on 15 December 2012)

Schonhardt, Sara, "Amid fear, Indonesian Atheists Build a Community of Support," *International Herald Tribune*, 26 April 2013, http://iht.newspaper direct.com/epaper/viewer.aspx (accessed on 07 May 2013)

Schonhardt, Sara, "US, China vie for influence among Indonesian riches," *Asia Times Online*, 06 May 2011, http://www.atimes.com/atimes/Southeast_Asia/ME06Ae02.html (accessed on 15 March 2012)

Schweller, Randall L., "Managing the Rise of Great Powers: History and Theory," in Alastair Iain Johnston and Robert S. Ross, Engaging China: The Management of an Emerging Power (New York: Routledge, 1999), pp. 1-31

Schweller, Randall L., "Unanswered Threats: A Neoclassical Realist Theory of Underbalancing," *International Security*, vol. 29, no. 2 (Fall 2004), pp. 159-201

Scott David, "The Great Power 'Great Game' between India and China: 'The Logic of Geography," *Geopolitics*, vol. 13, no. 1, 2008, pp. 1-26

Scott, David, "The twenty-first Century as Whose Century?", *Journal of World-Systems Research*, vol. 13, no. 2, 2008, pp. 96-118;

Sebastian Leonard C. and Imran J. Lanti, "Perceiving Indonesian Approaches to International Relations Theory," in Amitav Acharya and Barry Buzan (eds.), *Non-Western International Relations Theory: Perspectives on and beyond Asia* (London: Routledge, 2010), http://www.ditchley.co.uk/assets/media/7%20Indonesia-Sebastian%20and%20Lanti.pdf (accessed on 28 May 2013)

Sebastian, Leonard C., "Domestic Security Priorities, "Balance of Interests" and Indonesia's Management of Regional Order," in Joseph Chinyong Liow and Ralf Emmers, *Order and Security in Southeast Asia: Essays in Memory of Michael Leifer* (Oxon: Routledge, 2006), pp. 175-195

Severino, Rodolfo C., "Indonesia and the Future of ASEAN," *ASEAN Secretariat*, 26 August 1999, no. 3312, http://www.aseansec.org/3312.htm (accessed on 25 October 2012)

Severino, Rodolfo C., "The Year in ASEAN: the Charter, Trade Agreements, and the Global Economic Crisis," *Southeast Asian Affairs*, vol. 2010, pp. 60-68

Shekhar, Vibhanshu, "A Sino-Indonesian Push for APEC," *CSIS Asia House*, 22 November 22 2013, http://cogitasia.com/a-sino-indonesian-push-for-apec/ (accessed on 12 December 2013)

Shekhar, Vibhanshu, "Polarised ASEAN: 'Reverse Enmeshment'," *IPCS Article*, no. 3685, 31 July 2012, http://www.ipcs.org/article/southeast-asia/polarised-asean-reverse-enmeshment-3685.html (accessed on 14 October 2012)

Shekhar, Vibhanshu, "Address by H.E. Dr. R. M. Marty M. Natalegawa Honourable Foreign Minister of Republic of Indonesia," *Indian Council of World Affairs*, 27 July 2012, http://www.icwa.in/crindonesia.html (accessed on 21 October 2012)

Shekhar, Vibhanshu, "ASEAN's Response to the Rise of China: Deploying a Hedging Strategy," *China Report*, vol. 48, no. 3, 2012, p. 263

Shekhar, Vibhanshu, "TPP: A step towards integrating continents," *Business Standard,* 27 November 2011, http://www.business-standard.com/article/opinion/vibhanshu-shekhar-tpp-a-step-towards-integrating-continents-111112700014_1.html (accessed on 14 October 2012)

Shekhar, Vibhanshu, "SBY's visit and the Delhi-Jakarta Paradigm," *The Jakarta Post*, May 09 2011

Shekhar, Vibhanshu, "India and Indonesia: Reliable Partners in an Uncertain Asia," *Asia-Pacific Review*, vol. 17, no. 2, 2010, pp. 76-98

Shekhar, Vibhanshu, "Indonesia's Military Modernisation," *ICWA Issue Brief*, 11 February 2013, http://www.icwa.in/pdfs/VPIndonesiamilitarymodernisa tion. pdf (accessed on 17 May 2013)

Sinaga, Andre, "Income, a perilously widening gap," *The Jakarta Post*, June 05 2012, http://www.thejakartapost.com/news/2012/06/05/income-a-perilously-widening-gap.html (accessed on 18 December 2013)

Singh, Anoop, "Indonesia: Resilient Growth to Continue," *The Jakarta Post*, 2 May 2011, http://www.thejakartapost.com/news/2011/05/02/indonesia-resilient-growth-continue.html (accessed on 28 December 2012)

Siregar, Andre Omer, "SBY's strong message, sense of optimism at the UN," *The Jakarta Post*, 05 October 2012, http://www.thejakartapost.com/news/2012/10/05/sby-s-strong-message-sense-optimism-un.html (accessed on 16 December 2012)

Smith, Anthony L., "Indonesia's Foreign Policy under Abdurrahman Wahid: Radical or Status Quo State?," , vol. 22, no. 3 (December 2000), pp. 498-526

Snyder, Quddus Z., "Rising Powers and International Politics: A liberal systemic perspective," *APSA 2010 Annual Meeting Paper*, 2010, http://papers.ssrn.com/sol3/papers.cfm?abstract_id=1643369 (accessed on 14 November 2013)

Spero, Joshua B., "Great Power Security Dilemmas for Pivotal Middle Power Bridging," *Contemporary Security Policy*, vol. 30, no. 1, 2009, pp. 147-171

"Surana buys 49% in Indonesian coal mine," *The Hindu Business Line*, 10 January 2008,

Sukma, Rizal, "ASEAN and Major Powers in the New Emerging Regional Order," in Jun Tsunekawa (ed.) *Regional Order in East Asia: ASEAN and Japan Perspectives*, NIDS Joint Research Series, no. 1, 2009, http://www.nids.go.jp/english/publication/joint_research/series1/series1.html (accessed on 13 October 2012)

Sukma, Rizal, Indonesia needs a post-ASEAN Foreign Policy, *The Jakarta Post*, 30 June 2009, http://www.thejakartapost.com/news/2009/06/30/indonesia-needs-a-postasean-foreign-policy.html (accessed on 12 December 2013)

Sukma, Rizal, "Domestic Politics and International Posture: Constraints and Possibilities," in Anthony Reid, *Indonesia Rising: The Repositioning of Asia's Third Giant* (Singapore, ISEAS, 2012), pp.

Sukma, Rizal, "Indonesia Finds a New Voice," *Journal of Democracy*, vol. 22, no. 4 (October 2011), pp. 110-123

Sukma, Rizal, "Strength in Numbers: Indonesia's Multiple Defense Relationships," *Strategic Review*, 27 March 2013, http://www.sr-indonesia.com/in-the-journal/view/strength-in-numbers-indonesia-s-multiple-defense-relationships (accessed on 19 May 2013)

Sukma, Rizal, "the Evolution of Indonesia's Foreign Policy: An Indonesian View," *Asian Survey*, vol. 35, no. 3 (March 1995), pp. 304-315

Sukma, Rizal, "Indonesia's *bebas-aktif* foreign policy and the 'security agreement' with Australia," *Australian Journal of International Affairs*, vol. 51, no. 2, 1997, pp. 231-241

Sukma, Rizal, "Indonesia-China Relations: The Politics of Re-Engagement," *Asian Survey*, vol. 49, no. 4 (July-August 2009), pp. 591-608

Suryodiningrat, Meidyatama, "ASEAN 9, Human Rights 1," *The Jakarta Post*, 24 July 2009, http://www.thejakartapost.com/news/2009/07/24/asean-9-human-rights-1.html (accessed on 20 December 2012)

Tammen, Ronald L., 'The Impact of Asia on World Politics: China and India Options for the United States', *International Studies Review*, vol. 8, no. 4, 2006, pp. 563-580

Tammen, Ronald L. and Jacek Kugler, "Power Transition and China-US Conflicts," *Chinese Journal of International Politics*, vol. 1, no. 1, 2006, pp. 35-55.

Tank, Pinar, "The concept of "rising powers"," *NOREF Policy Brief*, June 2012, http://www.peacebuilding.no/var/ezflow_site/storage/original/application/aa7c23bf5887ab060f1af737a39a000a.pdf (accessed on 02 November 2013)

Tarling, Nicholas, "'Ah-Ah': Britain and the Bandung Conference of 1955," *Journal of Southeast Asian Studies*, vol. 23, no. 1 (March 1992), pp. 75-79

Taylor, Ian, "'The South Will Rise Again'? New Alliances and Global Governance: The India–Brazil–South Africa Dialogue Forum," *Politikon: South African Journal of Political Studies*, vol. 36, no. 1, 2009, pp. 45-58

Tedjasukmana, Jason, "In Indonesia, Corruption Scandals Plague Anti-Graft President," *Time*, 26 September 2011, http://www.time.com/time/world/article/0,8599,2094188,00.html (accessed on 23 May 2013)

Terada, Takashi, "Constructing an 'East Asian' concept and growing regional identity: from EAEC to ASEAN+3," *The Pacific Review*, vol. 16, no. 2, 2003, pp. 251-277

"The Importance of the Asia-Pacific Region," Voice of America Editorial, 24 September 2012, http://editorials.voa.gov/content/the-importance-of-the-asia-pacific-region/1514099.html (accessed on 11 23 December 2013)

"The Indonesian example: Remember 1998," *The Economist*, 07 February 2011, http://www.economist.com/blogs/asiaview/2011/02/indonesian_example (accessed on 20 December 2012)

"The U.S.-Indonesia Comprehensive Partnership," Press Release, US Embassy, Jakarta, 28 June 2010, http://jakarta.usembassy.gov/pr_06282010.html (accessed on 29 August 2012)

Tjhin, Christine Susanna, "Indonesia's Relations with China: Productive and

Pragmatic, but not yet a Strategic Partnership," *China Report*, vol. 48, no. 3, 2012, pp. 303-315

Umar, Ahmad Rizky Mardhatillah, "A critical reading of 'Natalegawa doctrine," *The Jakarta Post,* 07 January 2011, http://www.thejakartapost.com/news/2011/01/07/a-critical-reading-'natalegawa-doctrine'.html (accessed on 21 May 2013)

"UN reports subdued Asia-Pacific growth in 2013 as region faces developed world uncertainty," *United Nations Department of Economic and Social Affairs*, http://www.un.org/en/development/desa/news/policy/un-reports-subdued-asia-pacific-growth-in-2013-as-region-faces-developed-world-uncertainty.html (accessed on 16 December 2013)

Varadarajan, Siddharth, "From IBSA to CHIBSA? BRIC to BRICS? Not yet," *The Hindu*, 16 April 2010

Vaswani, Karishma, "Poor infrastructure curbs Indonesian growth," *BBC News*, 07 October 2010, http://www.bbc.co.uk/news/business-11483541 (accessed on 22 May 2013)

Verra and Fitriani, "Indonesia's Rising Middle Class: Tweeting To Be Heard," *RSIS Commentaries*, no. 104/2012, 19 June 2012, http://www.rsis.edu.sg/publications/Perspective/RSIS1042012.pdf (accessed on 27 December 2012)

"Vietnam accuses China in seas dispute," *BBC News*, 30 May 2011, http://www.bbc.co.uk/news/mobile/world-asia-pacific-13592508 (accessed on 07 October 2012)

"Vietnam says China Fishing Boat Rams Research Ship," *The Straits Times*, 9 June 2011, http://www.straitstimes.com/BreakingNews/SEAsia/Story/STIStory_678024.html (accessed on 12 October 2012)

Wallerstein, Immanuel, "East Asia and the World: The Decades Ahead", no. 157, Birmingham University, 15 March 2005, http://fbc.binghamton.edu/157en.htm (accessed on 21 September 2012)

Wanandi, Jusuf, "Indonesia: A Failed State?" *The Washington Quarterly,* vol. 25, no. 3 (Summer 2002), pp. 135-146

Weck, Winfried, "ASEAN and G20 – Indonesia 's Foreign Policy Perspectives," *Konrad Adenauer Stiftung International Reports*, no. 2, 2011, http://www.kas.de/wf/doc/kas_21871-1522-2-30.pdf?110209123433 (accessed on 17 December 2012)

Widjajanto, Andy, "Indonesia's Military Doctrinal Stagnation," *Strategic Review*, 20 March 2012, http://www.sr-indonesia.com/2011-08-09-22-09-10/commentaries/157-indonesias-military-doctrinal-stagnation (accessed on 19 May 2013)

Wiharja, Maria Monica, "Indonesia and the G20: a door left half open," *East*

Asia Forum, 29 June 2012, http://www.eastasiaforum.org/2012/06/29/indonesia-and-the-g20-a-door-left-half-open/ (accessed on 17 December 2012)

Wirajuda, N. Hasan, "The Democratic Response," *The Brown Journal of World Affairs*, vol. IX, no. 1 (Spring 2002), pp. 15-21

Wright, Tom, "Indonesia: Indonesia's Commodity Boom Is a Mixed Bag," Corp Watch, March 24th, 2008, http://www.corpwatch.org/article.php?id=14988 (accessed on 30 December 2012)

Yudhoyono, Susilo Bambang, "Indonesia in 2045: A Centennial Journey of Progress," *Strategic Review*, vol. 1, no. 1 (August 2011), p. 47

Zagorodnov, Artem, "Apec summit: Vladivostok talks reveal Russia's eastern trading plans," *The Telegraph*, 01 October 2012, http://www.telegraph.co.uk/sponsored/russianow/business/9578664/apec-summit-vladivostok-russia.html (accessed on 07 October 2012)

Zainuddin, Shoeb K., "Middle Class Growth Fuels Lippo," *The Jakarta Globe*, 06 November 2012, http://www.thejakartaglobe.com/business/middle-class-growth-fuels-lippo/554413 (accessed on 27 December 2012)

Zamroni Salim, "Indonesia in the G20: Benefits And Challenges Amidst National Interests and Priorities," in Wilhelm Hofmeister (ed.), *G20: Perceptions and Perspectives for Global Governance* (Singapore: Konrad Adenauer Stiftung, 2011)

Index